Meet These Women

Chapter 1

When the military drafted and deployed servicemen to Europe, the Pacific and even stateside during World War II, American women became active in military-related auxiliary groups such as Women's Army Corps (WAC), Women Accepted for Volunteer Emergency Service (WAVES), Women Air Force Service Pilots (WASP) and the Coast Guard's women's reserve (SPAR, which is named after the motto "Semper Paratus – Always Ready"). Their role in these organizations varied as some women test-flew airplanes and others test-drove tanks. Dedicated to their country, even civilian women worked on confidential military projects in secret settings without questioning what they were doing.

Eager to serve their country in another way, many women flocked to factories and took the places of men called to serve in the war. Factories that once manufactured automobiles were converted into tank-making plants. One-time dress manufacturing facilities were turned into military-uniform factories. And of course, there were aircraft-manufacturing plants where planes were riveted together by women referred to then and now as "Rosie the Riveters." Working 10 – 12 hours a day, often six days a week, American women proudly "manned" the country's manufacturing plants in order to support the war effort.

Still other women served as air-raid wardens, worked for the rationing board, volunteered for the United Service Organizations (USO) and the American Red Cross. They nursed wounded soldiers, taught the nation's children, worked the farms and did countless other jobs to support the war effort. During the World War II years, it seemed that every woman on America's home front served her country and did so in order to "bring the boys home."

Vena was in the Navy WAVES. Her base was at Whiting Field in Pensacola, Florida. There she slept in the barracks for two years, six months and 21 days. At Whiting Field, Vena taught some 200 new pilots the "new instrument-flying technique" for navigating airplanes. She worked in a flight simulator called a Link Trainer and instructed students on how to use the instrument panel so they could find their bearings without having to rely on the ability to see the landscape.

"Although I did not work in an aircraft plant, I did join the U.S. Women's Marines in January 1944. I worked on airplanes and served for the duration of World War II."

Vena Bryant
Atria Kennebunk
Kennebunk, Maine

"I was selected for aircraft training and sent to Norman, Oklahoma with male Marine and Navy trainees for six months. I loved learning all about Corsairs and numerous other planes. All of us learned to work on engines, change flat tires and fold parachutes correctly. We also learned how to jump off towers and perform correct landing maneuvers. Everything the men did, the women did. Marching day and night, staying afloat in water long enough to be rescued and staying up all night learning how to do an about face and march in cadence so that our platoon would look as good as the men's were just some of what we learned. My training and experiences were very valuable and contributed greatly to my maturity. I wore my Marine uniform with pride and knew I was contributing to the war effort in my own way.

During the war years, I lived at Camp Lejeune in North Carolina, Norman in Oklahoma, Quantico in Virginia and Ewa Air Station in Hawaii. Hawaii qualified me as an overseas veteran and earned me another medal.

I had many friends while in the Marines, some with whom I kept in touch after the war ended. Some of us agreed that after discharge, we would meet in San Francisco and attend college together. Using our GI bill, about five of us attended San Francisco State College. I considered that the greatest gift the government gave me. I never could have attended college without it. College changed my entire life, enriching it beyond my expectations.

I am a representative of Women in Military Service of America (WIMSA), an organization that encourages women to join the military. I enjoyed celebrating in Washington, D.C., at the dedication of the Women's Memorial in 1997."

**Marie Fennell
(AKA "Gallie" in the USMC)**
Atria Chateau San Juan
San Juan Capistrano, California

"In 1941, I was teaching at McKinley Elementary School in Alton, Illinois, when President Roosevelt announced the attack on Pearl Harbor, which galvanized the whole country. I considered the Navy, but at the time I didn't like to wear navy blue with my coloring. I didn't want to join the WACs. The Marines were the hardest to get in, and I liked their forest green uniforms. I soon passed all the requirements to be in the U.S. Marine Corps.

I was sworn in on March 25, 1944, but because I was teaching, they put me on inactive duty until school closed in early June. School closed on Friday. I reported to camp in North Carolina the following Monday. At camp, they asked for our work experience, so I listed teaching and my various summer jobs. They asked where we would like to serve. I chose Hawaii and was assigned to be a file clerk at Schools Training Regiment at camp.

I had been there a short time when a lieutenant asked me to do some illustrations for a book he had written, which I did. The woman who had been the regimental artist left the service, and I soon took over the position. I had my own office, about the size of a gear closet, which accommodated a drafting table and a stool. I produced training aids and whatever art projects were needed. One especially complex project had me crawling across a large table with my pantograph. As the only woman in the unit, I was a prime target for pranks. One day I couldn't move across the table because my Marine 'friends' had thumb-tacked my fatigue jacket to the table. Another time, their fiendish creativity inspired them to booby trap my pantograph, so when I moved it, there was a mini-explosion.

In May 1946, the war was over and the Women Marines detachment at camp was closed. Those of us still there were sent to Washington, D.C., and advanced to the rank of sergeant. I was a file clerk once again. In September, I was discharged and returned to Carbondale, Illinois. The GI Bill's financial help for veterans going back to school allowed me to enroll at Pratt Institute in Brooklyn, New York to study advertising design.

I've been actively involved with our local chapter of the Woman Marines Association since its inception in 1974. On November 10, 2001, I attended the 226th United States Marine Corps Birthday Ball in Houston. Upon my arrival, it was indeed a surprise to have a red rose corsage pinned on my shoulder and to see that page five in the event's program was all about me. It had been kept a secret from me that I was to be the honored guest at the ball because I was the oldest Marine living in the Houston area and the first lady Marine to be honored at the annual event."

Marion A. Harrison, USMCWR
Atria Westchase
Houston, Texas

"The series of drawings of Women Marines I did in my free time while in the service helped raise money for our Women Marines Association. They are now in the Marine Corps Museum in the Washington, D.C., area." Graduating in 1943, Laurie joined the Navy Nurse Corps and was stationed near the Great Lakes. She had many patients who were casualties of the war's biggest naval battles. They included many injured men from the Solomon Islands battles who jumped from their sinking ships only to land in water covered in burning oil. Quite often, whole shiploads of patients arrived at the same time. The nurses worked 12- to 15-hour shifts to care for them.

After one year of service, Laurie was ready to go to the hospital ship, Hope. However, she had become engaged. Since naval nurses were not permitted to marry, Laurie left the service.

Laurice "Laurie" Tappan
Atria Chandler Villas
Chandler, Arizona

In 1945, Elsie began to work as a draftsman in the Navy. She and the other women were rapidly trained to fill the vacant positions left by the men drafted into war. Elsie took a mathematics exam, completed weekend coursework and passed further examinations. She was assigned to work at Hunter's Point near San Francisco, where she made blueprints to repair submarines that had been damaged. Her first assignment was to revise the foundation of the target-bearing transmitters on a submarine. Not knowing what this should look like, Elsie took a hands-on approach and went to the submarine to see for herself. She also solicited advice from the men on board about any changes they thought necessary. Upon her high stool at her long table, Elsie went to work making the changes. She completed the project successfully and continued with this work until the men returned from war a year later.

Elsie Stebbings
Atria Covell Gardens
Davis, California

Ann worked as a secretary at Fort Mammoth during the war. Night vision equipment was developed and tested at this site. At times, Ann was not allowed in the hallways because of the confidential nature of some of the projects.

Ann Lenner
Atria Tinton Falls
Tinton Falls, New Jersey

After her husband went overseas, Estelle wanted to help with the war effort as well as occupy her time while her husband was gone. A friend told her that the Army Air Force was looking for volunteers for a special project. Estelle wasted no time inquiring about the project and was immediately hired as a volunteer.

It turns out that this "special project" was a highly classified experiment involving the airplane that would later carry the H-Bomb. At the time, there were no planes that could fly above 25,000 feet. The plane that carried the H-Bomb needed to fly at least 35,000 feet in order to transport its load. According to

Estelle, everything was at the strictest level of confidentiality. No one ever discussed anything while at work. They left their emotions at the threshold when they entered the work site and they resumed their personal lives only after they exited the building at the end of the day. Some of Estelle's coworkers consisted of many conscientious objectors who had served time in prison for refusing to be drafted, but wanted to serve their country in a different capacity.

Estelle's job consisted of enduring all kinds of testing on her body to see what it could withstand under certain compression conditions. Testing was done in a chamber similar to those used by New York's underground-tunnel workers. A physicist worked with the Army to develop the chamber that became the cabin that carried the crew and its contents on the special plane.

One of Estelle's most vivid memories is when she was finally able to physically move two huge oxygen tanks by herself to the constructed chamber, which was quite an accomplishment for a woman who is barely five feet tall. According to Estelle, women simply did whatever they felt they had to do. No one held back.

Estelle never told her husband that she worked on this project, but she felt very proud to contribute to such a critical effort for the security of the United States.

Estelle Rosenbloom
Atria Tamalpais Creek
Novato, California

"I learned about the bombing of Pearl Harbor from a friend and enlisted in the Navy soon after. I first applied for an officer's position, but found out that the only positions for officers were in the physical education training department. I knew that this was not a position that I wanted, so I joined as an enlisted woman. I worked as a secretary, typing papers for the enlisted men and women upon discharge. The high point of my service was the day I marched down Fifth Avenue in New York City where President Roosevelt was standing. It was a day that I will never forget.

After returning home from my enlistment in the Navy, I went to work at the local library in my hometown. I remember everyone having to use ration stamps for sugar, gasoline and other amenities, but don't recall having to use them myself."

Ann Beath
Atria Collier Park
Beaumont, Texas

"From 1941 to 1944, I worked as a nurse in Youngstown, Ohio. In 1944, I strongly felt the call of duty, enlisted in the Army and became a second lieutenant.

I went to basic training in Indiana and afterwards was sent to Fletcher Hospital in Ohio. From there, I was assigned to the 93rd Field Hospital going overseas. After much more training to prepare for military life overseas, I boarded the Holland-American ship Hollandia. The ship was a former commercial liner that was converted for the Army's use. The dining room was the only place in the ship that maintained its original look. It still had beautiful chairs, nice tables and fancy tablecloths. As a nurse, I was privileged to eat in the dining room.

When we landed in Manila, Philippines, we discovered the Japanese were there before us. I was assigned to Bilibid Prison, which was converted to a hospital. The Japanese destroyed the pipes, so there was no water. Other conditions, such as sleeping in the gym, made working in the converted prison very challenging.

After my term at Bilibid, I was assigned to a number of work sites—an inter-island hospital ship, a field hospital in Malolos, Bulacan, a general hospital in Quezon City and, finally, back home at Camp Butner in North Carolina."

Martha Sauer
Atria Daly City
Daly City, California

Harriet grew up in Detroit. She graduated high school with honors and was recommended for Officers Candidate School (OCS). After OCS training, Harriet moved to San Francisco, California, where she became a member of the Women Accepted for Volunteer Emergency Service (WAVES) organization. She landed a job in the Federal Building in San Francisco, in the decoding department for the Navy.

Highly classified information was handled in the decoding department, and Harriet's job was to read messages passed to her through a special window and decide to whom the messages should be delivered. Harriet was sworn to secrecy to never discuss her job or the messages with anyone.

One day, Harriet received a message about a ship in the harbor waiting for the go-ahead to be deployed. As far as Harriet knew at the time, all battleships were named after a state. Because the ship did not have a name she recognized, Harriet put the message aside and did not deliver it right away. After an hour or so passed, the ship notified the command center that its deployment had been delayed for more than an hour. The command center realized Harriet had not delivered the message promptly and delayed a very important mission. Harriet remembers getting "the full treatment" for that big mistake.

Harriet Turner
Atria Tamalpais Creek
Novato, California

"I was out on my own working as a telephone operator in California when World War II began. I was 26 years old and not married. I had a sister in the Navy, two brothers in the military and a boyfriend in Ethiopia, and I wanted to do my part for my country, too.

With 28 other girls, I signed up to go into the Women's Auxiliary Corps (WAC). We were sent to Des Moines, Iowa, where we had to wear heavy overcoats over our winter woolen suits, but I was proud to wear the uniform as a PFC.

I was stationed near Alexandria, Virginia. I was assigned to a group of girls and each day we were given sheets of paper with groups of five or six random numbers on them. Even though the numbers were meaningless to us, we typed them into a special machine. We were emphatically ordered not to discuss the numbers in any way with anyone.

We were given one change of fall dress uniforms: shirt, tie, skirt and shoes, all of which we took care of and cleaned ourselves. Our caps were pointed in the front and back, just like the men's. Everything was rationed. Winter dress uniforms were ugly brown; summer ones were light tan. Time in the service changed me. I became more independent."

Charlotte Withycombe
Atria El Camino Gardens
Carmichael, California

Dorothy served in the Navy during the war. She worked in Washington, D.C., in the communications department, and had the tedious job of encoding and decoding messages. She served in the Navy for two years. After the war ended, Dorothy's work slowly decreased as did the need for decoders. After her service in the Navy, Dorothy went back to teaching.

Dorothy Johnson
Atria Springdale
Louisville, Kentucky

"I was a secretary for the Army Engineers in Seattle, and at the Army base in Juneau, Alaska. At the request of the FBI, I helped nail a German spy who worked in the Juneau office. He was whisked away and we never saw him again! Some of my coworkers later teased me by calling me the 'red-headed Mata Hari.'

Japanese submarines cruised the Alaskan coastline, and we had blackouts at night and a weekly siren-call test. When the test siren sounded, we rushed into a cave in the mountains and waited for the all clear signal.

I also edited the Seattle Army Engineers newspaper and even made up crossword puzzles for it (the answers were in the next issue). I feel that, as a woman, I contributed to the war effort with the skills I had."

Ethel Adams
Atria Acacia
Fullerton, California

"I was a typist at an insurance company in Toronto at the time of World War II. I was also attending radio school. When I was about 34, the Army called and said it urgently needed radio operators. I learned how to work the teletype and how to read and send Morse Code. I sent out a lot of hush-hush information to England.

I lived at an Army camp on a beautiful countryside on Lake Ontario. I was not allowed to say where I worked. The name of the camp was Camp X; it was a secret government camp. Many commandos were trained there. We kept our windows closed because of the bomb training. They were very interesting times. Once the Army hosted a dance and one of my roommates and I were the only girls there. They had us dancing until dawn! I learned a lot through my experience with the Army and I was paid very well. I stayed with the service for four years. I then went on a cruise to relax and met my future husband."

Marjorie Storms
Atria Encinitas
Encinitas, California

Grace was 20 years old when she went to work in the wood lab at the University of Wisconsin. It was a salary-based government position that paid $1,440 a year. Workers analyzed different types of wood, as well as cut it down to make into ply sheets. They also tested wood from different states to determine how many different uses it had. However, the wood lab primarily tested wood for use in airplanes.

Grace said there were only two women who worked there and she was honored to be one of them. She also served as a volunteer at the Red Cross.

Grace Brashears
Atria Sunlake
Las Vegas, Nevada

Rose married her husband, Frank, right before World War II broke out. He was an Air Force staff sergeant stationed at the Banksdale Field Base in Louisiana. The couple lived on base and Rose worked on base, too. She worked with land mine fuse powder, which was highly explosive. Prospective employees were told not to consider working in that area unless they were very stable and sure of themselves.

When workers arrived at their working area, they immediately changed into jump suits to eliminate static electricity. She will never forget the first time she experienced an explosion. She was knocked out of her chair and scared to death. After that, explosions were not that surprising for her.

PEANUTS @ United Feature Syndicate, Inc. Reprinted with permission.

Occasionally Rose went into a bomb-proof room to take apart defective hand grenades. She tried to keep her job a secret from her husband. He was very upset when he eventually found out she was working with such dangerous materials. In fact, he exclaimed, "Rose, in that job you are seeing more of the war than I am. My job in the hospital is easy compared to yours!"

"In those days, there were a lot of people who put their lives on the line. I was just one of many. I don't regret it because I wanted to do my part and it was really quite an experience," she said.

Rose Kalivoda
Atria Manresa
Annapolis, Maryland

Florence worked for the government, handling equipment, testing antennas and driving tanks to teach soldiers how to protect themselves in foxholes. (The tank she used was from World War I because she was petite and could not reach the controls of the World War II tanks.) "If the soldiers lived after I drove over them, they were sent to a foxhole overseas to take care of themselves," she said.

One time during a lesson, a young man looked to see if the tank was coming and Florence had to slam on the brakes so as not to run over him. He learned his lesson, and he was quite surprised to see a pretty blonde woman pop out of the tank and give him the "look."

Florence Krakaur
Atria East Northport
Long Island, New York

"I enlisted in the Air Force on September 1, 1943, while living in Chicago. My basic training was at Daytona Beach, Florida for two months. I really enjoyed training, except for all of the medical shots I had to have.

Just like in 'Some Enchanted Evening' from South Pacific, I remember being out for an evening of fun and dancing with two women, also WACs. I looked across the way and saw a handsome master sergeant sitting with two other WACs. I was smitten! The feelings left me with no choice but to send him a note saying, 'I think you're real cute and would like to meet you.' He came over to my table and we started a lasting relationship.

Lerroy and I were married in 1945 in Valdosta, Georgia. I had been transferred to Valdosta and worked as a secretary to a colonel. I worked for him for about a year, then was promoted to corporal. From there, I was assigned to recruiting women for the Air WACs. A lieutenant and I traveled in a motor bus driven by a male sergeant. We toured all through Florida making stops to speak on the radio and at lunches about the service and trying to get volunteers to help with the war efforts. When the war ended, my husband was discharged first. Four months later, I was discharged. On October 5, 1945, I received a medal for good conduct.

I feel as though I did help out, especially in the area of recruiting other women to enlist."

Drusilla McHenry
Atria Windsor Woods
Hudson, Florida

"World War II started in England on September 3, 1939. One night, the bombs dropped on the hospital where I was living as a student nurse in Liverpool, England. That's when I decided to join the Women's Auxiliary Air Force or WAAF. (This organization was referred to as RAF in England.)

After my physical, I was hired on the spot and joined RAF immediately. I served approximately four years. I was assigned to flying control at Bomber Command Headquarters in Lincoln, England, where we gave instructions to incoming bomber pilots.

One day, I called in an all-Australian crew to instruct them on which runway to land. The bomb aimer of the crew had just returned that plane from Nuremberg, Germany. He came into the control tower to meet the girl who talked funny. The man asked me for a date and three weeks later we were married.

Eventually I went to Australia as a war bride. It was a six-week journey from London to Sydney, Australia on a troop ship. For four years, we were occupied by the Nazis. We ended up speaking both French and English. By 1945, we were liberated by the Americans. My husband was awarded the Distinguished Flying Cross. We were sent to Buckingham Palace to accept the award. He was very happy and his award was well-deserved."

Eileen Murtough
Atria Valley Manor
Tucson, Arizona

"I joined the Army in July 1942. I was a lieutenant and was stationed at four different bases. As a nurse, my uniform was white and I wore white-soled shoes. At that time it was almost impossible to find white heels, so I wore what I had – black heels. My mother found some white ones and I replaced my black heals for white ones and felt properly dressed again.

The second base I was stationed at was Fort Warden, Washington, where I met Lt. Horace Schaefer. I remained at this base two years before I was sent to California. Horace heard that if he didn't ask me to marry him, someone else would. So he took leave, came to California and asked me to marry him. I said yes. We were married only days before we were sent our separate ways and didn't think we would see each other again. I soon received my orders to go overseas. I knew if I became pregnant, then I would not be sent. When I took my pre-overseas 10-day leave, I became pregnant on purpose knowing I would not have to follow orders. Nine months later, my daughter was born."

Alice Schaefer
Atria Sandy
Sandy, Utah

While working at the Second National Bank Philadelphia, someone came in and asked a young woman if she liked her country and if she would like to defend it. Virginia Povey answered "yes" to both questions.

The 17-year-old was told to report to a secret place downtown. This was a volunteer job. Virginia was not paid, so she kept her day job. When Virginia came home form the bank each day, her mother had dinner ready for her. In the evening, Virginia was either picked up and taken to her second job or she rode the train downtown.

There were 14 volunteers in all and they were told to ask any questions they would like, but there would be no answers. They were told not to tell anyone where they worked or what they did and they were searched every night before they left the secret plant. Virginia's job was to put together parts, sometimes with a rivet and sometimes with a soldering iron. Virginia worked at the secret plant for nearly two years. The long hours of working two jobs was very tiring, but also therapeutic in that

Virginia and other volunteers were so busy they did not dwell on hate for the enemy. Virginia received no recognition for her work, but she remained dedicated to her country. She felt she was protecting her boyfriend (who later became her husband), who was a sailor. When the war was over and the workers at the secret plant were told they were dismissed, they all shouted for joy. Virginia was so exited she could not sleep. It was not until after her job ended that she learned she helped make bombs.

Virginia Povey
**Atria Mallard Cove
Cincinnati, Ohio**

"During the war, I lived with my parents in New Albany, Indiana and attended college. But during my second year at college, I got patriotic and dropped out of school to work in a defense plant in Charlestown, Indiana. Because of my home economics background, which included chemistry, I got a position in the lab working with chemicals and making

smokeless powder. Our uniforms consisted of wool pants and shirts and steel-toed boats, in case we dropped something on our feet. There was not any air conditioning at the time—you can imagine the heat of working in wool!

We worked all three shifts on a rotating basis and then got a couple of days off. Although we never knew where the powder went or how it was used to advance the cause, we did know one thing: we were doing our part, no matter how little it seemed, to help our country win the war.

I met my husband, a chemist, who transferred to the Indiana lab from New Jersey. You could say that the defense plant not only gave me an opportunity to help my country, but it also served as a matchmaker!"

Kitty Russell
**Atria St. Matthews
Louisville, Kentucky**

"I was an Army nurse, and signed up in 1942 for the duration of the emergency. I shipped out to Camp Pickett, Virginia. A typical day was 12 hours at the hospital with times during the day that the nurses were sent for various training, such as gas mask drills. Our everyday uniforms were white, our dress uniforms were two-toned navy, and later drab olive. Our unit was very close and we often took the bus from the base into Blackstone or Petersburg for a movie. Sometimes we also went to the Officers Club.

In November 1942, they told us we could come to the office if we wanted to sign up for overseas duty. I thought I'd wait a little while before traveling that far, but about four months later my name was on the bulletin board list of those scheduled to go overseas.

Nurses from several hospitals were sent to join the 78th Station Hospital. Army hospitals were on the front lines. The station hospitals had about 500 patients and received them after surgery and treatment in the front-line hospitals. Soldiers stayed there if they were able to return to duty within 30 days. They stayed at the general hospital if they needed longer treatment. Patients from there either returned to active duty or were sent to the states for more treatment.

The 78th Station Hospital was sent to North Africa in May 1943. We were in a tent hospital for about 10 months. I worked on medical wards that had patients flown in from Italy with conditions like malaria, hepatitis and frostbite. In April 1944, we were sent to Italy, just inland from Naples. We took over an Italian Army barracks and turned it into a hospital. We treated many German soldiers who were severely injured and left in the fields as the Germans were pursued by the Americans. Some surgical teams worked 24 hours a day, with each member working a 12-hour shift. Penicillin was used only for the most severe infections; others were treated with sulfa drugs.

In September 1944, we were transferred to southern France. We took over a hotel on the Riviera and made it into a hospital. When we arrived, we were warned to stay on the path as there were probably land mines on the side that could blow up. We later moved to a tuberculosis sanatorium that was beautiful up in the hills overlooking Cannes on the Riviera.

We had all kinds of injured and ill soldiers. I returned to the states in September 1945 and was discharged from the service in June 1946. It was hard to have an ocean between me and my home for more than two years, but I was glad to do my part during the war. I was amazed at the shortage of nylon hose, bed linens, towels and other items in stores. I took advantage of the GI bill and got my degree and worked in a VA hospital for five years before I got married."

Teresa Kaufmann Salchak
Atria MerryWood
Charlotte, North Carolina

"I was eating lunch at a restaurant when I heard the announcement about entering the war. I knew it was important that I enlist in the service because I knew nurses would be needed. I stayed in the states, but left my husband to be stationed in Fort Benning, Georgia. Soldiers came in from all over to be treated. I nursed German prisoners as well. One of the German prisoners said the best time he had was when he was in American hospitals.

By the end of the war, I had been away from my husband for eight months. I stayed in the reserves and was later stationed in Germany during the Korean War. They needed surgical nurses very badly.

Women proved to men during those times that we could be responsible in a lot of new and different ways."

Margaret Hodges
Atria Primacy
Memphis, Tennessee

Marguerite felt the call of patriotism while she was a nurse in Washington, D.C., she felt compelled to do something for her country and joined the Navy. Her service in the Navy took her to Walter Reed Hospital, where she was a nurse. There Marguerite had an extraordinary experience that involved a very special general who was not only a World War II veteran but a World War I veteran as well. General John Pershing became one of Marguerite's patients on the night shift.

During a visit to a friend who was in the Army, Marguerite decided to give the Army her loyalty. The only thing the Army needed to do was examine Marguerite's feet. She passed with flying colors, probably because of the pedicure she gave herself just before the exam.

At 24 years old, she found herself in Camp Lee, Virginia, in charge of a ward filled with German POWs. Marguerite kept the men in line and tried not to let them intimidate her, though they certainly tried. After Camp Lee, Marguerite found herself volunteering as a nurse on the trains transporting soldiers. She slept on an upper bunk while the men slept on the lower bunks.

As if she didn't have enough on her resume, Marguerite joined the Army Air Corps. While in the Army Air Corps, she served as an air evacuation nurse, helping evacuate wounded soldiers everywhere from the Philippines to Alaska. The Army Air Corps was the air division of the Army. It became the Air Force after the war was over. Thus, Marguerite can say she has served in the Navy, the Army and the Air Force!

It was at Army Air Corps training that Marguerite met her future husband, Daniel Tobin. The couple was married in November 1946 at Randolph Field's School of Aviation Medicine.

Marguerite Tobin
Atria St. Matthews
Louisville, Kentucky

"I will never forget Pearl Harbor. My family and I were listening to the reports on the radio because there was no TV and we couldn't believe what we heard. I was living in Texas and teaching fifth grade. Many men volunteered at once. When the Women's Army Auxiliary Corps (WAAC) was founded, I signed up in April 1943.

In June of the same year, I was sent to Ft. Devens in Ayers, Massachusetts for basic training. I remember Ft. Devens as a place of sand and rocks. Sometimes we had to go out of the barracks and rake the sand smooth because a general was coming to inspect. If someone got a demerit, they had to go and pile up rocks from the parade grounds.

Our company was made up of 120 women plus officers. We lived in barracks that had been built for men. They added curtains in the latrine for a little extra space. There were blacktop roads connecting the main buildings.

WAACs were commanded to stay on the black top roads away from the wooded areas. If a WAAC was accompanied home by a man, he had to stay on the blacktop road and go no closer than 150 feet of the barracks.

We took turns on kitchen police (KP) duty. We set tables, washed dishes, mopped floors and cleaned the grease trap, which was a dreaded chore. I caught on quickly that the sergeant in charge picked someone who was

not busy to clean the grease trap. So I polished the dinner table, swept the floors or dried dishes when it was near time for this job and thus escaped the dirty task.

There were problems getting uniforms, so we were issued men's shirts. Each of us had so few uniforms that we had to wash them with a wash board and iron them dry (there were no dryers or washers in 1943) because the laundry took so long to return them. To complete our uniforms, we wore high-top shoes because the post had so much sand and rocks.

On July 3,1943, I went with 30 other WAACs to Walter Reed Army Medical Center in Washington, D.C. An officer at Walter Reed told the existing soldiers before we arrived that the WAACs were coming, but they wouldn't stay long. It is now 2004 and WAACs are still at Walter Reed!

July 30, 1943 was our first day as the first WAACs at Walter Reed Hospital. I was assigned to work in the office, and I was the registrar much of the time. I learned how to operate the telephone switchboard. I also filed records and sometimes pushed patients in wheelchairs to their wards. WAACs had other duties, such as running the projector for training films, driving in the motor pool and working in the kitchen. In the fall of 1943, WAAC was changed to WAC, Women's Army Corps.

Walter Reed had a non-denominational chapel that is still there today. I met my husband, Herman, at Walter Reed in the PX and a year later we were married in the chapel – me in my WAC uniform and he in his Class As. I soon became pregnant and was given an honorable discharge."

Jean Streeter
Atria Highland Crossing
Ft. Wright, Kentucky

"My husband, Clarence Lindsay, worked at Oak Ridge at the Atomic Plant as a foreman. He was a hard worker. One night while he was at work, he had a severe stroke and never recovered. Because of his poor health he wasn't able to work anymore, so I knew I had to find work.

I went to Oak Ridge and was hired. I made 96 cents per hour. All new workers had to go to a special school for six weeks to learn the job. We were told not to discuss what we did at work with anyone, not even our coworkers. When we arrived at the plant, we changed into a blue uniform. My job involved sitting in front of a large cubicle with a lot of gauges. The gauges measured temperatures and my job was to graph the readings every 30 minutes. To this day, I'm still not exactly sure what it was that I was doing, I just did as I was told.

I worked at the plant for two years until the war was over. I didn't find out what had been going on at Oak Ridge until after the atomic bomb went off at Hiroshima. I felt bad for all the lives that were lost, but I was also glad it was over."

Grace Williams
Atria Cordova
Memphis, Tennessee

Virginia enlisted in the Navy and in 1943, went to Hunter College in New York for boot camp. She worked in personnel with military records. She was moved around a lot in her job, from Los Alamitos NAS to Seattle NAS to the Great Lakes.

Her typical day was like any other work day, filing and more filing. She wore a blue uniform skirt suit during the winter; during the summer, she wore grays. After work, she and her coworkers went to the clubs for fun.

When the war was over, it was not different for Virginia, she just went home and kept working. She took a job at North Island NAS and from there went to DCAS San Diego.

Virginia Dunkle
Atria Buena Vista
Vista, California

Muriel had five brothers in the military, so in 1944 she got permission from both of her parents to enter the Marine Corps. Muriel was in the last big battalion to enter the war shortly before it ended. After boot camp, Muriel considered being a plane dispatcher, but decided she loved driving more and went into motor transportation. She went to a six-week school to learn to drive various vehicles up to two and a half tons.

Muriel was transferred to the El Toro Marine Base in California and first drove a truck delivering laundry to officers' quarters. She then drove a bus of injured Marines from the Marine base to the Corona Navy Hospital.

Muriel said she suffered through aches and pains because she didn't want any demerits that would put her out of commission. One time she and a friend went to the beach to lay out in the sun. With her fair skin, Muriel was severely sun burned and her back was covered in blisters. She recalls driving a group of officers to a site where they wanted to check for water contamination. She was in so much pain, her back couldn't come close to touching the back of her seat. Even one of the medical officers on the bus asked if he could look at her back because he could tell she was really uncomfortable. That was real dedication!

Muriel served a total of 18 months in the services. After she was discharged, she drove an additional six months at El Toro. Muriel is very proud of what she did, but says it is one of those experiences she would not want to have to do again.

Muriel Williamson
Atria Fullerton
Fullerton, California

"I joined the Women's Army Auxiliary Corps (WAAC) in January 1943. I took my basic training at Daytona Beach, Florida. I was there for six weeks and then transferred to Chanute Air Force Base at Chanute Field, Illinois, where I stayed until 1944. I was then sent overseas and stationed at a base near Salisbury, England. After D-Day, I was sent to South Hampton for about two months. From there, I headed for Normandy. What I remember most about Normandy were the bees. I remember going to lunch and being surrounded by them.

From Normandy, I headed to Paris. It was a long ride! We left Normandy early in the morning and arrived in Paris around midnight. We made that trip in an open truck. We were tired and very dirty when we arrived. Some of us had to sleep in the corridor of the hotel. The next day we were assigned to a hotel in Montemartre, where we had a beautiful view of the Sacre Coeur Cathedral.

My first six months in Paris were busy ones. I was with Graves Registration and we had quite a backlog of work. We hired four very bright Parisians and in no time they mastered American typewriters and Army correspondence. It was a unique experience for me, and one I'll always treasure. I would gladly do it again."

Mary Lawson
Atria Golden Creek
Irvine, California

"I worked for the Transportation Unit of the Quartermaster Corps. It was a small unit with half a dozen men. All of us had taken a difficult entrance exam and felt fortunate to be selected. After December 7, 1941, the workload increased tremendously and the Transportation Corps moved to larger quarters. When I went to work at Harborside Terminal in Jersey City in 1942, there was a huge cadre of women hosing down the spent engines. Unfailingly cheerful, they greeted me with bursts of sunny smiles and foreign blessings. They were dressed in what seemed to be their husbands' clothing.

Upstairs, the women were taking off their white gloves and substituting slacks for skirts. There was rationing, but now the mood was willing compliance. Each of the employed women had a husband, son or sweetheart overseas fighting the evil adversary, and they were determined to do their share.

The freight consigned for shipment through the Port of New York was handled well. Every time the phone rang on my desk, I had a new file. A new unit, OS&D (over, short and damaged shipments), was created and I was put in charge. Once there was a shipment of three dozen Chevy chassis that broke loose in the East River. The call came in at 5:30 a.m., 'What can I do?' was the wail. I told the caller, a second lieutenant, there was too much traffic on the East River and that we would send a driver down to rescue the shipment. For all I know, the auto body parts are still down there. Then, there was the shipment of two truckloads of toilet paper heading for Georgia. We never located this shipment – the TP was never claimed."

Adele Fisch
Atria Lynbrook
Lynbrook, New York

Marie enlisted in the Navy and met the man of her dreams, who was an officer. Her husband left for two years to go overseas. Upon his return, Marie still worked in the Navy. Marie and her husband did not notice any hardships other than her husband having to report for duty so far away.

Marie Riley
Atria Collier Park
Beaumont, Texas

"While in nursing school at Memorial Hospital in Houston, I joined the Cadet Nurse Corps training for the Army, which paid a salary while I was going to school. I graduated in 1945 and went directly into the Army Nurse Corps. I served one and a half years and, in 1946, signed up to go overseas. While in training to go overseas, the Japanese surrendered, so I didn't have to go."

Lelia Harding Harris
Atria Willow Park
Tyler, Texas

Chapter 1

The following article was written by Amy Cavalier, a reporter for the Penfield Post Reporter, a Messenger Post Newspaper. It appears here courtesy of the reporter and the publication.

Ruth Patzwald and Helen MacPherson are patriots.

While American men fought overseas in World War II, the women both did their part helping the war effort back home. Patzwald worked at an optical company, Ilex, and then Eastman Kodak Co. making parts for gunsights for the war. MacPherson joined the U. S. Navy's Women's Auxiliary Volunteer Emergency Service, or WAVES, as they were called.

The two women, now residents at Atria Penfield, say they were just doing their part. "The men were at war and the women had to do what they could," Patzwald said. "I needed the work and, of course, it was helping out the war efforts."

MacPherson joined the WAVES after seeing an ad in the newspaper recruiting women to join the service.

"I guess I signed up for the adventure of it," she said. "I have been an adventurer all my life. I wanted to do it for my country. I've always been patriotic."

In signing up for the Navy, MacPherson also helped carry on a family tradition. Someone from every generation of her family has been in the Navy since the family arrived in America in Colonial times. After six weeks of boot camp in the Bronx, MacPherson was sworn in on March 1,1943, in Rochester. For her first year, after intensive training, she was stationed at a Naval air station in Atlanta, Ga. where she was in charge of training pilots how to use a flight simulator called a Link Trainer.

After a year, MacPherson was reassigned as a celestial flight simulator trainer at Quonset Point, R.I. There, she taught pilots how to use the stars to plot their flight course. MacPherson was responsible for putting pilots through a six-month course in less than 10 weeks. "The chief of our department hated the WAVES because we were replacing his fellows," she said. "So as soon as one of us was trained, one of his men was sent overseas."

Overall, though, MacPherson said the WAVES were treated with respect by both the public and the military. MacPherson was discharged when the war ended. She spent a total of two-and-a-half years in the Navy. "I did make a contribution and I was very proud of myself," she said.

Patzwald, along with the many other women who took jobs in factories doing war work, was told that when the war ended she would lose her job in the Kodak factory. Fortunately, she said, the photography giant kept her on. Shortly after the war, Patzwald said she learned how to type and left the factory for secretarial work in the Kodak offices. She was employed with Kodak for a total of 28 years.

Ruth Patzwald
Helen MacPherson
Atria Penfield
Penfield, New York

"I think I represented nearly all the women's roles in World War II. I followed my husband until he went overseas, then went to Portland, Oregon, and worked as a pipe fitter's helper at the Willamette Shipyard. I later joined the Navy and took boot camp at Hunter's College in Brooklyn. I went to storekeeper's school in Milledgeville, Georgia. I reported for duty in Seattle, where I worked for the captain in the port director's office."

Annorah Leach
Atria Willow Park
Tyler, Texas

"In 1942, after the fall of the Philippines to the Japanese and the loss of many of the islands in the Pacific, my father asked me if I might consider helping the war effort by going to work for the Navy. My brother had joined the Air Force and I had just finished two years of college. The Navy was advertising jobs in welding and sheet metal. After thinking it over, I signed up for testing and training. There was a six-week training period that consisted of learning the tools of the trade, the vocabulary and the math involved. About

12 women composed the class, which was taught in Palo Alto, California. Following completion, we were assigned to either welding or sheet metal and placed in our first assignment, which was at Moffit Field Naval Air Base in Mt. View, California. We had to wear coveralls and tie our hair in a bandana so it wouldn't get caught in the drills and other tools.

I became a sheet metal apprentice and worked on the Navy blimps, which were used as aerial surveillance over the waters of the Pacific Ocean. Their mission was to radio the ships at sea if they spotted any submarines.

After achieving the rank of journeyman sheet metal worker and earning $2.35 an hour, I didn't mind being called Rosie the Riveter."

Mary Ellen Sciarini
Atria El Camino Gardens
Carmichael, California

"I worked at the Brooklyn Navy Yard in 1943 as an assistant draftsman working on ship plans. In 1944, I worked at the Army camp at Fort McPherson in Atlanta as art director, making

decorations and teaching a class of soldiers. There were German POWs at the camp. When a truck of prisoners rolled by, everyone stood still and gave them glares of hatred until they passed."

Harriet Eisenberg
Atria Riverdale
Riverdale, New York

"From 1942 until 1947, I worked for the government and was stationed in Atlanta, Washington, D.C. and Cleveland. As a statistical assistant to the agricultural economist, I was reassigned to various locations frequently. I compiled figures for agricultural needs in production for European countries post World War II. Later, I worked for the legal enforcement department of the Office of Price Administration. I was a supervisor for more than 20 employees at that time. We kept records and files of every lawsuit documented."

Sandy Portnoy
Atria Willow Park
Tyler, Texas

During World War II, while her husband served in the Air Force, Lorraine volunteered with the Red Cross in Carrollton, Illinois. Lorraine worked in an office and helped flood victims in the community. In that part of the country, there was a lot of flooding in the river bottom, and the Red Cross collected clothing and food. Lorraine was also responsible for notifying the loved ones of soldiers who had been killed or wounded in war. This was the most difficult part of her job.

"When folks fell on hard times, everyone in the community pulled together," Lorraine said. Women gave up their family duties and sacrificed to keep the country going while the men were drafted and fighting the war. It didn't matter who you were or what you had, the goal was the same: to bring the boys home.

Because of the war and the tight economy, we learned to turn off lights and became much more conservative in our daily living. We learned not to waste anything and to make everything count. There were block police who patrolled the neighborhoods and you couldn't have lights shining from the houses at night because that was a threat and a potential target for the enemy.

Lorraine Jones
Atria Woodstock
Woodstock, Georgia

Amy saw an ad in the paper for Colgate Aircraft in Amityville, New York on Long Island. She applied and was accepted for a position as a welder, but first she had to attend a training program.

Amy worked Monday through Friday, 8 a.m. – 5 p.m. and earned 90 cents an hour. She wore pants, a turban on her head to protect her hair, a heavy-duty apron to protect her from the sparks, goggles, heavy-duty gloves and closed-toe shoes. She shared a room at a boarding house with another girl. The lady who owned the home prepared a brown-bag lunch every day for Amy to take to work as well as a full dinner when she got home!

Welding became too hard on Amy's eyes, so after two years, she left Colgate and became a checker for Harrison Radiator in Lockport, New York. After the war, her boyfriend returned from the Marines and they were soon married.

Amy Augustin
Atria Chandler Villas
Chandler, Arizona

"My husband was drafted during our first year of marriage and it was necessary for me to find employment. I started working at the shipyards where landing ships for tanks (LSTs) were being built. These ships played a big part in World War II because they carried tanks and soldiers to battle.

I worked in the business office of the subcontractors who did the electrical work on the LSTs and it gave me the satisfaction of helping in the war effort on the home-front.

I also had the thrill of watching the launching of each of the LSTs as they left the assembly line for the war-front.

Kit James
Atria Bell Court Gardens
Tuscon, Arizona

Darlene Anderson was 22 years old when she worked at J.I. Case Company in Rockford, Illinois. J.I. Case riveted parts together to be assembled on military airplanes. She worked 3 p.m. – 11 p.m. five days a week for seven months, but then moved to Sioux Falls, South Dakota, to be closer to her husband, who was in the Air Force.

Darlene wore pants and goggles as a uniform, noting that this was the first time the United States said women should wear slacks or pants.

Darlene Anderson
Atria Chandler Villas
Chandler, Arizona

Betty's contribution on the home-front was as a volunteer for the USO. Nearly every night, she took the red car from Venice to Santa Monica to a large upstairs room in a building near the ocean. There she joined other young ladies and danced, played games and served refreshments to the servicemen. Most of the boys were assigned to camouflage the Douglas Aircraft plant. She recalls one time the girls were taken to Catalina Island to visit and dance with the men stationed there who were not allowed off the island.

There were rules when you worked, such as always wear a dress and heels, there was no alcohol and no dating, and you had to have a membership card.

At the USO, you could have a good time without drinking and carousing. It was a fun atmosphere and you felt safe. It was a time when morals and patriotism were very high. Betty was involved with the USO from 1942 through 1944 until the time she started to date her future husband.

Betty received cards and letters from some of the boys up until about 10 years ago.

Betty Brown
Atria Colima
Walnut, California

"Both of my parents worked in the arms plant with other patriotic citizens of Salt Lake City for the entire time the war was going on. Little old me went on attending school as if nothing had happened."

Theresa Shannon Carlson by Donald Carlson, son
Atria Del Sol
Mission Viejo, California

"I suppose it would be correct to say my mother was a 'Rosie' during World War II. When war was declared by President Franklin Roosevelt, it was a very patriotic day in Salt Lake City.

My parents wasted no time severing themselves from employment with the Denver and Rio Grande Railroad and starting a tour of duty at the arms plant located nearby. They both were busy doing something they had never done before – making ammunition for

the war effort. At the time, I didn't know what a bullet was, but I soon became acquainted with them. My parents brought some home to show me, and even went so far as to make miniature bullets for me. These were attached to long, dangling key chains, which were very popular along with the 'Zoot Suit' around that same period of time."

After Wilma completed college in 1938, her first job was in the Nassau County, New York, Department of Social Services, where she worked as a social worker for four years. During the war, Wilma joined the Red Cross as a social worker and worked at the hospital at Camp Kilmer; a first stop for many soldiers returning from overseas.

At the hospital, Wilma's primary duty was to contact family members of the soldiers and inform them if the soldiers were being discharged or transferred to other facilities. As a social worker, she often talked with and tried to help the soldiers in the hospital as much as possible.

After the war, Wilma continued to work as a social worker for the Red Cross for another year or so.

Wilma Day
Atria Briarcliff Manor
Briarcliff Manor, New York

"I worked at Montgomery Ward department store in Fort Worth, Texas while my husband went to Bible Baptist Seminary. He signed up for the draft, but was unable to be enlisted due to migraine headaches. They told him that his migraines would be detrimental because he wouldn't be able to aim his gun. We both were on staff at First Baptist Church in Fort Worth. There was a military facility located nearby and we ministered to many soldiers in need and numerous young people as well. We wanted to do God's will and help all these young people in their time of need!"

Lillian Sudduth
Atria Willow Park
Tyler, Texas

A single woman in her 20s, Esther wanted to see the country, so she took a Greyhound bus from Ohio to Florida. Esther asked the bus driver if he knew somewhere she could get a room. He directed her to a friend's house, where she was welcomed by the couple who lived there. They told her the naval base was hiring factory workers, so she applied for and got a job. Esther was trained as a riveter, working on parts to be used on Navy ships. She trained on the day shift and after that worked the swing shift for three years.

She remembers sailors sometimes coming into the factory and the fun they had telling stories and jokes.

Esther Edmonson
Atria Colima
Walnut, California

Helen worked for the State of New York in the fingerprint identification bureau. She continued working there during the war and took on a volunteer position two days a week. She took a course through the Red Cross and trained as a nurse's aide. She worked at Albany Hospital making beds, emptying bedpans, giving baths and taking vital signs to help the nurses. She was required to wear a white blouse, a navy blue bib apron, a navy blue skirt and a navy blue nurse's cap. She remembers having to purchase this uniform herself and also having to pay for her physical exam for this volunteer position.

There are two memories that stand out in Helen's mind about her experience at the hospital. The first one was a rule that she always had to wash her hands after every patient. The second was an experience that she found a little embarrassing because she was told to go take the rectal temperature of a patient while he had a visitor. Helen did as she was asked – with the visitor present during the procedure!

Helen said her home-front experience gave her an opportunity to meet different people, learn different skills and realize that everybody has some sort of a "cross to bear," regardless of their differences. When the war was over, she left the hospital and returned to doing her regular job.

Helen Fontana
Atria Shaker
Albany, New York

Margaret had numerous jobs during the war. At one position in a Motorola Plant, she started as an inspector and was promoted to group leader. Her duties included making radios and walkie-talkies for the war effort. She worked seven days a week from 5 a.m. - 2 p.m. and earned $400 a month. She was 24 years old, married and had a one-year-old daughter. Her mother-in-law lived in the same building, so she took care of her daughter during work hours. When her husband came home from overseas, Margaret states she had saved a lot of money!

Margaret Busk
Atria Chandler Villas
Chandler, Arizona

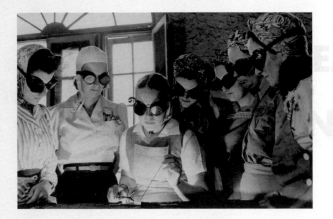

"From 1944 to 1946, I worked for Alcoa Aluminum Corporation. I had a two-year-old daughter to care for, so I went to work making 'Mae West vests' for the sailors.

I walked to work, and a typical day was eight hours long. We all never gave it a second thought. We had a job to do, so we did it. When the war was over, we were all very happy and went our separate ways."

Doris Ormsbee
Atria Bell Court Gardens
Tuscon, Arizona

During World War II, Violet worked at the Nabisco Cracker Factory in Denver. As an assembly-line worker, Violet broke up the crackers and packaged them. She made 50 cents an hour and worked full time at the factory for more than a year. She was 28 years old, married with no children and her husband was in the Air Force. Violet followed her husband wherever he was stationed. At one point, her husband broke his collarbone and Violet visited him in the hospital daily. She ended up being an errand runner for other hospitalized soldiers.

Violet Mullen
Atria Chandler Villas
Chandler, Arizona

In a time when women wore dresses and mostly worked in the home, Rose put on her pants and cap and went to work in the Keystone factory, making aerial cameras for bombers. Rose's main job was to make all the little parts. Once they were built, the two-foot tall cameras came back to Rose for packaging and shipping.

"Sometimes while we worked we sang that Rosie the Riveter song," said Rose, laughing at the memory.

Rose remembers the hardships of getting even the most common necessities, such as shoes, sugar and gasoline. "You had to have a stamp for everything," she recalled. "So I used to get all dressed up and go down on the trolley by myself to the ballrooms. The Marines and Sailors would get off the boats and go to the ballrooms. They would have dance contests, so I would keep my eye out for a young man who could dance. Once I got someone to dance in a contest with me. I reminded him that I got to keep the prize, which was always a stamp for something you couldn't get easily."

Rose Kontoff
Atria Hillcrest
Thousand Oaks, California

From 1942 to 1945, Lela Mae worked at Convair, a large plane factory in San Diego, where she helped assemble B5 military planes. Making 86 cents an hour, Lela Mae drilled holes and bucked rivets. The men put the panels on the side of the plane and Lela Mae and another female coworker assembled them. Lela Mae was the smallest woman and crawled inside the wing of the plane and bucked the rivets. Lela Mae said it was such a tight area that there was barely enough room to move around in. Lela Mae continued working for Convair until the war ended.

After the war was over, Lela Mae continued working on aircraft as an assembler until she retired in October 1974.

Lela Mae Miller
Atria Encinitas
Encinitas, California

"I learned how to use a lathe in Boys High School in Brooklyn when I was 26 years old. The purpose of learning this trade was to send me to Sperry Gyroscope Company in Brooklyn. There I learned how to operate a large engine lathe and an electric drill. I made rotors and various mechanical parts needed for the war effort.

Sperry moved out to Lake Success on Long Island, which was really too far for me to travel, so I went to work in the Navy Yard in Brooklyn. There we repaired binoculars by cleaning out the lenses and giving them new parts wherever needed. Later on, I started to inspect the binoculars. Each ship had a case with the ship's name written on it. When the binoculars were all inspected, they were packed in the case and placed in a closet until the men called for them before the ship left again for another trip.

At the Navy Yard, I worked from 6 p.m. until 4 a.m. There was a carpool because some of the men had cars. They took us to the bus station, trolley car or the Long Island Railroad. Going to work at those hours was terrible.

I appreciated having the work, as it kept my mind busy while my husband was in the Philippine Islands. I also felt that I was helping him and the others by doing this."

Margaret Rogers
Atria Windsor Woods
Hudson, Florida

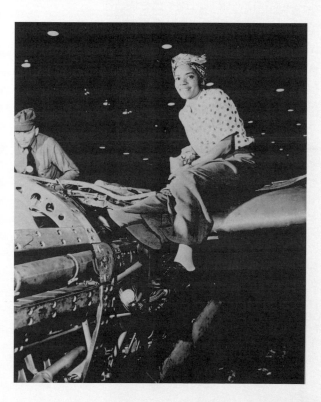

Betty worked for Hammond Aircraft in San Francisco. Hammond Aircraft produced and repaired military aircraft. Her main duties were in the personnel office filing, typing and answering employment questions. She was paid weekly, working six days a week, 48 hours per week. Her husband flew on sea planes as a radio/radar controller and helped rescue downed aircraft in the Pacific.
Right after the war, Betty remembers everyone in the streets of San Francisco celebrating. Betty and her husband then moved back to Los Angeles and Betty soon became pregnant with their first baby.

Betty Lewis
Atria Chandler Villas
Chandler, Arizona

During the war, Eva had many jobs. Her first was working for Morgan Knight, a company that made carbon brushes for planes and war equipment. Eva worked in the personnel department and helped sell war bonds. It was

there that she met her husband, Christopher. Eva helped the armed forces when they came to New York, making phone calls, writing letters, providing a listening ear and feeding many soldiers their favorite meal–hot dogs and soda.

Today, Eva values the influence that her experience had on her life. It has shaped Eva as a woman of knowledge and power.

Eva Passmore
Atria Lynbrook
Lynbrook, New York

"I worked in the Navy Yard in Portsmouth, New Hampshire, as a welder. When workers were hard to find, I went and asked if there was some way for me to help.

There were a lot of other women workers, and the leading man was young, but very appreciative of all we did. I did not have to wear a uniform, but had to supply my own

heavy clothing, gloves and helmet. A typical day was to rise early and walk to work. The best part of my job was admiring my work when it was all done.

We were all happy the war was over, but sad for the ones who did not see their loved ones return home."

Mary Stewart Welch
Atria Bell Court Gardens
Tucson, Arizona

"World War II was a very difficult time for my family. My husband was sent to New Guinea for three years. His family owned a country store, which is where I worked during the war. I worked for $75 per month. I lived with his father and mother. My husband's father passed away while he was gone, so his sister and I ran the country store until he returned."

Agnes Oates
Atria Cordova
Memphis, Tennessee

Among the unsung heroes of World War II was my mother, Antoinette Buchner. At the beginning of the war, she took classes at the American Red Cross and became a full-time volunteer who helped with the preparation of bandages and other Red Cross supplies.

My mother had five children—four sons and a daughter. Three of her sons were in the military service. At the beginning of the war, two of them were sent to the Pacific. As the war continued, the third one was sent too. My mother continued to work for the Red Cross, giving her time to those who needed help. She found a way to distract her mind from worrying about her sons. When her fourth son was drafted and sent to the Pacific, my mother got sick and had to stop her volunteer job for the Red Cross."

Norma McCrellis
Atria Daly City
Daly City, California

During the war, I worked for Western Electric and AT&T in Kearny, New Jersey as a blueprint inspector. My duties were to check the blueprints for legibility and corrections. After I reviewed them, the blueprints were counted and sent out. I also worked as a replacement layout operator for vacationing operators and assisted my boss in various clerical duties.

Peggy Peters
Atria Cranford
Cranford, New Jersey

Agnes Caviezel, my mother-in-law, was a remarkable woman. During World War II, she was 55 years old and yet she was working and holding down a job that needed full concentration and sharpness of vision. She was a supervisor at Fabner Bearing Company in New Britain, Connecticut. This company manufactured bearings that were used in airplanes.

I remember once there was a strike at Fabner. My mother-in-law left the company for a time to be with her ailing mother. When the strike was over, the company called Agnes and offered her the same position she had when she left. She must have been really good at what she did for the company to rehire her!

During the war, some items that we needed were rationed. Agnes would stand in line for hours during the day to get everything we needed. She would come home loaded with chocolates for her grandchildren, milk, coffee, sugar and every item that was difficult to get. Then, she would work her shift, which was 3 p.m. - 11 p.m. Agnes' job was good for her because when she started working, she transformed from being dowdy to a blossoming woman. I believe that she contributed a lot to the welfare of her country by being a part of the work force at a time when our country was at war.

Dorothy Caviezel
Atria Daly City
Daly City, California

"My wife, Dorothy Eva Conner, was a civil service employee and worked in San Francisco, for the government.

Dorothy was a hard worker. She had to wake up early because she took public transportation to work. Wartime was a difficult period for almost everyone, Dorothy included. Gasoline and food was rationed. During her days off, she had to fall in line to get the things she needed. Despite all the hard times, Dorothy's account of her wartime experience was relatively pleasant. In all the stories she told me about the war, she never complained about doing without or being deprived of the things she needed."

Wayne Conner
Atria Daly City
Daly City, California

I grew up in Santa Monica, California, graduated from high school and went to business college. Then the war came and my father had to close his plumbing business of 10 years because there were no materials. He went to work for the government and my family moved to Richmond, Virginia. We lived in a motel until we found a house to rent. There was a large victory garden on the lot next door. It was beautiful!

I went to work in the shipyard in the materials control office as a clerk of 40 people. We handled hundreds of items I'm sure Rosie the Riveter would use. I was soon given the job of secretary to the head of the department because of my typing and shorthand skills.

I felt I wanted to do more, so I went to San Francisco and passed all my written and physical tests for the Navy WAVES. I was 19, and I had to wait three months until I was 20 and had my mother's consent before I could join.

My boyfriend from school came in at Valley on the submarine Tautog and we were married 10 days later in Reno, Nevada. He asked me not to go into the WAVES, so I didn't report in. I wrote a letter saying I was sorry and I went on working at the shipyard with all the Rosies."

Barbara Frenkel
Atria Hillsdale
San Mateo, California

My husband was a Merchant Marine overseas during World War II. I was employed at the post office in San Francisco, when the war broke out. I was a mail-sorting clerk assigned to the midnight shift.

After my job at the post office, I was hired as a civilian driver for the Navy. I was assigned to Treasure Island. My job was to pick up servicemen from the pier who were being relieved of their overseas duties. I drove jeeps, trucks, buses and cars, depending on what vehicle was assigned to me to drive. How I loved to see the happy faces of the servicemen who were so glad to be able to come home!

Life was difficult for me during the war. I had a very young son who was very sickly. I was working full time. My husband was always away, so I had to be both father and mother to my son.

Josephine Coco
Atria Daly City
Daly City, California

Pregnant and alone, Mary chose to move back to Louisville where she gave birth to her first child. She recalls the difficulty of giving birth and raising a child without her husband. Her work was taking care of her new family while her husband fought for the cause.

Besides her new baby, Mary had the "war widows" to occupy her time. Once a week, these women got together and played bridge. The company was nice, but it couldn't replace the companionship of her husband. So when he returned to California, she packed up and joined her husband once again.

Mary Stahl
Atria St. Matthews
Louisville, Kentucky

Margaret Cooke worked at a defense plant in Brooklyn. She had a very important job as a first piece gear inspector. She inspected the first piece made by a machine with a microscope for perfection. If the piece did not meet the high quality standards, then she would not approve the part. Of course, this would cause production to come to a halt until the part was produced correctly. Margaret enjoyed her job and felt very important. Her supervisor encouraged her and praised her work.

Margaret Cooke
Atria Kingwood
Kingwood, Texas

"During World War II, I worked at Lockheed Aircraft factory, a company that manufactured airplanes. I was secretary to the 'big wig' and made sure that his office had everything it needed. My job consisted of typing, answering the phone, making appointments for my boss, ordering office supplies and making sure that office equipment was in working order. My boss hated unpleasant surprises, so I had to make sure that all of his schedules were accurate.

People always talked about the war in the Pacific and Europe. We were afraid that if the war did not end soon, there would also be bombing in America. I was truly glad that, though life was a little more difficult and we had to tighten our belts, actual combat did not reach us here. Sure, we sent our men to the war but it would have been more difficult had the war escalated and reached our shores.

Dorothy Cox
Atria Daly City
Daly City, California

"I was born in Idaho. My family had about 2,000 acres of wheat lands. During World War II, I worked on the farm just like my mother, brothers and sisters. My job consisted of feeding the animals, saddling the horses and doing other chores my father told me to do.

I know that in urban places, life during the war was very difficult. There were blackouts and food rationing, and some items were difficult to get. Some people felt that they were deprived of things they needed and wanted. That was not the case on our farm in Pocatello, Idaho. We had nearly everything we needed.

My father did not encourage talks about the war. He told us to work the farm, tend the animals and before we know it, the war would be over and everything would be normal again. Time flew by and the war ended just as my father predicted."

Zola Elsenpeter
Atria Daly City
Daly City, California

In 1942, Isabel worked at Douglas Aircraft in Long Beach, California. There she and the other women worked on the assembly line. Isabel earned $1.25 an hour. Isabel also worked at Bellaire Aircraft in Niagara Falls. During World War II, this company made plastic ailerons for airplanes. Isabel learned a lot working there and loved to work on the assembly line because it was much easier to work as a team.

The plastic the company used came in large sheets and then it was melted down to the shape that was needed. Isabel once was employee of the month. She was very thankful she was given the opportunity to work with aircraft and be a part of something really important for our country.

Isabel Oliver
Atria Sunlake
Las Vegas, Nevada.

According to Lorraine, companies were crying for people to work during the war. She was patriotic and unmarried, so she answered an ad and went to work in a bullet factory in Randolph, Massachusetts. Lorraine had to get up at 5:30 a.m. to be on the job at 7 a.m. She worked at a conveyor belt behind a piece of glass and a machine cut the bullets. She worked at this job until she found out that she was allergic to the metal they used to make the bullets and had to quit. She enrolled in nursing school and worked in a hospital until her retirement.

Lorraine Noonan
Atria Woodbriar
Falmouth, Massachusetts

Beverly lived in Junction City, Kansas, a small town that happened to be home to Ft. Riley, one of the largest Army bases in the United States. Beverly was involved in the effort to build and expand the base to accommodate the enlisted men who trained there before

Chapter 1

they were shipped overseas. Beverly, and most of the women she knew who were already working in a bank or an office of some kind, immediately signed on to be the support staff for the military personnel.

Beverly worked for the engineers who designed the expansion of the base. Her duty was to process all of the contracts for the base expansion for the chief of engineering.

Beverly Huffman
Atria Tamalpais Creek
Novato, California

Edna had her hands full providing care for five elderly people during the tough times of World War II. But she somehow found the time to bake cookies every week for more than two years. Edna took the cookies downtown to the center where the soldiers congregated.

Edna Hessler
Atria Heritage
Indianapolis, Indiana

During World War II, Dorothy worked with the USO and the Red Cross. Her duties entailed secretarial work and knitting. Her secretarial work consisted of communicating with soldiers on the front line who needed to come home due to sicknesses or deaths in the family. She also spent a lot of her time knitting sweaters and caps for the soldiers in a factory with 30 women. Sewing and altering uniforms was a big job for her. Dorothy did not think of this as work; it was simply her contribution to the war effort.

Dorothy also worked during World War I as a small child. Dorothy worked with her mother and brother and sold war bonds. Her mother played the piano and Dorothy and her brother sang. The purpose of this was to draw the crowd's attention and sell war bonds.

Dorothy Wyatt
Atria Montego Heights
Walnut Creek, California

During World War II, Muriel was employed at a guayule farm in Indio, California. Guayule is a natural source of rubber.

If the war lasted for a long time, the plan was to make rubber from the plants. She earned 50 cents per hour, which was a good wage at the time. Muriel's husband was in the service and stationed at Thermal Air Base near Indio, California.

The farm provided sleeping quarters, a bathroom, an oil stove and a crude bed with a mattress. Muriel went to work early in the morning and worked until noon. Workers crawled around the field pulling weeds, so they wore long pants, long-sleeved shirts and hats to protect them from the sun.

Muriel's job at the guayule lasted approximately two months, until the time her husband was transferred to a new location.

Muriel Hyer
Atria Kingwood
Houston, Texas

31

"When my brother joined the Army, I quit my job in Dallas and returned home to take his place on the farm. I operated every farm machine my father owned to keep the farm going. America needed food. There were no young men left on the farms, they were all serving on the front lines, manning guns and ships or some other vital job. Many farm-raised young ladies did what they had to do because we were needed so badly and we were at least partially trained."

Maxine Lester
Atria Willow Park
Tyler, Texas

Madeline McCarthy was an inspector at an airplane base. Her husband was drafted into the service, but was denied due to being over age.

Madeline McCarthy
Atria Westchase
Houston, Texas

Rachel Joyner was a "Gray Lady." The Gray Lady organization supported the war in many ways, such as rolling bandages from old white sheets into strips to be used by wounded service men. Rachel also gave blood on a regular basis. Rachel's two young daughters, Sue and Alice, also helped the war effort by picking flowers to be used in pillows by the service men.

Rachel Joyner
Atria Kingwood
Houston, Texas

Ethel Lawrence was born and raised in Indiana, but went to Texas when she married her husband, a rice farmer. Ethel's husband wasn't drafted so that he could stay home and grow the food for a country at war. Ethel and a helper cooked every day for the field workers, and Ethel drove the food out to the workers in a

pickup truck. There were German POWs who worked on their farm and Ethel remembers feeding them just like everyone else.

Ethel remembers many families growing "Victory Gardens," small vegetable gardens they used to supplement the few groceries they could buy.

Ethel Lawrence
Atria Cypresswood
Houston, Texas

"I was in Hawaii during World War II. My husband, Walter, was a certified professional welder working at Pearl Harbor. When Pearl Harbor was bombed, my husband was there. He was at the wrong place at the wrong time. Normally, my husband did not go on duty on weekends, but that weekend he was asked to work Saturday and Sunday. When the attack on Pearl Harbor happened, we thought hell broke loose. We lost electrical power and there was absolutely no communication because phone lines were not working. I was crying for my husband. I was almost sure he was dead. I felt like my heart was in my throat. After three days, my husband came home. I could not believe my eyes – I was ecstatic! My husband was a Pearl Harbor survivor! He told me that many of his coworkers were killed during the bombing.

My daughter, Sybil, was born on June 26, 1942, six months after the attack on Pearl Harbor. During World War II, I had a full-time job as a wife and mother. I took care of a professional welder, who almost lost his life while making sure war ships were seaworthy and battle-ready. My job was not easy. It needed full concentration, attention to details, wholehearted dedication, patience, commitment, loyalty and a willingness to work 24 hours a day with no days off. My job was not just a regular, ordinary job. It was my life.

Olivia Mendonca
Atria Daly City
Daly City, California

During World War II, I worked in Detroit for Packard Motor Car Company, which had started making ambulances for the war. I was a secretary and took shorthand. We used colored ration stamps, red was for meat and blue was for flour and sugar. My uniform was navy blue with gold letters and a hat that resembled an army hat. WWMDC was in gold lettering (Women's Willys Motor Defense Corps). We were in parades wearing our uniforms. Those are good memories!

Beth Rosen
Atria Bayside Landing
Stockton, California

Dorothy worked the swing shift at Plant One for Hammond Aircraft in San Francisco in 1944. She did not want to work in the office when she applied, she wanted to work on the line and did so for two years making tail cones for airplanes. Dorothy did such good work that her story, along with four of her coworkers, was written up in the Hammond Aircraft News.

Dorothy and her friends achieved a level of excellence and earned the Gold "E" in every Hammond department. The "E" objectives were safety, production, conservation, attendance and suggestions.

Dorothy Shrader
Atria Carrollton
Dallas, Texas

"I worked in Corpus Christi, Texas in the ship service store as a clerk. My husband was enlisted in the Navy. We lived in the naval housing facility, where we were able to be together every day. What a blessing!"

Armine Franks
Atria Willow Park
Tyler, Texas

"My wife, Katherine Folbert, was born in America and raised in Paris. When she was in her teens, she returned to America. During World War II, Katherine was in Rochester, New York, working at a private company that made the nose cone for the 20mm navy shell. She was a lathe machine operator.

Like everyone else, Katherine also experienced rationing of food, gasoline and other commodities during the war. After I got back from the war in 1946, we got married."

James Bruce Southard
Atria Daly City
Daly City, California

"I taught home economics at Troup High School during World War II. I had about 100 students daily with one "off" period to make lesson plans, grade papers and shop for supplies. When World War II began, male teachers quickly left schools for active military service. This was the case in our school, except for the superintendent, who was too old to serve. He assigned all female teachers extra classes and duties, and we accepted them graciously. I was assigned a biology class with a lab during my off period.

There was no increase in salary or perks with my new responsibilities, just an increase in studying, course-planning, shopping for lab supplies and paper-grading on the side. I burned the midnight oil for a great cause!

I don't know how much biology those 30 students learned, but I learned a lot!"

Mary White
Atria Copeland
Tyler, Texas

"In 1944, I lived in Des Plaines, Illinois, a town of 9,000 people. At the time, Douglas Aircraft was building a new plant in order to assemble C-54 cargo airplanes. Everyone in town was very eager to work there. In addition to the assembly plant, there were many offices. I got a job in the controller's office. My boss was in charge of analyses and reports. I wore skirts without nylons to work because there weren't any nylons available in those days. All the women who worked at the plant felt like Rosie the Riveter, but I felt like Rosie the Typewriter."

Marguerite Strand
Atria Bayside Landing
Stockton, California

"After high school, I worked as a private secretary for two lawyers. I hated it. I heard of an airplane-parts factory called N.A. Woodworth and I applied for a job – any kind of job. I got a job and was to work on the midnight shift. I worked on the spark-plug line, counting and packing. After about a week, there was an opening in the office, so I started to work there. I kept a nightly record of parts produced and employees working.

The women who worked at Woodworth were mostly wives and mothers. My own mother was a drill-press operator. We all loved being a part of the defense effort. During the day, I helped collect pots and pans to be melted down and produced into armor.

In 1943, I quit N.A. Woodworth and got married. I then became a part of the civil defense team. We canvassed all of the neighborhoods and kept a record of the residents in each home – those who would need assistance, those in wheelchairs and those with small children."

Lillian A. Axelson
Atria Windsor Woods
Hudson, Florida

"I graduated from the Methodist Hospital School of Nursing in Memphis, Tennessee, at the outbreak of World War II. There was a shortage of nurses and our graduating class was told we could volunteer for the service or be drafted. I joined the Army Air Force and was sent to Greensboro, North Carolina, for my basic training. Following my training, I was sent to Keesler Field in Biloxi, Mississippi, and assigned to surgery.

I met my husband in an operating room – Dr. James Williams. We were married in 1944. My husband was sent overseas and was in command of a Medical B.N. 369th Infantry Division. This division was in the Battle of the Bulge.

I remained at Keesler Field until the end of the war."

Wanda Williams
Atria Copeland
Tyler, Texas

Charlene was ready to jump in and make a contribution to the home-front work effort. She went to the offices at the Wright-Patterson Air Force Base in Dayton, Ohio, looking for work almost immediately after the war started. She filled out an application and sent it in, but didn't hear back immediately. One day she marched into the office of the colonel asking about a job and he put her to work right away. Charlene eventually gave the Air Force 15 years of service as a secretary.

Charlene Hufford
Atria Heritage
Indianapolis, Indiana

"I was 20 years old when World War II started. My husband was drafted into the service, so I went to work at Firestone Tire and Rubber Company in Akron, Ohio. I started as a riveter on the Atiron section of an air wing. Over time, I was promoted to supervisor over six rigs. I worked from midnight until 8 a.m. I was able to get my work done by 7:30 a.m.

I didn't have enough ration stamps to get gas enough to take me to and from work, so I used a bike for my transportation. After I got off work at 7:30 a.m., I went downtown to eat breakfast. Then I went to work at Goodrich Tire & Rubber from 8 a.m. until 5 p.m.

I worked on the draft board drawing parts for dicers for air wings. This was a secret program and I was chosen to do the printing of the drawings. I was locked in a room to do the printing and no one could come or go without the supervisor letting us out. There were six large wooden boxes in the room. I was to print a certain number of copies of each drawing in the boxes. Sometimes it took me two or three days to do it. When I finished the copies, I rang for the supervisor. He and I fastened the wooden lids on the boxes, wrapped them with two strings around the boxes, then armored trucks transported the boxes. They were sent to six different parts of the country. This was done in case one box was destroyed. There would be copies elsewhere. I did this until my husband came home and the war was over."

Delma Semenas
Atria Summit Ridge
Reno, Nevada

"As a nurse's aide, I worked in an Army hospital and at a blood bank in Dallas. I was also an air raid warden for Lot 10, Block 10, of University Park in Dallas. I was issued a helmet, gas mask and a pump for extinguishing incendiary bombs! It was a very frightening job."

Lometa Ackley
Atria Willow Park
Tyler, Texas

During World War II, Florence worked for Pratt and Whitney in Kansas City, Missouri, a company that produced airplane parts. Florence met her husband, Glenn, at Pratt and Whitney. They were married in 1944.

Florence Slocum
Atria Kingwood
Houston, Texas

During World War II, Edith and her sister Thelma worked at Ball Crank near Cincinnati in a factory that made ammunition shells for the Navy. The sisters lived together along with her sister's child. For extra money, Edith's sister made purses and hats.

When the war was over and Edith's husband came home, they searched for an apartment. The couple settled on an attic apartment in the same building in which Edith's husband's father lived. At this time, her husband worked for Philip Carey and brought home gauze, used for pipe covering, from which Edith made curtains. After about four years, Edith and her husband were able to buy a home.

Edith's sister Thelma went on to work at Gruen Watch Co., making small parts used for engines, and then at General Electric, where they were working on "something special." The other employees called the room in which Thelma worked on small parts "untouchable." Only high-ranking service men had access to the room.

Edith Schmit
Atria Mallard Cove
Cincinnati, Ohio

"When I was in college at the University of North Dakota, the school closed so that the students could help gather in the potato crop. My roommate's father owned a big farm, so we worked there for 10 days until school opened again. It was hard work, but we earned $60 plus room and board. We also helped save the potato crop from ruining."

Maurine Clopton
Atria Willow Park
Tyler, Texas

Joan's father was the head of civil defense in Iowa. He was in charge of rationing stamps. Joan's mother worked and made things for the Red Cross. Joan learned to knit at age 10 and worked alongside her mother for the Red Cross.

Joan Henke
Atria Carrollton
Dallas, Texas

"I graduated from college in 1939 and taught home economics. I ended up in Holton, Maine doing extension work for the state's agriculture department. At this job, I went out to area farms and held meetings with the women. This was in a rural community, way up near the Canadian border.

There was an airport right on the state line. I remember that servicemen were sent from our area over to fight in Italy. When one group returned, they would bring prisoners of war back with them. Another group would then go back oversees. We had five different POW camps around our area, from Maine to New Hampshire.

After leaving work at the extension service, I went to work at one of the bases as a short-wave radio operator. The POWs who were in the camps had to go out into the woods and cut down trees, chop them in pieces and stack the wood into cords. I kept track of all of the wood being cut in all five POW camps. I reported to an officer every day. If anybody tried to steal any wood, the wires hummed."

Mary B. Pattberg
Atria Windsor Woods
Hudson, Florida

"I lived in Nashville, Tennessee during the war and worked at Castner Knott Company as a secretary and department manager of a clothing store. I also organized U.S. Saving Bonds and was a volunteer at the USO. There, I danced with the soldiers, and many of us cheered the men on when they left to return to duty."

Lillian Arnold
Atria Willow Park
Tyler, Texas

"I went to work for Hammondale Crafts, which made nose cones for fighter planes. We were put on assembly lines to rivet the small parts of the nose cone.

I had the good fortune of meeting two very wonderful gentlemen, Bill and Al. Metal was so hard to get in those days and every piece counted. I taught Bill and Al how to sort rivets according to size, length and width. Bill was blind, but he wanted to work on riveting, so I took him to a separate assembly line and taught him how to put small pieces into the nose cone.

Soon I moved to the electrical department and made electrical harnesses to be posted in the nose cone for the machine gun and camera wires. One necessary component was a toggle box, which had to be assembled. I taught Al how to put them together and we became best friends.

I also remember a certain incident when a load of sheep overturned in front of our plant. It was a hot day and the doors were open. Pretty soon a bunch of sheep came into the plant and ran around everywhere. This was a very unusual event and it made us all laugh."

Mary Gadd
Atria Hillsdale
San Mateo, California

Even though she was only 14 years old, Terry played a major role in her family. Terry and her family lived in North Dakota. She had three older brothers and one older sister. When the war began, Terry's mother had just passed away, her father had a heart attack and two of her brothers left home to fight for their country. This left Terry, her older sister and a brother to manage the farm. At her young age, Terry took charge of the house and farm work.

On a typical day, Terry got up by 6 a.m., fixed breakfast, did household chores and worked out in the fields with her brother. At midday,

Terry returned to the house to fix lunch and to get dinner started. Then, she went out to the fields to work some more. A few hours later, Terry went to the house to finish dinner and any other household chores. By the end of the day, Terry was exhausted.

According to Terry, there were lots of celebrations when the war was finally over. For Terry, it was a relief because it meant her older brothers would be coming home. One brother was missing in action for a time, but was found wounded. Fortunately, he recovered and stayed in the Army for many more years.

During the war, Terry had to work so hard that it made her realize she wanted to be someone in life. She left North Dakota and moved to California. There she attended college, met her husband, got married and had a family of her own.

Terry McKay
Atria Campbell
Campbell, California

Charles and Mazelle fell in love. The war began, and Charles and his friends felt they must do their patriotic duty and enlist in the Army. Soon Charles was stationed in Florida. He wrote Mazelle and asked her to come to Florida and marry him before he shipped out.

Mazelle's parents bought her a black trunk and filled it with wedding gifts, trousseau and other items their daughter might need. Mazelle rode the train from Bowling Green, Kentucky, to Stuart, Florida, and was met at the station by Charles. The couple went directly to be married. It was a simple ceremony in the presence of four men: the chaplain, two male officers and Charles.

Daughter Patricia was born in Stuart and Charles was shipped overseas. Mazelle and her new baby boarded the train and traveled back to Kentucky to live on the farm until the war was over. Those were different times. Mazelle's parents had not yet even met Charles.

Mazelle kept the home fires burning until her husband returned. Charles was the only one of the four men present at the couple's wedding who returned from the war alive.

Mazelle Allen
Atria Westchase
Houston, Texas

"I met my husband, John, one summer at Fair Park in Dallas. Ordinarily, I would not have gone with a man under those circumstances, but I believe we fell in love at first sight. He was in the Air Force and was stationed at Sheppard Field in Wichita Falls, Kansas. I remember he would ride the bus holding onto the pole just to see me if there was not a seat nearby.

I went back to teaching at Big Sandy. On April 8, John and I were married at Brother Adam's house in Dallas. Four days later, John returned to duty. He was soon sent to England to be in the 8th Army Air Corps, 100th Bomb Squadron. On August 17, his plane, a B-17, was hit and he was missing in action until

January. In February, he came home. What a joyous reunion!

We had 36 1/2 happy years together."

Mary Lou Burgeon
Atria Willow Park
Tyler, Texas

"At the age of 16, I worked in New York at a factory that made belts for the soldiers in the Army. My job consisted of punching three holes in the belts. One of my hands ran the machine while the other one held the belt. I pulled the belt through the machine to make the holes in it.

I loved working for the company and was very proud to be doing something to help the men in the service."

Charolette Karlin
Atria Stone Mountain
Stone Mountain, Georgia

"During the war, I taught school, worked in an office and helped with rationing and registration."

Lois Patterson
Atria Willow Park
Tyler, Texas

During World War II, Christina Brenner was raising her family and volunteering for the Red Cross. She mainly worked in the bloodmobile for four to eight hours a day and traveled to various factories and did blood work for the employees. Christina recalls one time when they were at Camp Pendleton, a marine base in Oceanside, California. She said that is the day she saw how weak men were when it came to having blood drawn. She says so many men fainted that she could not believe it.

Christina said that during World War II, women could give blood at the age of 18, but men couldn't give blood until they were 21 or married. She thought that was interesting. A lot of women worked for the Red Cross because everyone wanted to do their part to help during

the war. She was a proud volunteer for the Red Cross for 35 years and said that it was a honor to serve her country and would do it all again if she could!"

Christina Brenner
Atria Sunlake
Las Vegas, Nevada

"I lived in Rockford, Illinois where I worked as a bookkeeper for Beaver Gear Corp., a subcontractor who furnished small radio gears for Collins Radio Company in Cedar Rapids, Iowa, and a prime government contractor.

During those days we worked six days a week and sometimes longer than eight hours for the war effort, as many other people did."

Eleanor Russell
Atria Willow Park
Tyler, Texas

"I was a 28-year-old teacher at the time and, quite by accident, I became involved in war preparation, even though we were not yet at war. I taught school on the south coast of Long Island, which was a very vulnerable spot.

Always being in a hurry in the morning at school, I automatically signed all letters and read them later. One day, I received a letter from the Civil Defense Committee thanking me for volunteering. I asked the principal, 'What's this all about?' She said, 'You signed the letter saying you would like to volunteer.' Because I could not admit to her that I didn't read the letter, all I could say was that I was happy that they would take me.

Soon, I received another letter telling me where to join the group for instruction. For one year, I dutifully went to classes to learn how to be of help in case of war. I learned how to be an air raid warden, including how to help children in case there was a raid during school and how to help the general public protect themselves. The day after the bombing of Pearl Harbor, I received a phone call to appear that evening and give instructions to the general public about who would go to a certain school. We patrolled the streets every night and checked to see that families were following directions. If one speck of light shown on the street, we knocked on the door and asked to have it fixed.

During the week, I continued teaching school. On Saturdays, I went to the rationing quarters in a neighboring town and handed out permits for gas and tires. In my spare time, I wrote letters to soldiers I had met at the USO."

Elizabeth M. Arendt
Atria Windsor Woods
Hudson, Florida

"In 1942, my husband was employed as an agricultural extension agent in Lee County in Geddings, Texas. He was drafted into World War II and I was left with a five-and-a-half-month-old baby son. I was unemployed.

The Prairie View Nursing Department called and asked if I would be interested in working as a Red Cross nurse in the Houston area. I accepted, and in this role I conducted classes on first aid and demonstrated how to make and apply bandages to all parts of the body. I also worked with physicians, nurses, school employees, housewives and even prisoner employees."

Marian G. Westbrook
Atria Willow Park
Tyler, Texas

Ellen worked for the New Mexico State Department of Health in a treatment center where patients often stayed for an extended period of time. She worked five and a half days a week, and states that her pay was excellent. Ellen's position as program director was to get to know all the patients and keep them busy during their stay at the center. Crafts, games, cards, puzzles, books and movies – anything was made available to Ellen to help make the patients' lives more enjoyable. Ellen taught the patients and, in return, she learned a lot, too.

Ellen Buckley
Atria Chandler Villas
Chandler, Arizona

"I worked at the Intercontinental Factory in Garland, Texas. I inspected missiles and made sure that they were in mint condition before they were sent out. If I found any problem or detail that was not perfect, I sent the missile back to be repaired. I also reported and documented the number of hours that each person worked on each missile."

Mona Price
Atria Willow Park
Tyler, Texas

"I was employed by the Clayton- Lambert Manufacturing Company in Greenup, Kentucky. The company produced 40mm shell casings for the Navy. I worked on an annealing furnace heated to 1,600 degrees. This started the process of producing the shell casings. A roller ran through the furnace carrying the round blanks. My job was to place blanks on the roller to carry them through the furnace, which was about 20 feet long. I don't recall how many stages it took to get to the finished casing, but I was always proud that

my partner and I "started the ball rolling" for that 40mm shell casing.

I managed first and second shifts easily, but oh my, when it was my turn to work the third shift it was a different story. I was okay until about 4 a.m., but for the next hour I was an absolute zombie. After that, I always recovered to complete my shift. My coworkers got a lot of laughs at my expense. In those days, we needed a good laugh now and then."

Ernestine Barbiea
Atria Highland Crossing
Ft. Wright, Kentucky

"During the war, my husband and I joined a civil defense group and became air raid wardens. We were issued gas masks and hard hats for our use when we patrolled the streets. Thank God we didn't have a real raid. During the air raid demonstrations, we canvassed the neighborhood watching for lights coming from different homes, as this was supposed to be a complete blackout. We alerted any homeowner with lights on to participate in the blackout.

I was also the block secretary. My job was to write to our boys in service who were members of our block area and send them gifts for their birthdays and holidays. It was not a paying

position, but it was very gratifying to do something. One of my letters was found on the nightstand of a soldier in an English hospital. It just so happened that my family physician, who had volunteered his services, was also a doctor for this patient in England. He wrote me and told me about finding one of my letters. I felt that there was an attachment between this patient, my doctor and myself. Thank God the boy did get home safely. In 1944, my brother-in-law was killed flying over Germany. The plane was shot down. He was killed during the crash and five other crewmembers were taken prisoner. It was a very sad day for the Bauer family when we got a telegram from the War Department. I remember it well."

Violet L. Bauer
Atria Windsor Woods
Hudson, Florida

"During the war, I was the secretary and office manager for Rodgers Engineering Company in Dallas, Texas, a company that sold equipment to air bases. During my spare time, I helped entertain and wait on soldiers during their leave of absence."

Jane Savage
Atria Willow Park
Tyler, Texas

"My husband, John, and I had only been married two weeks when he was called up to active duty. He was here in the United States for at least a year, but he never got home. I traveled after him as often as I could to see him. After our baby was born, I had to go to work. I went to Jack and Heinze, a company that produced airplane parts. Jack and Heinze was known for hiring Army wives, but you had to prove you were one.

I worked from 7 a.m. until 7 p.m., seven days a week. It was alot of work! We were paid $1.05 an hour for eight hours plus four hours of overtime every day. On Saturdays, we got time and a half for 12 hours and on Sundays we got double-time. In total, I made $113.24 a week for 84 hours of work. Back then, that was very good!

When I decided I wanted an easier job, I went to night school, learned how to type and got a job as a clerk typist. My husband was released from the Army three and a half years later. My baby was already 25 months old when his father returned home."

Gertrude Bukovac
Atria Windsor Woods
Hudson, Florida

"I had been married only a short time when I was hired by Goodyear Tire & Rubber Company in St. Mary's, Ohio. There was a good-sized group of women hired at the same time. I was placed in the brass-plating department where tractor blocks were made. Tractor blocks are linked together to make up the tread on military tanks. The blocks were strung on wires and brass plated first so the rubber would adhere to the metal. The metal was then coated with rubber and sent to the steam-press room for bonding. I had the honor of making the first tractor block made at that plant for the Chrysler M3 tank.

I was also responsible for doing the timesheet checks to see how many pieces were being sent to the press room. We were required to make a certain number per hour and I had to make sure the count was correct. Once in a while, some of the girls would pad their timesheets because we were paid by the piece, but not very often."

Donelda Grassley
Atria Eastlake Terrace
Elkhart, Indiana

44

"My husband was at Camp Campbell in Kentucky and the nearest housing we could get was one room in Clarksville, Tennessee. I heard that the Goodrich Rubber Tire Company was not getting orders for tires, so the government took over the building and manufactured gas masks for the military. I needed to do something, and they needed people to assemble the gas masks.

My first day there was a disaster! Turning the rubber pieces over the metal nose pieces was very hard to do. At the end of the day, the supervisor came by to ask me how I was doing. I told him I was fine. But when he saw my bloody fingertips, he said, 'I guess you haven't been doing work like this, have you? Come with me.' He took me over to a conveyor belt and told me that I could be the inspector and that I would inspect the wiring on the gas masks. That was a lot of fun, yet I had to be very careful and make sure all of the wires were properly in place. As workers, we knew that our husbands would probably be wearing these gas masks.

This work was a whole new ballgame for me, as I was used to polished floors and not concrete floors like the ones in the factory. The people were very different. I was used to associating with business people and many of the factory workers came from the mountains of Tennessee. The work was interesting and difficult, yet I enjoyed it.

I stayed with Goodrich until my husband was transferred. In those days, he was transferred very often. I went to South Carolina next and my husband was immediately transferred to flight school in Kansas, where he went into flight training. Wives were not allowed there, so I went back to Connecticut. As soon as my husband earned his flight wings, I followed him wherever he was transferred. He went oversees and I worked as a secretary for the manager in a department store until my husband returned at the end of the war. When the Korean War broke out, being an officer and a pilot, they called my husband to serve again. That's how I became an Army wife."

Agnes E. DuPont
Atria Windsor Woods
Hudson, Florida

"I was 23 years old, just graduated from nursing school and newly married when I got a job as an industrial nurse at Wright Aeronautical Plant at Lockland, Ohio. World War II was in full force. Wright Aeronautical consisted of north and south plants and two foundries where they cast molds for airplane engines. The plant had an assortment of blue and white-collar workers plus a team of midgets whose small-sized bodies fit into places where average-sized bodies could not. I worked 11 p.m. to 7 a.m. and averaged 75 patients a night.

Many women were employed at the plant. I remember they had a lot of skin problems due to the materials and solutions with which they worked. Everyone was working under bad conditions, but we wanted to do our part to win the war."

Marcella Harding
Atria Highland Crossing
Fort Wright, Kentucky

Pauline went to work because she needed the money. It wasn't until much later that she realized what a considerable contribution she made to the war effort.

Pauline worked for a plant called Weir Cook, where she built cells for walkie-talkies and inspected pull cords for parachutes. Pauline learned skills at the plant that would last her entire lifetime, including learning to get along with people, taking orders and following rules. She worked for Weir Cook for three years.

Pauline Hatchett
Atria Heritage
Indianapolis, Indiana

According to Helen Daniels, everyone had to register during the war to see what jobs they could perform. Because most of the young men were off fighting the war, the women had to chip in and do jobs that were considered men's work. She worked in a factory in Danville, Pennsylvania that made bullets.

Every day she reported for work at 6 a.m. and stood at a conveyor belt that rolled bullets that had to be cut. The scrap metal fell under the belt into a pit. Then the bullets rolled on to the next person. The whistle blew at 4 p.m. when it was time to go home.

One day, Helen had an accident and chopped her finger to the first knuckle so that it was hanging off. She was rushed to the hospital, where doctors stitched it back together. Today her finger is a little crooked but works as good as new. Needless to say, she did not go back to the assembly line.

She missed her husband very much and wrote to him daily. The mail was slow back then and Helen didn't hear from him as often as she would have liked.

Helen Daniels
Atria Woodbriar
Falmouth, Massachusetts

In 1940, Gaye attended Santa Monica Junior College. She remembers one day the government came into her class and picked 12 students who had the highest grades to be recruited to learn how to fly planes for a semester. Gaye was one of the chosen students.

Gaye and her husband, Carl Lundgren, had just gotten married before the war and just two days later, he was drafted. While Carl was away, he asked Gaye not to join the service and fly planes because he didn't want to worry about her safety. So Gaye gave up on the idea of flying planes for the service, took care of the home and went to work. She didn't see Carl for five years.

Gaye applied for a job at a shipyard called Western Pipe & Steel. She worked in the office processing insurance claims.

Gaye Cutting
Atria Buena Vista
Vista, California

"Even before the war started, I was working. I was a secretary at Lockheed Aircraft in Burbank, California, where they made planes. After the war broke out, I went back to Salt Lake City, where I was a secretary for a major with the Army Engineer Corps. In 1943, the Army had transferred our whole office to San Francisco. This is where I met the young Lt. Devoe and soon became a bride. Wherever he was sent, I got a job as a secretary.

I had three brothers in the Army Air Corps and a husband in the military and I was very worried about their safety. Every night, my mother and I listened to the radio and we prayed for their safe return. Thank God they all came home safe.

I always admired the Army WACs and the Navy WAVES. These women went into the military at a time when not a lot of women did that, not like today."

Irene Devoe
Atria Sandy
Sandy, Utah

"I worked at General Instrument in Newark, New Jersey, as a solderer for airplanes during World War II. We were told by the company that the assembly line was to be kept a secret. We had to work at a certain speed to keep up with the line.

I worked as a solderer until the war ended in 1944. I lived with my parents and we adjusted to the black market, ration stamps and day-old bread and cakes. It was very difficult to buy sugar, bread, flour, stockings, etc., but we survived, and here I am."

Benita Henetaez
Atria Cranford
Cranford, New Jersey

"One day, as our family rode back from downtown Houston, we passed a large building. Inside the building, approximately 100 women with tool guns in their hands were busily and intently working, and I asked my father what the women were doing. He explained to me that they were in school learning to rivet.

After finishing riveting school, the women were going to Dallas or Ft. Worth to help make bombers using their new riveting skills. Our American soldiers would fly these bombers. The more bombers we produced, the better America's chance of winning the war.

This gave me an excellent idea! I would also help in the war effort and learn to rivet and make bomber planes. All I had to do was convince my father. When I told him what I intended to do, he came unglued at the seams. There was no way his baby girl was going to leave Sugar Land and make bomber planes in Dallas. All I had to do was cry a little . . . that was all it took.

I had a cousin, Elsie, who was a lot older than me, but we were very close. Elsie liked the idea of going to riveting school, too, and in less than two weeks, she and I were in riveting school and Dallas-bound.

Soon the two cousins found jobs and began riveting. In the morning when you picked up your tools, you'd better not forget your badge or your apron. The apron would save you a lot of trips if you filled your pockets full of rivets. The badge was your identification to be issued tools. Your tools consisted of a riveting gun and a heck of a lot of rivets. I would engrave my initials on the inside of the bomber plane's tail in hopes that some good-looking soldier would one day write me a love letter. (Needless to say, I never received a love letter!) The pay was good and we made a lot of friends as well as a lot of bomber planes.

My experience as a riveter has lasted me a lifetime. I wouldn't trade this part of my life for all the tea in China!"

Olivian Horak
Atria Sugar Land
Sugar Land, Texas

Jean played a big role as a home-front worker. She worked at Westinghouse in Fairmont, Virginia, as a plant worker making fluorescent light bulbs when the plant was turned over to make radar tubes for the war. Jean, who was a top-seniority worker, was fortunate to be able to pick her shift.

Jean and two of her best friends, Wilma and Lucille, chose the midnight shift so they could go out to the movies or bowling before work. The work uniforms were pink with a white collar, short sleeves with cuffs and a zipper up the front.

Jean stated that work at the plant was hard and tiring, but people were more patriotic than they showed. When the war ended, Jean's fiancée returned and they were married. She worked in the plant for about two more years.

Jean Johns
Atria Kinghaven
Riverview, Michigan

"I worked as a radio operator during World War II from 1942-1945. My husband was in the Army Air Force and I wanted a position where I could remain at home and not leave my mother, who lived with us and was not very well. I explained my situation to the officer who interviewed me at Camp Evans. He called me a week later and said they needed civilian radio operators. He also said they would train me, so I accepted immediately.

The headquarters where I was trained was only three miles from my home in Belman, New Jersey. I learned code, numbers and how to use military time.

There were 13 radio stations on the WVGL network, and I called each station on the hour and said something like, 'All stations, this is station WVGL operator one zero, signal 57-61-64-over.' I was requesting each station to report if the reception of headquarters was received. The answers were in code. If there were problem, the stations were to call my phone. Duty officers in their cars used the same radios. There were several operators to cover three shifts.

When the war ended, we utilized the radios for transportation of military personal and civilians until the camps closed."

Kathleen Murphy
Atria Richardson
Dallas, Texas

Mary graduated with a degree in physical education and got a job immediately as a basketball coach at a local high school near Columbus, Ohio. Her passion was basketball until she met the love her life, Leonard, who was an Air Force pilot. Mary and Leonard got married and she continued working until Leonard got called away for duty at the beginning of World War II.

Mary traded her coach's uniform and basketball for coveralls, low-heeled shoes and a bandana firmly wrapped around a sassy Page Boy hairstyle. With her husband away at war, Mary went to Curtiss Wright aircraft plant to train for riveting and bench assembly, a job she says was sometimes difficult and challenging to do

but kept her busy while Leonard was away. Mary spent many long hours riveting and making parts for the Hell-Diver Bomber. When the war ended, Mary and Leonard were able to start a family. They have two sons and one daughter. They enjoyed their life together and have many wonderful memories to pass on.

Mary Tone
Atria Buena Vista
Vista, California

"I was working as a secretary when World War II broke out. My husband and my three brothers were in the service. They were in four different parts of the world. I decided I wanted to do my part, so I gave up my job with RCA in Harrison, New Jersey. The company tested me on the riveting machine and gave me a position as a riveter. I lived in Union City and was picked up by the RCA bus at 6 a.m. to be transported to my job.

An epidemic of measles caused me to leave my job. In those days, we had no vaccines and I was told to stay home."

Agnes Kronmeyer
Atria Cranford
Cranford, New Jersey

"I left a job at a shoe factory for a better opportunity working for the government. An ordinance plant in Green River, Illinois, is where I found myself working, along with my sister and mother-in-law, for six months. At first I made ammunition for bazookas. I placed the finished product inside a netted bag and made certain it was tied correctly because when a soldier needed to defend himself, the weapon needed to work. From there I went onto operating a machine that carried bombs.

Times were so hard for us back then, but we still had time to enjoy ourselves. When I worked the night shift, some of us girls stopped and had breakfast at a local diner on our way home. We laughed together and enjoyed ourselves on those mornings."

Alice McConnell
Atria Sandy
Sandy, Utah

While working at the U.S. Rubber Company in Woonsocket, Rhode Island, Loretta worked on the Barrage Balloons and the Ten Men Attack boats. She was the recipient of her share of "E" awards, which was recognition given for extra effort.

Many Barrage Balloons decorated the countryside of England. Those high-flying balloons discouraged the low flying of reckon planes on bombing missions. Ten Men Attack Boats were very useful for night operations. These crafts were easily deflated and then buried while soldiers were on their missions and available for the return trip to waiting submarines or patrol boats.

Loretta Lambert
Atria Stratford
Stratford, Connecticut

"I worked on the payload for the B29 as an aeronautical engineer for Consolidated Aircraft, which later became Conveyor Consolidated Aircraft. I began working in July 1942 for $1.25 an hour. Consolidated Aircraft came to my college and interviewed many girls. Because I had a double major – mathematics and physics – they hired me.

I was 20 years old when I graduated on June 1, 1942. Conveyor paid my way to San Diego. I worked 48 hours a week. I was in the weight division and needed to know the weight of different parts in order for the planes to transport bombs, ammunition, etc. I didn't have to wear a uniform; I wore slacks or business suits. When the war was over, I remember clapping my hands because it meant that my husband wouldn't have to leave anymore. He came home from the South Pacific on August 6, 1945.

I remember when they invaded Europe in 1944. My brother and three cousins were in the army at that time. That day I went to church and prayed for them. My brother and one cousin made it home, but the other two didn't. One was killed in France and the other was killed in Belgium."

Iorice Irey
Atria Bonita
Chula Vista, California

Florence was teaching kindergarten and first grade in a small Connecticut town before her life changed forever with one decision. She longed to go overseas and support the war effort. In 1942 when she announced her resignation to her principal, he said, "If you want to do something for your country, then stay right here."

After applying for the Red Cross, Florence was sent to Washington, D.C., for two months of training. She was given a military driver's license, just in case anything went wrong, and she would be treated as a second lieutenant. She even learned how to drive on the wrong side of the road. The Red Cross was headquartered in London, and Florence was going there to drive trucks! They were called club mobiles then and she eventually followed the troops close to the front line.

At 26, Florence sailed from Boston Harbor on the Queen Mary. Winston Churchill was on the same ship, returning to London after a meeting with President Roosevelt. Soon the Red Cross workers and their vehicles were put on ships and transported to Paris, a safe area at the time. They drove their club mobiles into the field to help the wounded, later following the troops and the war into Germany. The "girls" lived in an old castle in Friedberg, Germany.

Even after the war, Florence remained in the area establishing canteens because the war still had not ended in the Pacific, and the troops stayed just in case they were needed. She also stayed because she had met the man she wanted to marry. He was a military lawyer. After the war in 1946, the couple returned to the U.S., settled in his home state of Arizona and established the first YMCAs in Arizona.

Florence Loshe
Atria Campana del Rio
Tucson, Arizona

In 1942, Verla was only 17 years old. Many of her classmates had gone into the service and her brothers had just joined the Marines. Verla felt she just had to do something for the war effort, so she got a job in Los Angeles, working in the wing division of the B-29 bombers and assisting with the nacelles, which are the bullet-shaped appendages located under the wings.

Verla worked inside the wing because she was petite – only 94 pounds wringing wet! She worked there bucking rivets. One day her partner was not there so they had another guy on the outside of the wing. It was so noisy at the plant that the one who shot the rivets on the outside would signal with a loud rap to let the person on the inside know where the drill was going to drill through. Verla couldn't hear his signal at all, and was afraid to move for fear he'd drill right through her!

There was a midget who worked inside at the other end of the wing, doing the same task as Verla. He saw her crying and climbed out of the wing to find out where her partner was. It turns out he was up at the tool bench "shooting the breeze" with some other guys and had never informed Verla that he was leaving for a break. The big boss came up to him and fired him on the spot!

Verla worked for more than a year inside those wings and also on the nacelles. She made 75 cents an hour, which was pretty good money in those days.

Verla Maroste
Atria Del Rey
Rancho Cucamonga, California

"During World War II, I worked for a government plant in Kankakee, Illinois. Before it was a government plant, it was known as Florence Stove Co., and was converted after the war started. I was in charge of inspecting 20mm shells for the Navy on a gauge, which came on an assembly line. I worked day and night shifts, two weeks on days, which was from 7 a.m. until 3:30 p.m. and two weeks on nights, which was from 3 p.m. until 11 p.m. Depending on how busy we were, at times I worked six days a week.

I can remember a song called 'Goodbye Dear I'll be Back in a Year,' and it reminds me of when my husband went away for the war, except he was gone for four and a half years. When the war ended, my husband was in Europe, and it was a wonderful feeling knowing that the war was finally over and he was finally coming home."

Inez Largen
Atria Summit Ridge
Reno, Nevada

Rose worked at Briggs in Detroit, where she riveted parts and made airplanes. She applied for the job with her girlfriend, who later became her sister-in-law. Rose worked on a press and still today can remember smashing her fingers in the press. Because of the work they did, Rose and the other workers were allowed to wear blue jeans. Approximately 60 percent of Rose's earnings were given to her mother who bought savings bonds as well as items for Rose's hope chest.

Rose Monoco
Atria Kinghaven Manor
Riverview, Michigan

I remember hearing the news about Pearl Harbor from my uncle. I was about 12 years old and I lived in Lexington, Tennessee. I couldn't imagine bombs at my young age. My mother's first cousin taught at the University of Hawaii at Honolulu, so we were all very concerned.

I remember going to the train station, watching all the troops go by and waving to the soldiers. My mother left us for a while to obtain work and I stayed with my grandparents. We listened to the radio and read the newspaper to keep up with the news. We even went to the movies to see a newsreel across the screen about the war.

We could only get so much sugar, gasoline and eggs because these and many other items were rationed. I did volunteer work at the VA hospital. I pushed veterans in their wheelchairs; they seemed to get a kick out of that.

Betty McNatt
Atria Primacy
Memphis, Tennessee

Beatrice passed a civil service test and was told to report to Wright Aeronautical. There she was assigned to the burr bench where she knocked off burrs with a hand grinder. After six months, she was made a lead woman where she supervised workers who were cutting out

gears. Beatrice checked the measurement on each machine to see if it was according to gauge. She worked 4 p.m. to midnight, seven days a week for three and a half years until peace was declared.

Even though every day was the same, Beatrice liked the idea of completing the work with the cooperation of the others workers. She earned $80 per week and bought savings bonds with the money. At this time, her husband earned $42 per week. She created a trust fund at the bank with the bonds she had purchased. She and her husband bought a house and later a farm.

Beatrice McVey
Atria Mallard Cove
Cincinnati, Ohio

Lauretta raised three children while her husband worked in the military with the ammunition department.

She remembers living in an unfinished house due to lack of building materials during the war. Even many years after the war, the family lived in a house where walls and ceilings weren't complete.

After the war, Lauretta's husband moved to the Philippines to work on restoring the country. He was there one year before Lauretta packed up the children and joined him. They remained there for three years before returning to the United States.

Lauretta Myers
Atria St. Matthews
Louisville, Kentucky

"When the war started, I was working in a little rural school as a principal and a teacher. My contribution to the war effort was to quit my principal job and go to Cape McCain to be a post dietitian. I went from one Army post to another. I was in charge of USO social dances for the servicemen as well as food service. I wound up at Samson Naval Training Station at Ithica, New York. I did this for about five years until the war was over.

In 1945, I married a man who served in the war. He didn't like to talk about it, but talked about how lonely he was."

Martha Rannels
Atria Primacy
Memphis, Tennessee

"When the war began in 1941, we were living in Kansas. My husband had registered to be called to serve in the war, but then they changed the age limit and anyone over the age of 26 was not to be called. He took a correspondence course and obtained a position with the USDA.

We then moved to Evansville, Indiana, where my husband became a government meat inspector.

At that time, we had to have stamps to buy beef, but we could get liver, heart, tongue, brains and sweetbreads. There were also stamps for shoes and gasoline. Once a week, we went to A & P grocery store where we were allowed one roll of toilet paper.

During the war, I took care of two boys, ages four and five, as well as a lady with a baby. They lived with us for seven months and I did the laundry for them. When the Welfare Department heard I was a nurse, they asked me if I would take care of babies of young women who were not married and did not want to keep their babies."

Caroline Neywick
Atria Richardson
Dallas, Texas

Before the war, Lorraine was a registered nurse at a hospital in Florida. When the war broke out and her husband was sent to India with the Air Force, she decided to help out at home. Lorraine changed her job and worked as a nurse at the veteran's hopital in Lake City, Florida until her husband came home.

Lorraine Mertins
Atria Encinitas
Encinitas, California

"I was born and raised in the country near Houlka, Mississippi. I was married during the time of World War II and had three boys and one girl. I was about 28 years old. I remember certain things were rationed, such as sugar, flour and coffee. We ate plenty of cornbread. I used sorghum molasses for sugar during those days and canned lots of beans, tomatoes, cucumbers and other vegetables for the family. Our dairy milk was used to make cheese for the boys in the service. People nearly starved to death during that time. These were hard times. We couldn't buy shoes and clothes.

That's when I learned to sew even though cotton material was also hard to get because the government bought cotton to furnish the war effort. We raised chickens and hogs and sold eggs and chickens to make a living. At that time, we sold a pig for 90 cents. Imagine that!"

Laura Norman
Atria Primacy
Memphis, Tennessee

Betty was a Rosie the Riveter on the home front. She worked in a dry cleaning plant in Minnesota where hundreds of uniforms were processed. For 13 hours a day and 85 cents to $1 an hour, there was no time for a social life. Brown outs were abundant, which meant covering all windows to extinguish any light in the event of an air attack. Betty's friends consisted of fellow workers, some of whom she remains in contact with and still enjoys their friendship. During the three years Betty worked at the dry cleaning plant, her husband was overseas with the Army Corps of Engineers. He worked on the China/Burma/India Road

(now called Lido Road), and was unable to come home this length of time. Betty was allotted $50 a month during his absence.

Betty Ready
Atria Maria Del Sol
Santa Maria, California

At the age of 19, Shirley was introduced to carpooling as she reported to her defense job from 1942 to 1943. This was all so new to Shirley, and she was shocked at the size of the buildings and the mass of people as she entered the Alcoa Company in Illinois.

Shirley's first line of duty was to wind wire on a machine. Small wires, big wires and strong wires were hanging, laying and stocked everywhere. Shirley transferred to a milling machine in the same company. Her definition and conclusion of this procedure is, "I did not know what I was milling or why." Alcoa's pay was 50 cents per hour and she worked a 40 hour week.

Shirley also attended night school. Her greatest memory is when Shirley's dear mother met her at the station after her classes each evening at midnight.

Shirley Phelps
Atria Maria Del Sol
Santa Maria, California

"I was living in Salt Lake City, Utah, when the war broke out. Because most of the men were away at war, the factories were hiring women to do jobs the men had been doing. So we went to work in one of the factories. We made something called UE2s. What the military used them for I really don't know, but we made a lot of them. We worked really hard for two months and finally had enough money saved to go back to San Diego."

Barbara Phelps
Atria Sandy
Sandy, Utah

"World War II changed my life. I was a young mother, a wife and a graduate of Linden High School. I had my first apartment in Roselle, New Jersey, which was in a four-family house. With the war getting worse, the men were drafted into service. I was asked to be a neighborhood watcher, so I walked the blocks designated to me.

My husband was called into service, as well as my sister's husband, so I had to give up my apartment and move in with my sister and mother.

With no income from my husband, I decided to go to work and put my daughter Sharon into nursery school. I had no problem finding a job. I went to work as a secretary for an airplane manufacturer. While on my job, I was asked to join the USO as an entertainer because I could sing and dance. I accepted and I entertained at Fort Dix, New Jersey."

Claire Pollakoff
Atria Cranford
Cranford, New Jersey

"When the war broke out I left my job at Saks to do my part for the country. I went to work in a factory making bazooka shells for flame-throwers. I was also a subway bomb shelter volunteer. Because there weren't any bomb shelters, we were to use the subways in case of attack. When the sirens went off warning us of a possible attack, I went to my subway shelter post ready to show the way to a safer place than the streets of Long Island. I remember hearing there were Japanese submarines off the coast of New York.

Six million people died during World War II and it was a very scary time for everyone. For two years, we heard the worst and thought we were going to lose the war. We were all so frightened, but we pulled together and did what we had to do."

Francis Puzio
Atria Sandy
Sandy, Utah

In 1939, when war was declared, the boys in Canada rushed down to enlist in the military and the girls rushed to marry them before they were shipped out. Sally Pyper was 18 years old at the time and was one of the girls to marry. Sally's wedding took place on April 6, 1939. The Canadians with their caring thoughts believed it was proper to have someone at home waiting for their enlisted fellows upon their return. Sally's new husband and some of his friends were deployed to Italy and Germany. He was overseas for six years, with no visits home during this time.

During this period, the factories were turned into war plants. Sally became a turret lathe operator and was employed in one of the plants for five years. Her duties were cutting and drilling holes in Bren (machine) guns where the bullets were lodged. It was a nine-hour-a-day position at 25 cents an hour, six days a week. The long tedious days left her tired and ready only for rest at the end of the day. There was never any definite news about the whereabouts of any of the boys. The media censorship added to the anxiety of those waiting at home.

Upon the return of Sally's mate, they became the parents of four children. They shared stories of his experiences in the Canadian Tank Corps as the driver in a tank and her duties at the war plant on the turret lathe on the assembly line.

Sally Pyper
Atria Maria Del Sol
Santa Maria, California

Pat was only 11 years old when World War II started, but she was able to do her part protecting her hometown of Huntington, West Virginia.

Every city in the country, including Huntington, was required to observe the no-lights policy to protect against air raids. Pat was part of a volunteer group that mounted their war vehicles – a.k.a. bikes – and rode around an eight-block radius to make sure all the blinds were shut in those homes. Pat remembers the group riding out at dusk with a volunteer air raid warden. She doesn't recall feeling frightened about possible air raid attacks; she simply remembers the fun of it. Her mother, however, could be seen on the front porch, eyes plastered to her watch, waiting for Pat to return home.

Pat Jones
Atria St. Matthews
Louisville, Kentucky

Arlene worked as a Red Cross volunteer at hospital in the Bronx, New York. She wrote letters, gave back rubs, planned parties and just about anything else she could do to cheer the soldiers. Arlene said many of the servicemen were very young and often bitter, and it was very important just to sit and talk with them. She even helped them write songs to boost their morale.

According to Arlene, it was very rewarding and wonderful when the soldiers left to go home. Sadly, some never left and she tried with all her might to lift their spirits and do things for them.

Arlene Manaker
Atria East Northport
Long Island, New York

During the war, Margaret's husband and her two brothers went off to the war. When many of the men left the American Can Company, women took over their jobs. Margaret became an inspector of the cans. She was also responsible for keeping the key to the cabinet where the lead was stored. This metal was rationed, so this was an important responsibility. She also said that they used to have to feed aluminum into the punch press to make small parts for airplanes (which they did not do before the war) and she was injured doing this.

At this time, food was rationed and by the time Margaret got off work, the food was gone. She became anemic while she was dealing with the injury to her finger from the punch press. Her physician told her not to work any longer, but she did not want to stop. Instead, she took the office job, which she considered to be "lighter work." She stayed there for 32 years.

Margaret did volunteer work as a member of the Women's Ambulance and Defense Corps. This was an organization of women who were trained by the Army to be able to help evacuate and care for people in case the United States was bombed. Margaret was a lieutenant and a leader in the organization.

Women in the corps went to work every day and then at night and on weekends they met to be trained in ambulance driving, first aid, fixing motors, mess-hall cooking, factory evacuation and many other emergency-type skills.

During their time training for mess-hall cooking, Margaret was one of the leaders because she was used to cooking for 13 in her family.

Margaret Randolph
Atria Del Sol
Mission Viejo, California

"During the World War II years, my husband, Wagner, and our four boys, ranging from age two to 12, lived in Pennsylvania. "Wag" was employed at SKF Ball Bearing Company, a vital defense industry located 12 miles from our home in City Line at the north end of Philadelphia.

Early in the war effort, probably in 1942, our community began to hold twice-a-month meetings where local residents had the opportunity to sign up as volunteers to help protect our neighborhood homes during enemy alerts. The women rolled bandages, and some were designated to patrol the streets over a several-mile area.

My husband worked nights. I volunteered as a neighborhood night patrol, and when the silence was broken by the penetrating and eerie sound of the Civil Defense sirens, my children knew what to do. We knew that unidentified aircraft were headed our way inland. After we had turned off all the lights, gone into our basement and secured our homemade blackout curtains, I locked our home and walked my assigned block to be sure that everyone's home was completely darkened, with no light visible from the outside.

For about three years until the war was over and our neighborhood was safe again, regardless of weather conditions, or how I felt, or what I happened to be doing, when we heard the sirens, I dropped everything and walked our block in pitch-black darkness. I was glad to be able to add my contribution, along with other women across the country, to our national security."

Marie Schorr
Atria Campana del Rio
Tucson, Arizona

Myrtle was born in 1927 on a farm in Plant City, Florida. She had four brothers. At the beginning of World War II, all four of Myrtle's brothers decided to join the Navy. The depression had just ended and the family was still affected by it, and the boys thought joining the service was a way to bring home some money.

While her brothers were off at war, Myrtle was at home doing what she could to help out the family. At age 16, Myrtle had her first job at a canning plant. She stood on the dock and caught the boxes of food. Then she loaded them on the trains that were sent to the troops.

When asked if all four brothers made it home, Myrtle with a wide smile on her face said, "They certainly did."

Myrtle Lia
Atria Golden Creek
Irvine, California

Virginia worked as a stenographer during the war, eventually becoming the executive secretary to General Scillwa of the Joint Chiefs of Staff. She held this prestigious position during the crucial years of 1941 to 1945. She really enjoyed the work because she always got immediate results and she was happy to be able to serve her country during this very difficult period.

Virginia Curtin
Atria Manresa
Annapolis, Maryland

"During World War II, my husband and brother both served in the Navy. We lived in Portsmouth, Virginia, which is a big Navy town. My husband, Dave, was sent to Europe and my brother, Philip, was sent to Panama. It was so hard having two men I loved so much being shipped off to war. I knew I had to do something to help out and to keep busy.

I knew the headmaster of the accounting department of the Naval Yard at Portsmouth, so I asked him what I could do to help. He put me to work in the payroll department. I became friends with some of my coworkers. We liked to go out after work when one of us could borrow a car, but that wasn't too often because of gas rations. I was a college graduate and I was only making $1,260 per year, but I felt that I should do my part to help out.

I lived with my parents during the time that Dave was away. They had a large home and they opened it to other wives of servicemen and didn't ask for a dime. When the war was over, my husband and brother came home. There were parades to celebrate."

Peggy Lou Spence
Atria Cordova
Memphis, Tennessee

Mary worked for Chase Vought during the war. The name has since been changed to Sikorsky Aircraft. The company made fighter planes such as the F4 fighters and aircraft carriers. Mary worked in the experimental department. In her role, she came in contact with generals, admirals, servicemen and pilots. Mary enjoyed working there. Now that she lives at Atria Stratford, Sikorsky Aircraft is directly behind the street from her home – what a coincidence!

Mary Thompson
Atria Stratford
Stratford, Connecticut

"I was a block warden during World War ll. We had to make sure that all blinds were drawn and no light could be seen from any window. It was an eerie feeling to be out on the street alone in complete darkness and quite a relief when we heard the all clear signal and that it was only a drill."

Edna Tripp
**Atria Highland Crossing
Fort Wright, Kentucky**

"I went to work in a hosiery factory in Inverness, Mississippi, shortly after we married. We made silk hosiery. Sometimes I was an inspector; other times I was a hosiery model. When the war started, we began to make parachutes for the military."

Madine Trusty
**Atria Cordova
Memphis, Tennessee**

"When my husband, Bill, entered the service in 1943, I took a leave of absence from teaching so that I could be near him. When he was transferred to Camp Cook, California, I went to Los Angeles. At Hawthorne, California, I worked as Rosie the Riveter at Northrup. The plane I helped make was the Black Widow night fighter. I liked working there because I enjoyed working with my hands, doing mechanical work and reading blueprints.

Bill was then transferred to LaCross, Wisconsin. I got a job sewing netting for army tents. In November of the second year, he was shipped out to Europe, where he served in the Battle of the Bulge. At that time, I went home and back to teaching. Thankfully, Bill returned."

Laura Wood
**Atria Windsor Woods
Hudson, Florida**

Catherine was a secretary in a squadron at a gunnery school in Kingman, Arizona. Her husband, Nick, was in the service and they were stationed there. They lived in government housing on the base.

A friend told her about a job opening. Catherine applied and got a job as a secretary. A major was in charge of the office and there were all uniformed servicemen working with her. In her role, Catherine typed rosters and plans for the military. She was the only civilian there.

She started work at 8 a.m. and worked until 5 p.m. She walked a half mile to the bathroom. For lunch, she went to the GI mess hall. She did not wear a uniform.

"The generation of today wouldn't have the guts to do what we did back then. When the war was over, everyone was relieved. Our lives were put on hold because of the war effort," Catherine said.

Catherine Zakoff
**Atria Woodbriar
Falmouth, Massachusetts**

"My mother, Anna Janowski, was a farmer's wife. We had very large farmlands planted with wheat, barley and oats, and my mother worked on the farm just like the rest of us. Her job was to cook and feed her family and the farmhands. She also did farm chores, such as feeding the animals. My mother was a hard worker. I never heard her complain about the things that she had to do. She was always cheerful, and she was an inspiration to us, her family.

When the war broke out, I continued to do what I had been doing before the war, which was work on the farm. I woke up at 5 a.m. each morning, ate breakfast and I was off to work. We had tractors on the farm.

Life during World War II was not as difficult on our farm in North Dakota as it was in other places. In terms of food, we had everything we needed. While some commodities were rationed on other areas, we had them in large quantities on our farm. We had meat because we butchered our pigs and ate them. We had eggs from our chickens and milk from our cows. Farm work was not easy, but it gave us the things we needed.

During the war, we kept the economy afloat by providing people with food."

Lucile Gowan-Wipf
Atria Daly City
Daly City, California

"As a 16-year-old, I was a riveter and helped build B29s. I got the job by responding to an advertisement. I worked the 3-11 p.m. shift in a bay in a large metal building. I put armor plates around the pilot and copilot instrument panels. I didn't have to wear a uniform, only an identification badge. I want the younger generation to know that jobs would not have been filled during World War II if the women had not come forward."

Jimmie Campbell
Atria Cottage Village
Lubbock, Texas

"I was 18 and I had just graduated from high school. My mother could not afford to send me to college, so I went to the employment office. They sent me to an interview at a place called Midway, which is between St. Paul and Minneapolis. I was on my way there and just happened to see the Northwest Airlines sign on the side of the road. I said I'd try anything (including free travel!), so I pulled in, interviewed and got the job.

I was a secretary and I kept a record of all the planes as they came and went. I saw many troops coming in and going out. Some real interesting folks came through. I even had to interview pilots."

Eve Back
Atria Regency
Mobile, Alabama

Marie lived on and worked a 650-acre farm in Madison, South Dakota, with her husband and little daughter. Their foster son was off fighting in the Army, so they managed the entire farm alone. The farm was subsidized by the government to provide dairy and meat to the servicemen and women.

Marie and her husband worked long hours raising 50 hogs, 200 lambs and 25 steer. The 600 laying hens provided eggs to make dried eggs for the troops. They also raised all the feed for these animals: oats, wheat and corn. They had no running water, so they carried pails to many of the animals from wells on their property. In 1944, the Lindners won the Skelly Award in recognition for the most farm production for the war effort in the area.

Marie taught school before she was married. However in those days, once a woman got married, she could no longer teach. One day the principal from the school called and begged her to return and work as a substitute teacher. Marie said no because of all of the farm work that needed to be done. When Marie spoke to her husband about this, he said, "Marie, he needs a substitute for all of the female teachers who need to say good-bye or spend time with their young servicemen. Just think if that were you and I who needed the time together." She ended up substitute teaching and working the farm.

Marie Lindner
Atria Campana del Rio
Tucson, Arizona

"I worked in Denver at the Dupont Factory, and did several things there. We worked in groups of 10 and changed positions every half-hour. Later, I became a foreman and supervised eight groups. When I started working at the factory, I made 20 cents an hour; when I left I was up to 50 cents.

I went to work using public transportation. I worked 7 a.m. - 5 p.m. or so. I remember a number of things about my job, like using copper spoons for the powder and having Plexiglas between stations so things wouldn't get contaminated.

When I got to the Dupont Factory, I changed into my uniform, which included a cap, clothing and shoes. Once I was dressed, I had to be grounded to get the static electricity out of my body. I couldn't take the uniform home, I had to sign it out and return it at the end of the day. The Dupont Factory did the laundry. I was not allowed to wear nail polish or any type of jewelry. If I did wear jewelry, I had to remove it and put it away in my locker.

At the time the war was over, I was married and living in Washington, D.C. When I heard the news about the war being over, my husband and I ran down D.C.'s main streets, yelled with happiness and hugged people we didn't even know.

Harriet Nixon
Atria Bonita
Chula Vista, California

"I had just finished beauty school when the war broke out. Because there wasn't enough money for women to get their hair done, I went to work at an arms plant where my father and brother worked. I think I made about $1.50 per day and that was good money at the time. We took bullets out of a box and placed them into a belt and then packed the belts in army tins. Some of the girls wrote their names, addresses and phone numbers on a scrap of paper and placed the paper in the tins with hopes of hearing from a soldier.

My mother took care of my daughter while I worked. I told myself that as long as my baby didn't cry for me, I would work; but when she started crying for me, I would quit."

Kate Cook
Atria Sandy
Sandy, Utah

Diane worked in the Brooklyn Navy Yard during the time that her boyfriend served in the Navy. She felt the need to do her part to help our boys overseas. Diane took part in an assembly line that made Navy uniforms. Pants and shirts came to her on the line and she finished them by clipping off threads on the cuffs. From there, the uniforms were sent to the pressers, boxed and sent out to the servicemen. Every once in while, a few officers came in and modeled the 'stunning' uniforms for the ladies. According to Diane, "There's nothing like a man in uniform!"

Diane watched battleships coming and going in and out of New York Harbor from her window at the plant. It was a very exciting time. People were very enthusiastic and patriotism was at a high.

Diane Schlien
Atria East Northport
Long Island, New York

For your country's sake today—
For your own sake tomorrow

GO TO THE NEAREST RECRUITING STATION
OF THE ARMED SERVICE OF YOUR CHOICE

63

Everyday Life During World War II

Chapter 2

Rations, blackouts, war bonds, victory gardens, little money, cramped housing and the fear of losing a loved one to the war were part of everyday life for people on the home front. Long lines, meatless meals and the inability to buy a new appliance, let alone a pair of nylons, during the early 1940s didn't weaken the resolve of home-front women and men. Even though The Great Depression was still fresh in the minds of Americans, the inconveniences of having limited access to shoes, sugar and gas became part of normal life. People did without . . . and they survived.

"When World War II began in 1941, I was pregnant with my daughter. I wanted to continue to work, but I had to stop when the war broke out. I opted to stay home and be a full-time wife and mother. During those days, there were not enough people who wanted to work in other people's homes in San Francisco, where we resided. Even if there were people willing to baby sit for my kids, I didn't dare leave them with strangers at a time of war. I was very insecure and wary.

My husband worked as a merchant marine. Merchant marines supplied ships and crews to those who needed them. The war brought food rationing, blackouts and air raid sirens all the time. I remember the scariest time in my life. One day at around 8 p.m., I was coming home from grocery shopping and all of a sudden it was pitch black. I was on the street walking, and suddenly I could not see where I was going. You could not imagine how dark it was when there was not a glow of light from anywhere. The moon was not up and it was completely

black around me. I was shaking with fright when a strong light came upon my face hurting my eyes. Someone was shining a flashlight straight in my face. I shouted, 'Who are you? Why are you doing this?' He said, 'I'm sorry, don't be afraid, I am the block commander, I'm here to help you. Where do you reside? I will take you home.' Still shaking, I walked with the man until we reached my doorstep and my husband opened the door for me.

The wartime era was difficult for everyone, but I believe people were more helpful to one another during that time. What I did not like about what happened during the war, which was political, was the rounding up of all Japanese people here in America and putting them in concentration camps. Even American-born Japanese who did not know any other country except America were interned. I believe that was bad judgment."

Violet Rosenstock
Atria Daly City
Daly City, California

"I was 16 and it was my first job. Several girlfriends and I decided we'd apply for work at the German prisoner of war camp about 40 miles outside of Florence, Arizona. One got a job working in the laundry and one in the motor pool. Since I had secretarial training in high school, I was hired to work as secretary to Col. Ryan, commanding officer of the base. Several privates worked with us.

Some German prisoners were sent to Coolidge to help with farming, while others helped the civilian employees on our base. They were in their 30s and 40s (the youngest men were held at Litchfield Park in Phoenix, Arizona) and had to be well-proven before being allowed to work. They worked in the offices, in the fields and at the base hospital doing cleanup, laundry and other housekeeping duties. Because we ate in the officer's mess hall at the hospital, we saw them as servers, cooks, etc.

"The prisoners were well-behaved for the most part and we never had a bit of trouble. They were treated very well, and for some of them, life on the base was better than their life had been in their own country. I loved to hear the men march down the inner streets of the complex, singing German songs in beautiful harmony. Because I was so young, they treated me as if I was their little sister. I thought it was rather sweet that one of the men said I reminded him of his daughter; he always greeted me with Guten Morgan! and Auf Wiedersehen!

I served at Florence about two and a half years until the camp deactivated. I was the very last female to be employed there, gathering all the records and files and sending them away for storage.

After the camp closed, I transferred to Williams Air Force Base near Phoenix. By now I was 18 and living on base at a converted office barracks about the length of a football field from the office. I had a room by myself with MPs patrolling all night outside. Because I had the top secretarial job at the POW camp, a similar job was created for me as the first secretary in jet training. It was a varied job, working 9 a.m. to 5 p.m. for the commanding officer of the base. The only other girl in the office building worked in the legal department for the provost marshal.

One of my assignments was to keep a record of each jet pilot's flight hours. Our office was right on the very edge of the field where the planes landed. About once an hour, students who had just completed their training with an instructor came in for a solo landing in a one-seater. With only about five or six feet between our office and the plane, we often saw the planes of student pilots skidding on their bellies with the nose of the planes starting a curve straight toward the glass that separated us from the runway. We had to cover our ears to protect us from the roar. And yes, I witnessed some terrible disasters.

One plane skidded on the runway while landing and burst into flames, killing the pilot. I panicked and started running for my room at the barracks. One of the officers came after me and brought me back in tears. He told me, 'You have to expect this. It's a fact of life when you work with planes.' He brought me something to drink and the rest of the men came and comforted me. After that they let me take the rest of the day off. But none of us ever got used to it. I worked at that job nearly two years until the base closed at the end of the war, again helping to close all the files and ship them to their permanent destinations.

Meanwhile, a romance had blossomed with one of the pilots at Williams, and we were planning to be married. Those plans were interrupted when he was sent to Okinawa. After the base closed, I found a job in my hometown. But love found a way and we were married by proxy and reunited shortly thereafter when he was transferred to South Carolina."

Sylvia McMullen
Atria Campana del Rio
Tucson, Arizona

When World War II erupted, I did not yet live in the United States. I lived in the Philippines with my husband who worked at a large American firm there. My husband was at work when the bombs were dropped in Manila. I remember there was fear, confusion and panic all around us. My husband ran home from his office, which was more than three miles from our home in Lepanto, Manila. He said that everyone scrambled out of the building. They ran all directions as fast as they could.

During the war, I had three young sons, the eldest was seven years old, and I was a dressmaker. When the Japanese took control of the government, some Japanese Imperial Army officials lived in the residential areas. They mingled with the Filipino people in order to monitor their activities. They wanted to make sure there were no Americans around them and that the Filipinos were not hiding draftees to the U.S. Army.

We had a neighbor who was a Japanese Imperial Army officer. This officer was not like the other soldiers who were cruel. He was mild in manner and more respectful of the civilians. One day, he came to the house with a big white bed sheet. He wanted me to make him some boxer shorts and asked how many boxer shorts could be made out of the sheet and I told him two pair. I think he was a little stupid because I could actually make six or seven boxer shorts out of the big bed sheet. But I thought if he believed me, then he either had very poor calculations or he was dumb as a bell.

I said earlier that most Japanese soldiers were cruel. They were in the habit of hurting civilians who were not doing or displaying any aggressive behavior toward them. I remember an incident that happened to my seven-year-old son. He was playing outside the house when a Japanese soldier suddenly materialized from nowhere. He stood right there where my son was playing. The soldier suddenly slapped my son on the face accusing him of being on the soldier's path, blocking his way. Extremely terrified, my son ran home crying. My husband and I were fuming mad, having seen the red streak of finger marks on our son's face. What could we do in a situation like that? We took a deep breath and hoped nothing like that incident ever happened again.

When General Douglas MacArthur finally came to drive the Japanese forces away, the whole Filipino nation rejoiced."

Rosario Aldeguer
Atria Daly City
Daly City, California

"During World War II, all military personnel being shipped from one coast of our country to another passed through the north-central prairie land of Nebraska on the Union Pacific Railroad line.

Soldiers on their cross-country trek, whether headed for service in Europe or in the South Pacific, all knew about an important stop their train would make at the town of North Platte. The train would stop ten minutes for refueling, and all but the wounded would rush off to be greeted by women serving food and encouragement from the platform of a depot-turned-canteen. There would be coffee, sandwiches, cookies, candy and even birthday cakes for the men, as well as the warmest of welcomes, expressions of pride and hope and thankfulness, motherly hugs, and often a quick exchange of addresses with some of the very young and homesick. Occasionally a soldier would discover a piano there on the platform and would sit down to give a brief impromptu concert.

From Christmas Day, 1941, when the canteen opened, until the end of World War II, 3,000 to 5,000 men a day were served (even as many as 8,000 toward the end of the war). In all, more than 6 million were served. It was open every day from 5 a.m. until the last troop train departed at midnight and there could be as many as 28 trains in one day. Volunteers from different towns and the outlying farms took turns serving on assigned days, sometimes staying up all night cooking and baking.

For the sake of efficiency, anyone under 16 was not supposed to work at the canteen, but a few of us who were younger were allowed to watch with awe from the sidelines. Seeing the men tumble from the train for a taste of home cooking and to be cheered on their way remains a single lump-in-your-throat snapshot of history still vivid to me today."

Maurine Kish
Atria Campana del Rio
Tucson, Arizona

"My story is probably different from most. As a Jewish family, we survived the war living as Catholics in the so-called unoccupied zone of France. In reality Vichy, France, had been occupied since November 1942. Still, it was in Auvergne that we were freed by French forces when the Germans were hastily evacuating and the organized Underground came out in the open.

In September 1944 right after Paris was liberated, my family left the small village we had spent the war years in and decided to return to our roots. We tried to make a new and more normal temporary life for ourselves. We took the train to Paris and my parents, brother and I settled down in a small room that was located in some Parisian backyard. My parents decided that we would await the end of the war in Paris, so this room became our new home.

I was 18 years old at the time and was born and schooled in Belgium. English had been part of our school curriculum and I spoke it haltingly. Still the French employment office recommended that I apply for an English-speaking job. I had some secretarial skills, even though as Jewish children in Belgium, we had been forbidden to go to school and I mostly had instructed myself during the war years.

I got a job at Depot O-644 in Paris, where I did office work. The depot was an ordnance depot and contained all kinds of motorized vehicles, machinery, weapons and spare parts for everything imaginable. In addition to the American GIs, there were many French civilians working at the depot. There also were several hundred German prisoners with POW stenciled in big white letters on the back of their American fatigues loading and unloading the supplies under the strict supervision of armed soldiers. The depot consisted of an entire American Regiment and with all the French workers and the POW compound it was a small city covering many acres.

From the depot, materials and parts were distributed every day to the advancing armed forces. As a civilian employee working for the military, I was proud and happy to be part of it all.

The department where I worked consisted of one lieutenant and several sergeants. The informality with which everything was handled was a real surprise and novelty to someone like me, who had been brought up to believe in military class distinction. The lieutenant and the sergeants laughed and joked together, and if a sergeant thought the lieutenant was handling something the wrong way, he told him. Because of this I witnessed many arguments in our office. This kind of informality, where officers turned their heads to have to salute enlisted personnel and where they spoke to each other on an even keel, was a great eye-opener.

I was in Paris during V-E Day; a day that will forever remain sculptured in my heart. I continued to work at the Depot until our departure for the United States in February 1946."

Lea Berliner
Atria Kew Gardens
Kew Gardens, New York

Kay Orsini took to the General Electric assembly line as her contribution to the war effort. As the men left for combat, supervisors were needed at G. E., and Kay applied. Hired to inspect motors and generators, Kay became an expert in a field she never dreamed she'd be a part of.

Dressed in coveralls, her day consisted of checking the parts and workings of the machines. These machines were not only important to the population in general, but they were also vital to the overseas troops. Kay hoped her experiences during the war would help to bring troops home safely.

When her own dear husband returned home, he was never quite the same, having survived the Death March of Bataan. His health was forever compromised. When fellow soldiers fell by the wayside, Kay's husband stopped and picked them up in an effort to help them survive. For this, he suffered continual beatings at the hands of his captors. As a consequence of his bravery, Kay was left a widow much sooner than she might otherwise have been.

Kay Orsini
Atria Crossgate
Albany, New York

While her husband was in the Army during World War II, Eleanor applied for a job at Camp Anza prison camp in Riverside. She originally applied for a job as a driver in the convoy, but was too short for the position. Instead, she was put on an Army Jeep and given the job of chauffeuring the captain and other officers around the camp to meetings and appointments. Her day consisted of driving, waiting and delivering mail. She liked it and it was easy. Luckily, she didn't have to wear a uniform.

Eleanor recalls that there were many Italian POWs in the camp. She said they were very polite and friendly in spite of their situation. Eleanor was under strict orders not to engage in conversations of any kind while working around the POWs. It was hard to be surrounded by so many Italian prisoners and not be able to talk to them.

Some women who made friends with the prisoners in their own way eventually went to Italy and got married after the men were released from prison camp. When the war was over, Eleanor went back to life as usual.

Eleanor Ramirez
Atria Buena Vista
Vista, California

"Instead, she was put on an Army Jeep and given the job of chauffeuring the captain and other officers around the camp…"

In this section are stories from Atria residents who shared memories about their work and/or detention experience in internment camps during World War II. Internment camps were detention camps that held people of many different origins who were believed to be a threat to America during World War II. These camps were often called concentration camps and the majority of the people detained in them were Japanese-American. There were 10 internment camps in the United States in operation from early 1942 until 1946. They were located primarily in the western U.S.

"I was in Amache, a camp of 8,000 evacuees located in the eastern part of Colorado. The nearest town was Granada near the Kansas border. The area was desolate, arid and the soil was very sandy.

High wire fences enclosed appointed personnel and evacuees with barbed wire on top. Armed guards were posted at the corners of the enclosure. A pass was needed by every individual to leave and enter the camp with information-destinations, business, time of leaving and returning with a guard's signature.

I was asked to replace a teacher who was drafted. I was a teacher, certified with experience and could fill the position, but I also had a four-year-old daughter and a five-month-old baby girl. This proved to be no problem as I soon had a Japanese woman become our nanny, housekeeper and sometimes cook. She did not speak English and I could not understand or speak Japanese.

I was to teach 7th graders social science and U.S. history. In my class, I had the daughter of the Japanese nanny, who was able to be a go-between. She carried my wishes in writing to her mother, which she memorized and faithfully did the following day. My older daughter was delighted with her nanny, and called her "Totsy," as she couldn't say her Japanese name.

My four-year-old daughter went to kindergarten. Her teacher was a young Japanese woman who spoke excellent English. Four pupils were Anglo and the rest were Japanese in a class of 25 pupils. My daughter had only one complaint – she was blonde and the Japanese children couldn't keep their hands off her hair.

After the school terminated, I was given a secretarial position in the property department. We took care of the Japanese who were relocating to the Midwest and eastern states of the U.S. Our records were important to their destination, business, address, baggage, express and freight. Problems often arose from delays in the shipping and receiving of their belongings. The elderly did not want to leave the security of the camp. We received many letters saying they had not received their belongings. They were in need of most of their possessions as they were in colder areas than the camp. I remember one letter from a troubled Japanese man – "I do not get my brankets (blankets). I freeze, go dead."

My husband, Chuck, was the music director of band, orchestra and choir. The musical groups performed in concerts and parades, as well as at funerals for the bodies of returning soldiers.

Later, Chuck supervised a group of German prisoners as the camp was closing. They were brought into the camp to work in clearing and cleaning up the grounds and barracks. Then, he was later transferred to Fresno, California, to help the Japanese claim their property that was stored by the U.S. Army. He retired from the property department.

My family had a part in the war effort, and we were proud to be of service."

Doris Hinman
Atria Vista Del Rio
Albuquerque, New Mexico

"I lived in Lovell, Wyoming and my contribution to the war was something totally different than the rest of the country. We had Japanese internment camps in the area, and I went to these camps to entertain. Unlike the rest of the country, the Japanese people were able to leave the camp daily for visits to their banks, see a doctor or do daily errands. In the evenings, they returned and that is when I, and others, went into the internment camp and entertained them with singing and playing piano."

Gwenn Manning
Atria Sandy
Sandy, Utah

Marie was born in Vacaville, California, to parents who were citizens of Japan. From 1942 to 1945, she lived in an internment camp in Arizona, along with her six siblings. Marie has very little memory of those years.

Marie was born blind. At age seven, she lived at a school for the blind in Berkeley, California. It was from there that she was taken to the internment camp.

About eight years ago, Marie visited a military ship in Oakland's naval harbor. Collecting t-shirts has been her hobby. In the gift shop was a Rosie the Riveter t-shirt. The clerk explained who Rosie was, and Marie purchased the shirt. She had not thought about it again until the Rosie the Riveter project was brought to the attention of Atria residents.

Marie is now a retired teacher. She feels she contributed to the "Rosie" story by buying the t-shirt and being a good little resident in the internment camp during the war.

Marie Hatanaka
Atria El Camino Gardens
Carmichael, California

"All my life I have felt it wasn't fair that my father had been treated like he was just because he was Japanese. He was a very educated man and wanted to become an American citizen. My father had been taught English by a tutor from London.

I had just started going to the University of Hawaii when Pearl Harbor was bombed. The university closed and they took my father away. My father was quarantined (as they called it) for five-and-a-half years. We did not know where he was during that time.

I went back home to help my mother with my seven siblings. I was able to get a part-time job teaching English and Japanese. My father had taught my mother how to be self-sufficient and during the time he was gone those teachings came in handy."

Elsie Prosser (Aiko Hisatake)
Atria Sandy
Sandy, Utah

Born in San Bernardino, California, Florence and her husband owned a flower shop and had a daughter named Mildred in 1938. In April 1943, they were all taken to Arcadia Racetrack in California. They were put into horse stalls, where they slept on straw mattresses and cots.

In August of the same year, they were moved to a camp in Arizona. There were three different camps that were 10 miles apart. Florence's family was placed in Camp #3. According to Florence, they were given $16 a month. If she wanted to buy anything it had to be purchased through Sears Roebuck.

At the camp, there were men with machine guns watching in case someone tried to run away. The food was served at the cafeteria at assigned times. If they wanted to, prisoners

could work at the cafeteria. Schoolteachers had jobs at the camp, educating the children. The camp had toilets and a community shower stall with no sections. After many complaints, they decided to section them.

In September, Florence's husband and a few other men went sugar-beet-topping in Colorado. Florence was left with her daughter. After a couple of months, her husband sent for her.

When the war was over, Florence recalls having to start all over again, because everything was taken from them. Her husband started truck farming.

Florence Yamashita
Atria Bonita
Chula Vista, California

During World War II, I was living on the Island of Java, in the Dutch East Indies. Just before the war, I worked at the National Library in Surabaya. During the war, we all were taken as prisoners. I was taken prisoner because of being Dutch and because of where we were

living. We were able to pack only one suitcase and then trucks took us to our camp, which was ruled by the Japanese Army. When we met a Japanese soldier in camp, we had to bow to him and tell him in what portion of the camp we lived.

The Japanese did not tell us the war was over until September 1945, when the English rescued us from the camp. I do not have any photographs of my life prior to when I was taken to the Japanese prison camp. The soldiers took our pictures out of our suitcase, put them in a stack and burned them.

Johanna Garretson
Atria Rancho Park
San Dimas, California

> "At the camp, there were men with machine guns..."

> "When we met a Japanese soldier in camp, we had to bow to him..."

Margaret was attending school to learn machine-shop skills. In 1942 or 1943, Consolidated Vultee Aircraft contacted her school to locate candidates to work in its factory. Margaret was recommended and soon she, her husband and father were all working on the assembly line building B-24 bombers. Although the pay was less than $1 per hour, she worked the night shift because it paid an additional 5 cents per hour.

"I remember the women made just as much as the men," she remarked.

Margaret's job was working on a lathe creating bomb-release mechanisms, while her husband and father riveted wing sections. She produced about 50 to 60 mechanisms a day. By the end of the day, her blue coveralls were covered with cutting oil, to which she developed an allergy and was relocated to inventory. According to Margaret, she was strong enough back then to carry a nose plate to the assembly line!

One day stands out in Margaret's memory; the day she was able to tour a B-24 aircraft built exclusively for President Roosevelt. Inside, she recalls there was a beautiful United States of America emblem table made of inlaid wood. Margaret learned that the plane she toured was the same aircraft later used by FDR to take him to meet Winston Churchill during the war.

Margaret has another fond memory of waving to President and Eleanor Roosevelt as they drove down the assembly line in a convertible.

"No one had known they were coming, and it was very exciting!"

Margaret Kerbow
Atria MerryWood
Charlotte, North Carolina

Mary was a teenager in Baytown. She had five brothers in the service. She enjoyed entertaining servicemen and going to USO dances.

Mary Graham
Atria Westchase
Houston, Texas

Peg was a volunteer at the USO during World War II. She met her future husband at a USO function.

Peggy Lewis
Atria Kingwood
Houston, Texas

"It was Christmas Day 1942 and my parents decided to call the USO and invite two servicemen to have dinner with us.

Dad went to the USO and picked up the two gentlemen. Both were in the Army. One was a T4, which is a technician fourth class, and his name was Bill Mills. They spent the day with us, then Dad took them back to the USO. He also invited them to attend a party the following weekend at the home of my married sister. Bill Mills accepted the invitation.

Bill kept coming back weekend after weekend, and we eventually married on August 11, 1943. Bill was sent to California only a few months after our wedding. He also spent time in both England and France, helping move tanks to the front lines in the Battle of the Bulge.

When Bill returned from the war, we lived with my parents while we built a house right next door. We spent quite a few years there and raised seven children."

Thelma Mills
Atria Salisbury
Salisbury, Maryland

"I worked in the accounting department for Tidewater Oil Company located in Tulsa, Oklahoma. The company produced oil to supply the war. I also did volunteer work at the USO. I helped clean the facility where the soldiers were. I did a little dancing with the soldiers, dated a few and wrote to them."

Betty Rogers
Atria Willow Park
Tyler, Texas

"I lived in Lake Charles, Louisiana, down the road from Camp Polk during the war. I worked for the U.S. Employment Government Service. I rented a room in the home of a colonel and his wife. I volunteered for the USO and went every week to the dances. Camp Polk's enlisted men came to Lake Charles dressed in their uniforms for the dances."

Jean Holmes
Atria Primacy
Memphis, Tennessee

"I had a full-time office position in manufacturing during the day and I volunteered at the hospital in my free time. One day I was in charge of hanging the curtains between the wounded men to give them some privacy when I noticed a handsome soldier staring at me. I tried to make him stop looking at my legs, but he was pretty stubborn! It turns out that he was a paratrooper who had been severely injured overseas and was sent to that hospital to finish his recovery. He was in hospital for a very long time. We became very friendly and eventually married.

The hospital wasn't my first choice for service, but I stayed because I was, as was the entire nation, completely dedicated to winning the war."

Laura Lorentsen
Atria Kennebunk
Kennebunk, Maine

"In 1941, Dixie went to work at Point Mugu as a switchboard operator for Pac Bell. She was only 18 years old and had just finished high school. Most of the ladies who worked with Dixie were in their 40s. They made her feel right at home.

She met her husband-to-be in Long View, Washington. They were married in Pensacola, Florida, soon after. He was shipped out to sea right after they married."

Dixie Irene Gibbons
Atria Las Posas
Camarillo, California

Margaret worked at General Motors in Abington, Massachusetts, as a bookkeeper. She sold Chevrolets and was one of only two women in the office.

During the war, it was hard to get new cars so they did a lot of repair work on the old ones. Margaret drove to work in her own car, and the garage where she worked supplied her with the gas. Her future husband got his gas there, too, and that's how she met him.

Margaret Donovan
Atria Woodbriar
Falmouth, Massachusetts

"Margaret drove to work in her own car, and the garage where she worked supplied her with the gas."

"I worked for the government in Boston and helped make flight engineer boots. I put the soles on the boots. I was a 'stripper' because I had to strip off long pieces of tape and tie them around the boots to seal the soles. I got tired of stripping, and it was too long of a ride back and forth into Boston.

I got a job at Howard Johnson's Candy Factory in Quincy, Massachusetts. Howard Johnson's sent tins of candy to the servicemen and I was one who filled the tins. I had to be thumb printed in order to qualify for this government job. When I was a child, I cut myself with a razorblade and I had quite a scar. When the man from the government took my prints, he told me, 'Lady, never do anything wrong. With that scar, they'll get you in two minutes!'

All of the girls in the chocolate factory sent love letters in the cans of candy. I thought that was wrong. I just wrote 'Get Home Safe, God Bless You!' I really loved my work. I felt I was doing a great thing."

Shirley Lane
Atria Windsor Woods
Hudson, Florida

77

Chapter 2

"The aeronautical industry sent representatives to the Midwest to interview recent math and science college graduates to work as replacements for drafted engineers. I had been teaching college, but with so many being drafted there were not enough men to go to college.

The first of September, about 50 of these draftees started working at the aeronautical factories in various places throughout the United States. I was located at Wright's in Patterson, New Jersey. That's where they tested engines for airplanes.

We worked shifts and we had toolboxes. We did mechanical work on the engines and mounted them on test rigs and did endurance testing. We wore coveralls, which got greasy, and I still have my toolbox to this day. My father gave it to my husband when we got married. I worked there until after V-J Day.

I had a ball at this time in my life. I was with people my age and we were mostly single, doing interesting, stimulating work, and we felt we were helping the cause."

Frances B. Brooks
Atria Windsor Woods
Hudson, Florida

"When the war began, I was teaching school in Jacksonville, Arkansas, making $60 per month. In 1942, my brother, who lived in Little Rock, told me about an ordinance plant that was hiring women at $125 per month. The ordnance plant made detonators for bombs and my job was to walk up and down the aisles and make sure everyone was doing their jobs. As I recall, the only special clothing requirement was to wear rubber-soled shoes. I met my husband right before he was drafted. He spent time in Italy and North Africa. We were married after the war was over.

I was at work when they announced that the war was over. We were told that we could leave work, but if we wanted to get paid, we must stay and work until 11. I stayed."

Muriel Baber
Atria Cordova
Memphis, Tennessee

" I was teaching school in Jacksonville, Arkansas, making $60 per month."

Ceil lived with her husband in Waukegan, Illinois. Both of them worked at U.S. Steel and were glad they had jobs that paid $2.80 an hour. Ceil worked second shift, 3 p.m. to 11 p.m., as an inspector for bomb and grenade casings. The really hard work was placing the casings into the truck – that was very difficult!

At the plant, men and women worked side-by-side and became good friends. On Fridays when the checks were distributed, all of her team went to have a drink before heading home.

"I remember when the movie stars would visit on pay day to sell war bonds," Ceil said. "The men really bought when the beautiful starlets would sell them."

Ceil Zaleck
**Atria Northgate Park
Cincinnati, Ohio**

"I worked for the Selective Service with the U.S. Government in Springfield, Illinois. I put the men in different categories, such as Army or Navy. I was so bored that I asked to be transferred to Chicago, Illinois, where there was more action. There were really more boys there, too, which is why I really wanted to go! My girlfriend and I transferred to be there together.

After we arrived in Chicago, I worked for the U.S. Government War Finance. In the evening, we volunteered to become 'spotters' for friendly and enemy planes. It was very exciting. We also signed up to be hostesses at the Mayor Kelly Servicemen Center, which was like a USO. It was there that I met my husband-to-be.

As a plane spotter, I was on the beach at sundown when I saw my first enemy plane approaching. They had given us pictures of American planes and enemy planes and we had studied all of the plane outlines. I got very nervous, the plane sounded scary, yet I passed the responsibility on to my superior, which was my job to do. I also felt I was being patriotic.

After the evening's excitement on the beach, I went home with a Navy man as an escort. We stopped at a tavern on the way home and closed the place. This was against the rules, but it was love at first sight! Eugene and I have been married 59 years.

I remember the war bond rallies in Chicago, where we all worked so hard to get money for the war effort. I met so many movie stars. Bob Hope was wonderful! I remember him telling us he would keep talking until he was tired and then he'd lay down on the floor and talk from there! His wife was with him and she was knitting sweaters for her children – she was marvelous!"

Dorothy J. Snediker
**Atria Windsor Woods
Hudson, Florida**

At the age of 21, Wilma worked at a Lockheed plant in southern California. Her duties included assembly work for the interiors of B-24 bombers. Her hours were 8 a.m. to 5 p.m. five days a week and she earned $1 per hour.

Wilma met her husband at Lockheed. He was in the Air Force and supervised soldiers working on the B-24 bombers. Wilma's husband was transferred to Texas and she followed him there. After the war, Wilma and her husband enjoyed friendships with other soldiers and their wives.

Wilma Wood
Atria Chandler Villas
Chandler, Arizona

"In 1943, my brand new "Shavetail" husband was assigned to a Coast Artillery Corps anti-aircraft unit that guarded President Roosevelt and the Washington, D.C. area. While my husband's troops kept watch over the White House from their barracks built on the adjacent State Department lawn, I worked for the Treasury Department around the corner at 24th and Pennsylvania Avenue as a personnel clerk. In fact, the entrance to my office is still pictured on our $10 bills.

Six months later, we were transferred to Ft. Totten, New York. From there, we were sent to Camp Bell, an Air Force staging center located halfway between Buffalo and Niagara Falls, New York. It was easy to find work at Bell Aircraft Corp., the company that provided many fighters. I was a clerk-typist/secretary in the service department.

In addition to the 12 to 16 hour days I spent in the office, I was part of a USO group, which entertained the military bases throughout upstate New York. The troops awaiting overseas assignments seemed to enjoy our entertainment. That was a very enjoyable and gratifying time away from the stress of the wartime production activities.

It wasn't very long until my husband was shipped out. I returned to my job and entertainment activities for another year-and-a-half before the war ended in Europe and my husband returned safely home."

M.E. "Tim" Wallace
Atria Woodside Village
Columbus, Ohio

"…the entrance
to my office is still
pictured on our
$10 bills."

Jeanne was an artist in her 30s and sold her pictures on the lawn. She vividly remembers the day she heard that the war was over. Jeanne and her husband were in their garden. Just after the radio announced the news of the war being over, a white dove suddenly flew into their garden and then flew out. Moments later, it came back and stood on her husband's shoulder.

"I will never forget that day for as long as I live," she said.

Jeanne Cartledge
Atria Bonita
Chula Vista, California

An enlisted woman serving in the Navy and getting trained at Hunter College is where it all began. Dorothy was assigned as the secretary to the officer in charge of Lemington Hotel on the corner of Flagler and Biscayne. Because training was tough, many nights Dorothy joined the other enlisted young women in the barracks as they held one another and shed tears of sadness together.

As secretary, Dorothy was responsible for assisting the officer in charge with phone calls, responding to letters on other typical secretarial work.

Her normal routine changed while she was playing on a softball team and her first base coach insisted that she go watch the men's team play that night. He also told her to pay close attention to the first baseman. Dorothy took her coach's advice seriously and the first baseman of the barracks team ended up to be her husband.

"It's hard to believe that Earl kept me," she reminisces, "considering the first words out of my mouth were 'you smell bad' after a baseball game!"

Dorothy Brick
Atria Lawrenceville
Atlanta, Georgia

"During the war, I worked at the Grissom Air Force Base in Peru, Indiana. I rolled bandages with red crosses on them and I worked in the blood bank labeling bags of blood and taking temperatures. I also worked in the canteen selling donuts and cookies to the soldiers. All of these jobs were volunteer positions. I felt that every women should take part. It made feel that I was doing something productive.

My husband, Paul, owned a filling station. It was allowed to remain open because he re-treaded tires. We had a victory garden in our yard where we raised our own vegetables. We did a lot of canning. I even canned ketchup.

One of my best memories of that time was when the soldiers were home on leave. They came over to our house to play cards. I made Spam sandwiches for them, and we had a good time."

Wilma Fultz
Atria Cordova
Memphis, Tennessee

Back in 1936, Ortence Schmidt accepted an invitation for a double date to the Mayfair Night Club. Little did she know that she would be meeting her future husband . . . and he was not the gentleman from whom she had accepted the date! Ortence's eyes met Marion's, who was sitting with some mutual friends. Somehow that night, Ortence ended up seated next to him and never left his side.

Marion enlisted in the Air Corps and was sent to California. Ortence took her two-week vacation time and bought a ticket aboard the El Capitan bound for Los Angeles. This was Ortence's first time out of Michigan! Aboard the train, Ortence met another woman traveling to be with her husband, and the two women became life-long friends.

Once settled, Ortence set out to find a job. She had worked as a bank teller back home in Michigan. The very first bank hired Ortence on the spot, giving her the duty of writing up savings bonds. Ortence and her friend Louise from the train, found a room together in a boarding house.

Marion had begun pre-flight school and Ortence was able to see him only on Sundays. Ortence continued to follow Marion to other California cities. Finally the two ended up in Wichita, where she became Mrs. Marion Nowakowski. They were married at the army post with Louise serving as matron of honor.

Ortence Nowakowski
Atria Shorehaven
Sterling Heights, Michigan

Ginny was in her early 20s during the war years and often traveled to Fort Knox, Kentucky, on the bus and danced the nights away at the USO.

Although many names could be found on Ginny's dance card, only one name remained on that card well beyond those USO dances. Steve Hunt – the boy next door, her brother's best friend and her future husband.

When it came time to go to war, Steve was among those who fought overseas. The entire time he was gone, Ginny wrote to him and he wrote to her.

Ginny says life was dull during those years, meat was scarce and good times were hard to come by. But her patience during World War II resulted in the biggest award she could desire – a husband with whom she would waltz into the next stage of life.

Ginny Hunt
Atria St. Matthews
Louisville, Kentucky

USO dances were something everyone looked forward to attending. When the call came in for me to hostess a USO dance, I happily went and entertained the soldiers. Some soldiers had been wounded or were handicapped because of combat, but they still made it to the dances.

Norma Nelson
Atria Sandy
Sandy, Utah

"I was 27 and single when World War II started. I lived in Vicksburg, Mississippi, and worked as a telephone operator. There was one big USO place in town. I had the opportunity to meet a lot of handsome men in uniform and even dated a few of them. I volunteered to roll bandages with the Red Cross. I also volunteered to work the graveyard shift as a telephone operator, during which time we had blackouts to practice for air raids.

I met my husband at the end of the war at a big celebration party. He had been home since December 1945. He proposed to me in February 1946, and we were married in April 1946."

Gladys Pittway
Atria Primacy
Memphis, Tennessee

Angela worked for five years in Cicero, Illinois, for Western Electric Company. Angela's duties included assembling appliances and making sure the manuals were packaged with the correct appliances. She worked Monday through Friday, 8 a.m. to 4 p.m. Angela was married and had two sons. At times, she socialized with her coworkers and organized parties and dances to keep everyone happy and motivated.

Angela Barro
Atria Chandler Villas
Chandler, Arizona

Helen worked at a bank during the war. She was in charge of organizing a group of women to visit the canteens and USO clubs. Their job was to make the soldiers comfortable and welcome because many were far from home. The ladies went to the centers once a week and talked and danced with these brave young men. Helen felt great contributing to the war effort. Building morale was very important during those trying times – many of those men were never to come home again.

Helen Murphy
Atria East Northport
Long Island, New York

"I did volunteer work at the VA hospital in Denver. Each volunteer was interviewed and assigned to a veteran. My soldier was unresponsive. I was told that he had been a writer and had talked about the beauty he saw in Germany. At one time, his fellow soldiers resented him because they saw only the ugliness of war. I told my soldier that I hoped to travel to Germany someday, see its beauty, meet the people and maybe even write a story. He looked up. I asked him if he had ever written his story. Then I asked him if he would like to write a story and if he knew how to type. He smiled! This was the breakthrough we wanted! I motioned to a counselor and asked if my soldier could have a typewriter. She smiled and said, 'Tomorrow!' I hugged him and waved goodbye. I still can see his smile today!"

Elizabeth Locke
Atria Willow Park
Tyler, Texas

At age 18, Marty began working at Delco Radio. When the war began, Delco focused on making radios for the war. Marty worked on the production line for a more than eight years. To further help with the war effort, Marty joined the USO and helped entertain the servicemen in Bunker Hill, Indiana.

"A whole bunch of us gals got on a bus and we'd entertain the fellas, which I sure didn't mind at all. I met my husband at one of the dances. He was a sailor, and he sure could dance!"

Marty Peck
Atria Heritage
Indianapolis, Indiana

Mary worked in Windsor, Ontario, Canada, in a machine gun factory. She inspected machine guns to ensure they were assembled properly. She worked five days a week, 10 hours per shift. She wore slacks and a special smock.

Mary remembers that on her time off, she went dancing at the Coral Gables. The girls looked forward to meeting the 4-F men – those who were unable to be drafted due to poor vision or flat feet. They enjoyed dancing the Jitterbug.

After the war ended and on V-Day, the girls went out to celebrate at the Grass Rail, where Mary met her husband, who was home on leave from the Air Force. He couldn't bear to leave her and they were married six months later.

Mary Mattison
Atria Chandler Villas
Chandler, Arizona

"I worked in a garment factory in Tennessee making 40 cents an hour doing piecework on a sewing machine for six years prior to the war. My brother was on leave from the Navy and told me he was going to take me back to Detroit.

On Tuesday morning, my brother went to the Cadillac factory and got me a job there right away. We had a dressing room where they

furnished our uniforms and headpieces to cover our hair. I went right to work on the polishing line where there were burrs on the gears that had to be polished off.

One day, Mrs. Roosevelt arrived and walked down the assembly line. She went to every person on the line and pinned a little pin on every single worker. She was a lovely lady! She was a very smart lady, but rough looking, for she wore no makeup – she was just plain Eleanor.

I ended up working for another car company called Kelsey Hayes. I met my husband, Charles Thomas Rogers, there. Later, I moved to Ford Motor Company and retired from there. Who would have thought that my work at the first assembly line job with Cadillac would lead me to retire from the automobile industry?"

Hilda Rogers
Atria Windsor Woods
Hudson, Florida

At age 18, Velma began working at Ohmite Steel Manufacturing Company in Chicago. Ohmite produced the steel that went into the parts used for the war effort. She was paid $30 a week. In her spare time, Velma was a roller skating teacher, teaching her students the Fox Trot and the Waltz on roller skates. She had an organist who played live music while she and her students skated. She received medals for her teaching achievements.

Velma Lang
Atria Chandler Villas
Chandler, Arizona

"During that time, the USO was very prominent in entertaining the troops. I was a secretary to the president of the Wisconsin Electric Power Company, and the USO contacted us to use our auditorium.

We talked to several employees about creating our own entertainment for the troops in Milwaukee. About eight or so of us formed a group of pseudo-entertainers. Some performed comedy; others did impersonations and dance routines. A girlfriend and I did a song and dance routine to 'Bill Bailey, Won't You Please Come Home?' and other Mitch Miller-type songs.

For the troops, it was a break for them. It was different than going to a movie. They were so far away from home and the songs we did reminded them of their families. You could see the men cry. Sometimes the audience participated in our corny routines. It was a feeling of fulfillment, deeply gratifying. We felt their appreciation!

Once, a soldier came up to me, threw his arms around me, picked me up and turned me all around. Thinking I was his long-lost girlfriend, speaking in French accent he called out , 'Yvette!, Yvette, my dear, I have found you at last!' I said, 'Oh, I'm so happy you're happy, but I'm not your Yvette!' He was shocked because I looked identical to his girlfriend."

Eunice Mielke
Atria Windsor Woods
Hudson, Florida

Rose vividly recalls the day peace was declared at the end of World War II. She and her husband lived in Indianapolis, where he was stationed, and had plans to meet friends across town for the Barnum & Bailey Circus. The streets were packed with people celebrating the end of the war. According to Rose, it took quite a long time to get across town.

Rose's husband was discharged when the war ended and they moved to Danville, Kentucky, where she helped her husband work on her father's farm.

Rose Carter
Atria St. Matthews
Louisville, Kentucky

Chapter 2

As a very young woman, Ruby began working at the T & W factory in Elizabethtown, Kentucky. The factory was hiring people to make uniform khaki pants for all branches of the service. The entire factory staff, except the top management and two men in the cutting room, was made up of women.

Ruby's job was to face the hip pocket and the next person would bind the pocket. Ruby's day began at 7 a.m. and lasted until 4 p.m. On occasion, factory workers worked an hour overtime if the production was too slow for that day. Although it was a long hard day, during lunch some of the girls gathered outside at the picnic tables and ate together. Once in a while, they treated themselves to a stroll downtown for lunch in one of the local cafés. Talk of the war was rare; the ladies simply threw themselves into their work, were grateful to have a job and happy to help out with the war effort. "It was hard work, but we needed to keep our jobs," said Ruby. "The pay wasn't bad. We made $23 a week."

Once the war came to an end, the employees were very happy and a little afraid. After all they were sewing military pants. Fortunately, the factory was able to continue manufacturing pants for civilian companies and Ruby continued to work.

Ruby Mortensen
Atria Elizabethtown
Elizabethtown, Kentucky

Pearl left her family home in Milan, New Hampshire, to travel with her brothers to Connecticut to work for Hamilton Standard. In a production floor office, Pearl met her future husband – the true love of her life. This, Pearl said, "was the most important thing that happened to her during the war."

Pearl Fogil
Atria Kennebunk
Kennebunk, Maine

Young and in love is what Jeanette Allen was at the start of the war. As a high school senior, Jeanette had to say goodbye to her sweetheart when he went off to war. Riley Allen, was stationed in Alaska where he was responsible for fighting fires. While Riley was away, Jeanette volunteered at a hospital near her town. She still can't believe her mother allowed her to attend dances at the hospital and socialize with the wounded soldiers!

At the end of the war, she and her high school sweetheart, Riley, married after college in June 1947.

Jeanette Allen
Atria St. Matthews
Louisville, Kentucky

Josephine attended nursing school in Saginaw, Michigan, at St. Mary's Hospital and School of Nursing. Her training took her to basic training camp in McCoy, Wisconsin, and eventually to Camp Shelby in Mississippi where she served out her military service in a medical unit.

Jo's days were spent working 12-hour shifts that rotated monthly. She lived in a dormitory that had adjoining rooms. Helen McCoy, a nurse from Illinois, had the room next to Jo and they became great friends. The patients Jo cared for were those who had been abroad and were injured or became sick. One of her patients, Bill Prall, asked her out and she flatly refused him. Bill was the persistent type though, and unknown to Jo had talked to her friend Helen, who eventually talked Jo into saying yes for a date. Finally, Jo walked into Bill's room to accept the movie invitation and he already had his dress uniform ready on his bed.

The movie date was a big risk for Jo because it was against the rules to date a patient. When they arrived at the movie theater, two of the first people they ran into were the doctor in charge and the nursing supervisor, and not a word of their courtship was ever mentioned! Shortly after, Jo and Bill were married, and Helen McCoy attended the wedding.

Josephine Prall
Atria MerryWood
Charlotte, North Carolina

"The movie date was a big risk for Jo because it was against the rules to date a patient."

"Women during the war time did a variety of things. Many of them had to become the head of the household. There were hard times and the rations on items affected everyone, but you made do with what you had. If we couldn't get fresh meat, then we ate canned meat. We also grew our own garden to can fruits and vegetables because they were hard to get. Mostly it was business as usual for me.

Post-war was a time of jubilation of families coming back together and picking up where they left off. Fort Sill Military Post had a parade with floats when the soldiers came home. In all, it was a time of hardship, and then great relief."

Wilma Rigsby
Atria Richardson
Dallas, Texas

"When the war broke out, I was still in school and lived in Parkin, Arkansas. One of the first things we had to do was register everyone for the draft. The mayor asked if I would be willing to help, and I gladly did. There were many sharecroppers and other people living on farms who didn't have birth certificates and were essentially, unaccounted for. Every person had to have a birth certificate for various reasons, especially for rationing purposes. A government representative came to town and helped us get organized. We set up at the school and registered everyone.

There was a German POW camp near Parkin. We rode our bicycles there and even though I couldn't speak German, I could speak Yiddish. Because German and Yiddish are similar, I communicated with and interpreted for the prisoners. I helped the county nurse when she went to the camp to give shots. I also took histories for her.

Then came the food, clothing and gas rationing. Most people, especially the older ones, were scared to death. My parents owned a store. They told people to go to the school where I was and I would explain everything to them. That seemed to ease their minds. When their sons were drafted, some of them even came to me to help them mail care packages or write letters.

After I graduated, I moved to Memphis, Tennessee, and lived with my grandparents. I went to work at the Army Depot on Airways Boulevard. I later got a permanent job in West Memphis, Arkansas, at an engineering office, where I stayed for the duration of the war. Twice a week, I went with my friends to Kennedy Hospital where there were wounded soldiers. Some were paralyzed, some were missing limbs and some just needed someone to listen to them. Every Saturday night, all servicemen and women were invited to come to the Menorah Institute. If they needed a meal, we would provide one for them.

When the war ended, we all went downtown. Everyone was laughing, crying, singing and dancing in the streets. I thank God I was able to do something, no matter how small, to help the country that I love and have been privileged to live in. God bless America!"

Bertha Baer
Atria Cordova
Memphis, Tennessee

"...I communicated with and interpreted for the prisoners."

"On Valentine's Day 1942, my family moved to San Francisco, from a little town in Wisconsin. What a magical place San Francisco was! I had never seen a city as beautiful or clean in all my life. I was 15 years old and just soaked up the whole atmosphere. Of course, the war colored everything because of San Francisco's location as a point of embarkation on the Pacific Coast.

We were so patriotic and supportive of everything that had to do with the war efforts. One of my girlfriends belonged to an organization called the American Women's Voluntary Service. She was in the Junior Auxiliary and asked me to join. I was delighted and it ended up being one of the most memorable periods of my life.

At first, we rolled bandages, made sandwiches and visited servicemen in the hospitals. The wounded were already coming back from Hawaii and other places in the Pacific. In 1943, as more girls joined the auxiliary we started a new project. My friend's parents owned a big house in the Richmond District of San Francisco and offered it as a place to entertain the servicemen waiting to be shipped overseas. So every other Sunday, we girls put on our 'Sunday clothes' and gathered to help our servicemen forget for a moment that they were bound for a war zone and let them just enjoy being young men.

There were 12 of us and we usually had about 15 servicemen from all branches of the military who arrived at the house at about 2 p.m. A couple of times later in the war, we even entertained some British and Australian servicemen. My friend's father played the records while her mother, and other mothers, cooked in the kitchen. The boys who didn't want to dance played Ping-Pong, Checkers or Chess; some went out to the backyard and played Badminton or threw a ball around.

Usually dinner was at 6 p.m. Because so many of the boys came from the Midwest, we enjoyed their reaction to California foods, such as avocados, artichokes and tamale pie. After dinner, we gathered around the piano and had a songfest. Then we danced and visited some more until 8:30 or so when the boys left. Most of them had to be back on base at 10 p.m. on Sundays.

Several of the girls dated boys they met at the parties, mostly double-dating. None of us ever had to 'fight for our virtue' or had an unpleasant experience with any of the young servicemen.

Being in the AWVS gave me the opportunity to have a variety of experiences that I would never have had otherwise. For instance, when Madame Chiang-Kai-Shek came to San Francisco in 1944, I was able to see her up close and personal. She had the most beautiful skin I have ever seen on any woman in my life. I got a job at a golf tournament and met Bing Crosby and Bob Hope and our group went to Treasure Island to attend a show with Kay Kyser.

It may sound as if all these activities were just for fun, but during all of them, our underlying thoughts were for winning the war and helping our servicemen. It was a very special time."

Helen Lann
Atria Lanier
Buford, Georgia

"I worked at Wright Aeronautical in the early 1940s. Parts came to our department and we recorded and placed them. For three years, I ran parts to the planes. I was 27 at the time, married and I had one child. My husband was A1, which meant he was on the waiting list for the draft. One day he received a card from the Army that read, 'Do not report until further notice.' I was so happy that he did not have to report and that I had some time to spend with him.

My brother-in-law, Art, knew that the draft would not take two sons from one family. Art did not want my husband to go to war because we had a child, so Art joined the Seabees. The Seabees were the first servicemen to go in by ship and clear the ground for planes to land. I was very sad, but I was also very proud of my brother-in-law. As a result of my brother-in-law's kindness and bravery, my husband was never drafted. I wrote my brother-in-law as often as I could in my free time between working the third shift, seven days a week and raising a child. I thought this was the least I could do. My husband and I worried about him constantly.

The women in the factory often told me that I should work only six days a week because I had a family. I wasn't doing it for the money, I only wanted to get the parts to the plane and get this war over with.

Now, my grandson is a Special Ranger. So pray with us. By the way, my brother-in-law did come home when the war was over!"

Vera Ernst
Atria Mallard Cove
Cincinnati, Ohio

" Ann was two years old before she saw her father after the war."

When the war broke out in 1941, Jean was driving home from a teachers' convention in St. Louis. She stopped in a small town for lunch and received word that Pearl Harbor had been bombed. Her future husband, Malcolm, was on his way to Fort Barclay in west Texas, where he received his officer's training. He trained in medical services in the Army and left for England shortly after. Jean and Malcolm's daughter, Ann, was two years old before she saw her father after the war.

Jean remembers there wasn't much meat during the war years, so people ate rabbit. There wasn't any butter either, but they mixed margarine and a packet of yellow food coloring to make the margarine look more like butter. People collected scrap metal, such as cans, old machinery, car parts and anything else that could be melted down to make artillery for our forces. No effort was too small; people came together to contribute any way they could.

Jean Alloway
Atria Cypresswood
Houston, Texas

"I was already married to Frank Ammiro when World War II started. We had a house on Hyde Street in San Francisco. My eldest daughter was just 18 months old. My husband was not drafted into the war. He was on F-4 because he had only one kidney.

I remember we had what we called blackout curtains. We put them down at night, so that no light passed through them. The air raid marshals patrolled the block and made sure that all curtains were down. I also remember the food rationing of milk, butter, coffee, meat and gasoline.

I was afraid and worried during the war. Two of my brothers were already in the service even before the war. One of my brother's troops was the first to be sent to Italy. He got malaria and his hair grew white before he aged. My other brother was in the National Guard and sent to Alaska. I guess that wartime period was difficult for all of us."

Catherine Ammiro
Atria Daly City
Daly City, California

Charlotte's husband, Leonard, was the pastor of a Quaker church and the associate pastor of another church in Los Angeles. For several years, the Gilmours opened their home to soldiers, giving them free room and board. Most of the soldiers stayed a week or two, but some of them stayed two or three months. Charlotte and Leonard had seven children of their own, so they had a big house. During the war, Charlotte and her husband made six rooms available to soldiers in need of a safe place to lay their heads and a good meal.

Charlotte Gilmour
Atria Valley View
Walnut Creek, California

"As far as I can remember, my mother, Aida was always working. She used to be a real estate person even during the war. She owned properties that she rented out to people who needed temporary places to stay. There was a lot of movement during the war. People in other places came to San Francisco to work.

Mom was a hard worker. She cleaned her rental places herself. My sisters and I helped, but we also had our individual jobs. Life was difficult during the war, but somehow we were able to manage because we all worked."

Aida Blitz, by daughter Frances Pivnick, resident
Atria Daly City
Daly City, California

"For several years, the Gilmours opened their home to soldiers, giving them free room and board."

"I graduated high school on a Friday night in May 1941. On Saturday morning, I was in my grandmother's garden planting peanuts when a neighbor came by and asked if I would like to work in Port Arthur for the Texas Company, which made oil cans for Texaco Oil. Positions there were vacant because the male employees had gone to war.

I took a position on the lug line. I hated it, but I needed the money and there were no men to work in the factory. I sat at a conveyor belt with two other people around me. The first person put soap and water on the ears of the cans to see if they were leaking. Then, some other employees and I dried the cans off and put them in an oven. I worked shift work – either the 6 a.m. to 2 p.m. shift or the 2 p.m. to 10 p.m. shift. Both shifts involved either coming to work or heading home in the dark, and boy, it was scary! I had to walk three blocks to get to the bus stop and then I had to transfer to a different bus.

I was unhappy and homesick, but stuck with it for eight months until January when I was let go because the plant began making something for the war and didn't need me. I went home on a Saturday night and my girlfriend and I met some soldiers. They asked us out, but we told them we were not pick-ups! However, we did schedule a date for the next day to ride motorcycles. We wore red slacks, which was a no-no for girls back then. On the same day, we met four more soldiers; one of them would one day be my husband. We rode around all day in a car and we even took a picture and sent it home to his family. It was love at first sight for him, but he would never admit it. We were supposed to have another date a week later, but he showed up at my house the very next day only to discover that I was out on a date!

In March, I was called back to work at the Texas Company and asked to do a different job that I liked. This time, I cut corks and placed them in small oil cans.

Raymond Buck (nicknamed Buck) and I married in August of 1942. Buck was stationed at Camp Folk, about 30 miles from Burkville. One day in August 1944, I received a telegram stating that Buck was seriously wounded. Would I become a widow at 21? It was three weeks before I received word from him that he was okay. Even though he had been injured, he stayed in the service for 16 additional months to train other soldiers in France.

When the war was finally over, Buck returned home. We didn't recognize one another when he got off the bus.

Wartime was terrible – just awful. I actually prayed that the Lord would let me lose my mind and then get it back when the war was over."

Edna Buck
Atria Collier Park
Beaumont, Texas

Grace remembers rationing during the war, especially sugar rationing. For someone who likes sweets, it was a big sacrifice to give them up. To this day, Grace still takes her coffee without sugar because she learned to like it that way during the war.

Food was often scarce, too. Meat was rationed, but chicken wasn't because families could raise their own chickens. One time Grace's family was expecting guests for dinner. After a great deal of discussion about what to feed them, it was decided they would buy a chicken from a local farm and serve it to their six guests. When Grace's sister saw the guests arrive, she was crestfallen. The father of the family was a large man and she could only imagine how much of that chicken he was going to devour!

Grace Bohn
Atria Cypresswood
Houston, Texas

"We lived in Connecticut when World War II erupted. My husband worked for the defense department. I was a full-time wife and mother with two children to care for. I kept myself busy working around the house. I also had a victory garden, which was a government project that encouraged everyone to have a vegetable garden to help with food production. The government argeed to lend its land to those who wanted to have a victory garden. There were four of us who cultivated our victory garden. We shared the produce with the rest of our neighbors.

I also remember that the government encouraged us to collect aluminum products like foil and other aluminum wrappers. We turned these in to the government. I do not really know what they did with those but we just did what we were told to do. We were always careful to conserve food because we had food rationing then. We also had blackouts and we heard air-raid sirens."

Dorothy Caviezel
Atria Daly City
Daly City, California

Flo was just 17 1/2 years old in 1945. She had lost her father when she was 15. She dropped out of school to support the family and went to work as a drill press operator in a factory that made airplanes. Flo's job was to drill press a part of the motor on an assembly line. She made $35 a week.

Flo did not understand the war, but she knew what she had to do for her mother and the country. She worked at the factory for one year and then went back to school and completed her education.

Flo Miller
Atria Woodside Village
Columbus, Ohio

"I was already married to 1st Lt. Anthony Vincent Dominski during World War II. My husband was a doctor in the service and he was among the very first ones sent to war. He was assigned to the 3rd Army with General George Patton. My husband was shipped overseas to the Pacific.

I worked as a nurse assistant at La Grange Hospital in Illinois. There was a shortage because many volunteered to be sent to the war zones. The hospital needed a lot of women who might not be nurses, but who were willing to assist. I changed bed sheets and bandages and did other duties the registered nurses assigned me to do.

Wartime was a difficult time for me. I had no husband to help with the kids. I was nervous all the time because I was afraid for my husband's safety. In one of Anthony's letters to me, he said that he was in the actual battlefield. There were shootings to his left, right and above his head. All the time he was gone, I kept a star on the window for him.

When Anthony came home, he had battle scars. Oh, how I rejoiced and thanked God for bringing my husband back home to my daughters and me. Shortly after my husband came back from the war, I conceived and gave birth to a son. We christened him Anthony Jr., after his father, who was a World War II hero."

Pauline Dominski
Atria Daly City
Daly City, California

"My life changed during World War II. The man I married had a very dangerous job working in a bomb making factory. His long hours kept him away from home, which left me to raise the kids and take care of the house by myself.

Several times a year, I had to uproot my family and move because of something known as 'black market rent.' In black market rent incidences, landlords raised the rent after tenants lived on their property for more than two months, which left a lot of my family and friends constantly looking for new housing. In times like this, it wasn't unusual to see people sharing amenities. I lived in a duplex and shared the ice box with the neighbors.

Everything from food to clothing was rationed. I received two slips a year to buy my children shoes. As we all know, it was never quite enough. And, if you showed that you had enough money to purchase a second pair of shoes, then you had to deal with the 'black market renters' and then spend the next several days moving your family again. In this depression time, we were not allowed to buy a car. All metals were sent overseas to help with the war. When my kids were sick, I had to take them to the doctor by bus, which meant long hours of waiting at the bus stop.

All families had to make sacrifices until our loved ones were brought back to us safe."

Dicie Duke
Atria Collier Park
Beaumont, Texas

Florence was a military wife whose husband was an officer. Florence left her home in the Chicago area to follow her husband to different military bases. Florence was always able to work at the bases, usually at processing military questionnaires for the communications department.

Florence was not issued any kind of uniform and wore regular civilian dresses and low heels to work. Florence's husband was never sent overseas. The longest Florence worked at any base was when her husband was transferred to Texas. They lived in off-base housing and there were times when she did not see her husband for days at a time while he was busy doing his job.

Florence continued to work and follow her husband until he received a medical discharge from the service. Florence feels that the work she did for the military was always interesting and important, but the best part was that she could be near her husband.

Florence Edward
Atria Tamalpais Creek
Novato, California

"I didn't carry a gun, but I carried a ration book during World War II. Gasoline, sugar, nylon hose, shoes and other necessary things were in short supply. My husband worked in a refinery in Fort Worth, Texas. One brother helped build planes at General Dynamics and another was in the Air Force.

We had two girls to dress and dress material was in short supply. Everyone we knew was affected one way or another, so we learned to get along the best way we could. People were patriotic and supported our country."

Elizabeth Collins
Atria Willow Park
Tyler, Texas

"Gasoline, sugar, nylon hose, shoes and other necessary things were in short supply."

"In mid-1942, Schlage Lock in Bayshore hired me. My job was to inspect the parts used to make bombs. In 1943, I was hired by Butte Electric, which was located in San Francisco. I worked on the assembly line, making signals used by Navy ships.

It was a very difficult time for all of us during the war. There was food rationing. Butter, bananas, coffee, cream, sugar and other commodities were hard to get. We used tokens and stood in line to get some items that we needed. Even gasoline was rationed. I remember that we did not have nylon stockings to wear and painted our legs with make-up. Sure, our legs looked ok with make up, but it did not protect them from the cold. There were also blackouts during the night and we had to put our window shades down. Our shades stayed down until the air raid warden tapped on our windows to signal us that it was okay to put the shades up."

Grace Fardella
Atria Daly City
Daly City, California

"I started working for the government even before World War II broke out. I was a secretary at Fort Chafter in San Francisco. We did not have to wear uniforms in the office; only military personnel wore uniforms. As a secretary, I did regular office work, such as typing letters and memos, answering phone calls and requesting office supplies.

World War II was a difficult time for almost everyone. We had our own worries and concerns, even if we were not in actual combat. We knew that we were a nation at war and American soldiers were fighting in the battlefield. I had a boyfriend who was sent to war. I never heard from him again. I do not know if he survived or if he was one of those who died."

Geraldine Gallagher
Atria Daly City
Daly City, California

"I was married in October 1941 two months before the bombing of Pearl Harbor. My husband was drafted into the Armed Forces when I was six months pregnant with my first child. He went overseas and was gone for the first two years of his daughter's life. When my husband and all the men were overseas fighting for our country, the women received allotment checks in the amount of about $80 a month. It was extremely hard to stretch this money for an entire month. I was unable to work because I had a small child at home to raise, so all we had to live on was the $80 each month. These were very trying times for me and my family."

Tee Garner
Atria Collier Park
Beaumont, Texas

"I was in Minnesota when World War II broke out. I was a young girl then, living with my parents and still going to school. Although I did not work outside the house, I helped my mother with household chores.

I knew that my parents were worried about the war, but in Minnesota, it was not as bad as in other places. We had food rationing, but I do not remember going without the basics. We also experienced blackouts and heard air raid sirens. However as a young girl, I did not worry too much. Sure I heard about the war going on and about the government's encouragement to conserve food, but because I did not see actual combat I guess I was not really afraid. I simply did what I knew best to do during those times."

Carol Hanson
Atria Daly City
Daly City, California

Loubeth remembers gas rationing with a particularly vivid event. One day her boyfriend, Billy, took her to Paris, Texas. He drove a friend to the train station to leave for the Army and Loubeth rode along with them. Billy's car ran out of gas in Paris and they had a hard time finding fuel. Back then, you didn't go anywhere you didn't have to because of the gas rationing. Finally, Loubeth broke down and called her mother, who knew a man who was an executive with Sinclair Oil and Gas. He helped them out by giving them some gas so they could get home safely.

Loubeth went on to marry Roy Hames, who won the Silver Star for valor in battle. Roy served in the 90th Division under General George Patton and went into France at D-Day+6. Roy also served as company commander of POWs in Belgium. When he arrived, prisoners were eating grass, prompting Roy to set up a soup kitchen to feed them.

For her part, Loubeth moved into a garage apartment across the street from her parents and raised their small children. Raising children is hard enough for two people, but with only a mother it is especially difficult. For Roy to be effective in his Army service, he needed Loubeth at home holding down the fort.

Loubeth Hames
Atria Cypresswood
Houston, Texas

"I was working at Kaiser Hospital in San Francisco, when the war broke out. Life would have been pretty normal for me if the man who later became my husband was not sent to war. Matt Jasper and I were about to get married when he was drafted.

My mother did not want me to be married while Matt was off at war. She said that it would be difficult for Matt and me to withstand the separation as a married couple and that if we were meant for each other, we would find each other again when the war was over. Mother also told me that war was already complicated and getting married to a man, whom I know may not even return, will cause me a lot of heartaches. Obedient as I was to my mom, I told Matt that I decided to postpone our marriage until he came back from the war. Poor Matt did not have the chance or the strength to fight my decision. He had lots of other fighting to do.

Off to war Matt went. I was left worried and broken-hearted. It was a relief to be busy with my job at Kaiser. It helped take away some of my misgivings about not marrying Matt before he left. Matt and I wrote regularly to each other, though mail was terribly slow. When Matt returned from the war, we were married immediately. Boy, oh boy, – we were so happy; not only because the war was over, but also because we were in each other's arms again."

Violet Jasper
Atria Daly City
Daly City, California

Chapter 2

"Rosalie Hansen was my eldest sister. She used to live at the Atria Daly City with me before she passed away in March 2004. My sister was a beautiful person inside and out. She used to take care of me when I was growing up.

During the war, our mom and the two of us worked hard. Rosalie was a good salesperson. She rented a space at a building near our home and sold practically everything that she could. She also worked as a waitress in a big hotel in San Francisco. Rosalie was always busy. It seems like she did not have leisure time for herself.

Life was difficult during the war and things were difficult to get. Even though many items were rationed, Rosalie managed to get what we needed. She charmed almost everyone and she somehow managed to have a place in line ahead of the others. I do not know how she did it, but she did."

Rosalie Hansen, by sister Frances Pivnick, resident
Atria Daly City
Daly City, California

"World War II was a very trying time. Before the war, my husband was stationed in Battle Creek, Michigan, and during the war he was stationed in Paris.

When he went to war, I stayed with my parents and also with his parents for a while. He had a younger sister that I helped take care of.

Sugar was rationed and you could not get it without vouchers. Electrical appliances could not be bought until after the war. Even when the war was over, we had to put our name on a waiting list to get a refrigerator. Gas was also rationed. I can even remember a no-light policy where the lights would be turned off for a couple of hours at a time.

I was sitting on the front porch of my parents' house in Centre, Alabama when the war ended. Dad was listening to the news and he came in and told me that the war was over.

The war was hard on almost everybody, but some very important lessons were learned. I learned to exercise my faith. There were times when my father was weak and I watched his mother, whose faith was so strong, and it really helped me."

Katherine Johnson
Atria Weatherly Springs
Huntsville, Alabama

Lucille Johnson remembers running home when the newspaper announced the war and asking her parents if we had won yet. Her father didn't go to war because he was a doctor and had a wife and children to take care of. Even children worked in the war effort and Lucille was no different. She knitted wool washcloths and socks for the soldiers.

Lucille Johnson
Atria Cypresswood
Houston, Texas

Inice lived in Oklahoma during the war and sold Red Cross buttons as part of the war effort. She also worked for the rationing board.

It is hard for Americans today to imagine what it was like to have sugar, gasoline, meat, shoes, tires and stockings rationed. During the war years, mothers had to save coupons to bake birthday cakes for their children. People traded their ration coupons for other things they needed. Everyone worked together because everyone was in the same boat. Today, Inice is proud to have a grandson who is a Navy SEAL.

Inice Keltner
Atria Cypresswood
Houston, Texas

"It is hard for Americans today to imagine what it was like…"

"My husband was an Army Medical T-5 and went to Casablanca. I moved back to Los Angeles, and worked for Cannon Electric Company. My job was in manufacturing and design. I assembled prongs on the bottom of glass radio tubes and drilled holes in the end of the prongs. We had a bowling team; our leader was pregnant and we still took third place in a tournament.

During that time, I also attended night school and finished a class in mechanical drawing. Soon, I was promoted to product design for the Army and Navy. My wage was $1.15 per hour and my dress code was long pants, closed-toe shoes, hairnets (snoods were the rage!) and jeans were okay. My husband's nephew gave me a mechanical drafting set to keep me out of mischief at night and that is how I got started in drafting. It was very popular to make catalogs with parts and exploded assembly views, because at that time no one knew how to read blueprints for mechanical parts."

Ethelda Linville
Atria El Camino Gardens
Carmichael, California

"My boyfriend was sent to war in the Pacific. He was a chief petty officer and a captain's secretary.

From 1941 to 1945, I worked two jobs. From 8 a.m. to 5 p.m., I worked at the Industrial Indemnity Office in the financial district in San Francisco. Then from 6 p.m. to 12 a.m., I worked at the Stage Door Canteen as a junior hostess. There I danced with visiting servicemen, consoled them and wrote letters home for them. We were not allowed to drink or date these men – that was a no-no. Working at the Stage Door Canteen was fun. I loved to dance and the music was very good.

Meat, butter, cream, coffee, sugar, shoes and cigarettes did not come easy during the war because these items were rationed. I was lucky because my boyfriend, Louis Kirschner, came home alive when the war was over and we were married immediately."

Florence Kirschner
Atria Daly City
Daly City, California

99

Chapter 2

Gladys grew up in a small, rural farming community in Texas. When she was 17, she left home for Houston. It was there that she cared for the Baird family children, a family that owned Mrs. Baird's Bread. She met her husband in Houston and he was drafted into the Army. Gladys went back to the family farm, and worked hard doing the work of men.

Gladys's husband was killed in the war. Gladys never remarried. She has been in love with him her whole life and she still thinks of him all the time.

Gladys Knight
Atria Cypresswood
Houston, Texas

"My mother, Mary Kalafatich, and father had 12 children together. Life was difficult because food was rationed. We had to stand in line to get the things we needed. She was the one who put food on the table. I could not imagine the hardship my mother went through to feed all of her children.

My mother worked in a bakery as a kitchen helper. Her job was washing baking dishes and pans. It was not an easy job and when she came home, her hands were red and sore. She walked from home to the bakery, and from the bakery to home because nobody was kind enough to give her a ride. My mother was saving transportation money for food. At night when I came home from my work of cleaning other people's houses, I saw my mother massaging her feet with her painful hands. I felt so bad for her."

Mary F. Kalafatich
by daughter Katherine Swisher
Atria Daly City
Daly City, California

When the war broke out, Shirley worked with her family in their grocery store. There they sold fruits, vegetables, meats and other items to the local community. Soldiers from the Air Force base 50 miles away came to town regularly and the town provided free movies and other items for them.

Shirley met her soldier at a dance and he promptly asked her to marry him. She told him he was crazy and that she was only 18 years old. He persisted and the two married a year later.

Shirley remembers how hard it was to get work as a serviceman's wife because everybody assumed she would be gone in no time and leave them stranded. Shirley had business-school experience, but worked in a laundry using a mangle press. It was just part of doing what needed to be done.

Shirley Moreland
Atria Cypresswood
Houston, Texas

Dee was 16 when she met her husband Lawrence, and 17 when they married. When war broke out, Lawrence felt compelled to join the service. Dee hated the idea, but didn't try to talk him out of it because she felt they both would have suffered if she kept him from living up to his ideals. They had two sons, a four-year-old and a five-week-old, when Pearl Harbor was attacked. Lawrence signed up for the Navy as an enlisted man and later attended officer's training school, which prevented a tour of the Pacific, something Dee remains grateful for today.

Dee devised a code before Lawrence left so that she would know from where he was writing. If Lawrence said he had seen Mary, it meant that he was in France. This method of communication kept Dee somewhat informed of his location. Dee lived for Lawrence's letters, which took weeks to arrive after they were sent. She was visiting her parents one day when a call came from the Navy. Knowing inside that it was word of her husband's death, Dee let out a huge scream. She rushed home to find that Lawrence had only been delayed.

During the war, Dee remembers not being able to get shoes for her children. They seemed like they were made of pasteboard and only lasted three weeks. She also remembers not being able to get laundry soap. A grocer took her under his wing and always put aside a box of Tide whenever it arrived. Living on a serviceman's pay was not easy, but it was all part of Dee's commitment to doing the right thing.

Dee's efforts during the war were raising two sons on a serviceman's pay and learning to do all the things her husband had previously done. She took care of paying bills so well that when Lawrence returned, he never took the chore back from her.

De Alva "Dee" McAnnally
Atria Cypresswood
Houston, Texas

"I was married with children to take care of during World War II. I did not work outside the home because I was afraid to leave my kids with strangers. I was a full-time wife and mother and my job is a responsibility that was there 24-hours a day, every day of the week. I cooked for my husband and children, cleaned up after them and did the laundry. Life was not easy when there was war going on. There were things that we could not get as we used to get them. Butter was one of the things that I stood in line for. We loved butter around the house, so I made my own.

Everyone experienced difficulties during the war. Even then, I guess we were luckier here in America than in other places like Europe, Asia and the Pacific. Life was more difficult there because they experienced what it was to be in a place where there was actual combat."

Lorraine Murdock
Atria Daly City
Daly City, California

Chapter 2

"I first heard about the war from my husband, James Joseph Maher. He was riding a horse and he was shouting, 'The Japanese attacked Pearl Harbor.' I was scared because war is frightening. I did not know what would happen or what to expect.

My husband was not drafted to the war. He was deferred because he worked for a company that made gloves, uniforms and other military items. I worked at four different companies during the duration of the war. I worked for Kitchen Fresh Bakery in San Francisco, where we baked goods that were part of care packages sent to American soldiers. I also worked at American Can Company as a factory worker, Blum's Candies as a chocolate dipper and American Licorice Company as a licorice wrapper. Despite the stress of everyday life living in a country at war, I knew that I had to be strong.

I remember all the blackouts when we had to stay inside the house and be as quiet as possible. They told us that blackouts were happening so that planes dropping bombs would not see us. We heard air-raid sirens. It was very scary. Life was difficult and stressful."

Dolores Maher
Atria Daly City
Daly City, California

Pearl Harbor happened on Allene's 19th birthday. Allene remembers helping our troops by letting two soldiers stay with her family and by taking care of them in her home for the weekend. She also remembers that her family didn't have a car, so they traded gas stamps for sugar stamps.

Allene O'Neill
Atria Carrollton
Dallas, Texas

Pauline worked in downtown Houston at the Ben Milam Hotel during the war where soldiers transferred in and out constantly. Pauline kept everything running smoothly for the GIs who were a long way from home and about to go overseas, and often lonely and afraid. Helping keep morale up was a service in itself. A smile or a kind word to a boy far from home went a long way.

Sometimes we think the great heroic acts are the important ones. We often fail to realize that small, ordinary kindness can make a difference in someone's life. Pauline later married a man who served in Italy in the Army.

Pauline Morrow
Atria Cypresswood
Houston, Texas

"I was a young girl when World War II broke out in America. I lived with my parents in San Francisco, and I remember that we had air-raid marshals who went around the neighborhood and told us that we had to pull our window shades down at night. The same marshals came by in the morning to tell us that it was okay to pull up our window shades. I heard those shrill sirens and every time I did, I trembled with fear. I knew there was war going on because older people talked about it all the time. However, those were adult conversations that were done in whispers whenever children were present. I never really understood how dangerous it was for us. I was afraid and insecure, and my mother told me to stay home and not wander far from the house. During the wartime period, we could not have everything we wanted. Milk, eggs, coffee, sugar and butter were difficult to get. We had stamps for these and stood in line for hours to get them. I remember my mother used to make her own butter."

Joyce Nagel, daughter of Lorraine Murdock, resident
Atria Daly City
Daly City, California

"I was married to a second lieutenant and I traveled and lived with him in 17 different places. I rolled bandages and worked with the USO providing coffee and donuts to the soldiers. I once accompanied a military representative to visit a family to notify them of their son's death. World War II was unforgettable."

Katherine Griffith
Atria Salisbury
Salisbury, Maryland

"I was already married to Richard Pedranzini during World War II. We had two wonderful children, a boy and a girl. My husband was not sent to the war because it was more important to keep him here than to send him to war. Meanwhile. I worked in retail in one of the stores in San Francisco that sold wine and liquor . . . all the good stuff. I worked despite having children to take care of because everything was expensive. I left my kids with my relatives or sometimes with my husband's relatives when I was working.
I also kept a victory garden in our backyard.

I planted lettuce, tomatoes, corn, carrots, beats, cauliflower and broccoli. The government encouraged us to plant our backyards with vegetables to help in food production.

In the beginning of the war, I was so afraid. I did not know what would happen. I was always scared that San Francisco would be bombed just like Hawaii. We had to put our window shades down and cover them with black cloth to keep the lights out. At night there were air-raid wardens. These wardens patroled the neighborhood and they told us to raise our blinds when it was okay to do so. I think that we were fortunate we did not get bombed, as we had always feared. Nevertheless, I was so scared then. I was so thankful when the war finally ended."

Rosalie Pedranzini
Atria Daly City
Daly City, California

"When my husband was drafted to serve his country, we sold our established cleaning business and headed for Fort Dix, New Jersey, where he was to report for active duty. Upon arriving at Fort Dix, an officer checked his paperwork and said that there had been a mistake and that they had changed the age limit for being drafted and that he was now too old to serve. Therefore, he did not have to serve his country.

My husband went to work for Bethlehem Steel. He worked long hours that kept him away from home. To help with the family income, I began to take in typing jobs for extra money. I rode the bus downtown to pick up typing assignments. I was paid so much for every 100 pieces that I typed. I did not suffer as much as some others in those trying times – thanks to God's help."

Gertrude Petrova
Atria Collier Park
Beaumont, Texas

"During World War II, I worked at the military office in the Presidio in San Francisco, as an office clerk. I logged the names of the people who came into the office on official and unofficial business. I was later transferred to the water department in Van Ness. My job was the same there, mainly clerical.

My experience during the war was sad. I had a boyfriend, Mannie, who was drafted. I don't know what happened to us. It seems that we both lost interest in one another. We did not even write to each other. I think that the war changed people and how they felt.

I had a friend whose name was Hilda. Her parents were Japanese, but Hilda was born in America. During World War II, the Japanese were taken to concentration camps. I remember when Hilda and her family were taken from their home. I was very sad because Hilda was my best friend. I heard that they were taken to camp at Tanforan and I never saw her again."

Frances Pivnick
Atria Daly City
Daly City, California

Helen was a young lady during the war and lived with her parents in Petal, Mississippi, in a modest house in a middle-class neighborhood. To Helen, World War II was a time of great sacrifice.

"We had to learn how to live on a whole lot less money. If the men were lucky, they made only $2 or $3 dollars a week," said Helen.

Sugar and gasoline were rationed, and Helen can remember needing stamps to buy a number of necessities.

"People traded the stamps for different things, even whiskey," said Helen.

Because the food supply was so terribly low, her father plowed up the yard and planted a garden of turnip greens. Helen can remember him giving some to the local neighbors when they were in need. Supplies were short and prices were high. Even fishing hooks were expensive, so they bent straight pins and fished with them.

Helen remembers that the war was a time of sadness and stress. Although times were very hard, Helen came from a family that loved her very much and taught her the meaning of sacrifice.

Helen Price
Atria Weatherly Springs
Huntsville, Alabama

"My mother, who was a widow and in her 50s during World War II, lived in San Francisco and was a very strong, brave woman. In the face of difficulties, she was not fazed or rattled.

Life was difficult then because of food rationing. The government provided seeds to plant gardens in the backyards and these gardens were meant to augment food production. Some bought their own seeds to plant. My mother, who always kept a garden, took advantage of the government's victory garden project during that time. She felt that she contributed to making life easier during war times by supporting the government's food production project. She shared the produce from her garden with her neighbors. She did not sell her vegetables, instead she gave them to her neighbors free of charge.

My mother also sent clothes and goods to her family in Italy. My mother and her family did not experience any discrimination like some Italian families did during the war. My mother loved America, no matter how difficult the war period was."

Fortunata Pelligrini by Lina Ragghianti
Atria Daly City
Daly City, California

"My husband served during World War II and I worried myself to death at home. He was wounded and was in the hospital for three years."

Mary Pruitt
Atria Salisbury
Salisbury, Maryland

"My contribution to the defense of our nation during World War II was working in the personnel department of Kaiser Shipyards on Swan Island in Portland, Oregon. Numerous ships were constructed at that location for service in the Pacific war zone.

Throughout the war, the selling of war bonds often took place at the defense plants where some well-known (and some not so well-known) entertainers performed for the workers. It was early in my singing career that I was asked to perform in a bond drive. The song I sang was 'Night and Day,' which seemed appropriate for the nighttime shift. The actor Gene Kelly was the star performer at that event. It was one of the few happy memories I have of World War II. By the way, my uncle had me buy $10,000 worth of war bonds for him that night".

Sylvia Radovich
Atria Daly City
Daly City, California

Bonnie Pyle had a fit when her husband wanted to join the service in 1941, but Ernie won and entered the Air Force. The couple was sent to Victorville, California, but had no place to live because the base had so many servicemen looking for housing. They finally found a mountain cabin 35 miles away and shared it with another couple.

Bonnie went to work on the post in civilian personnel where she was responsible for the timecards of 800 civilians. Pilots trained at the Air Force base and Bonnie remembers them flying overhead, stirring up the dust after the women had hung the wash on the line. Bonnie also remembers rationing, especially of nylon stockings. Women painted lines down the backs of their legs to make it look like they were wearing hose.

Ernie was transferred to San Francisco to recruit WACS and was scheduled to go overseas the day the war ended. What a relief it was for Bonnie and Ernie when they found out that good news.

Bonnie Pyle
Atria Cypresswood
Houston, Texas

"When my boyfriend was drafted into the service, we agreed to marry when he became an officer, which I thought would take two years. Instead, it took seven months! He was supposed to go on maneuvers overseas and his buddy was going to the 97th division in Texas. His buddy got the measles so their orders were changed and my husband was sent to the Texas division instead. This change probably saved his life!"

Lucille Van Kirk
Atria Salisbury
Salisbury, Maryland

It was 1941. Marge was 18 years old and a music student at the University of Louisville. One year later, she married her husband who served as a Captain and later Lt. Col. Three years later, their daughter was born. War circled around them, but her husband was not forced overseas until after the war ended. His company was responsible for cleaning up the concentration camps in Europe.

Marge remembers the rationing and other lifestyle changes that occurred during the war. She recalls praying continually for her husband as well as others serving in the war. At some point Marge's husband was given a one-month leave that eventually became a permanent leave – the Japanese surrendered and the war was really over.

Marge Hewitt
Atria St. Matthews
Louisville, Kentucky

When World War II broke out, Rita was just 12 years old and lived in DePelchin's Children's Home because her mother had died when she was nine. Rita had two brothers in the service and remembers missing them horribly while they were away. The boys wrote to her older sisters, who kept Rita up to date on their location and news.

Rita remembers how much she loved hot chocolate and not being able to have any because of sugar rationing. Even at her age, Rita was able to make a contribution to the war. War stamps were sold for about a nickel. Rita bought them when she could and pasted them into a coupon book. When Rita had saved $17.50 she bought a war bond. These bonds financed much of the war. Giving up her nickels was a big sacrifice for Rita, but it was all part of doing the right thing for America.

Rita Reglein
Atria Cypresswood
Houston, Texas

"In 1941 during the war, I worked as a medical assistant for a doctor on Sutter Street in San Francisco. I also drove for the Red Cross. I think it was very important to work during World War II to support our country. Everyone did without some of the things we could normally have. In a way, we felt a little insecure because we did not know what would happen. We just did what we had to do, and hoped that the war would be over soon.

In San Francisco, we experienced blackouts. We heard air-raid sirens once in a while, and when we did, we had to stay where we were. Like everyone else, I was glad when the war was over.

I felt I was doing something good for my country by helping the people get medical attention."

Hazel Robinson
Atria Daly City
Daly City, California

"I was single and working in a bank in Worchester, Massachusetts, when a lady from the Red Cross came in and gave the female employees of the bank a lecture. She was recruiting volunteers to be trained to work as nurse assistants because there was a terrible nurse shortage. When she finished, she asked if anybody would be interested. Two of us offered our services.

We had probably two months training at night at the Red Cross headquarters. At the end of our training, we took a test and we both passed it. We worked at Worchester Hospital at night after working all day at the bank. We provided basic nursing care for the patients. It felt good to be doing something during the war. I volunteered my services for about two years, until the end of the war."

Norma Benjamin
Atria Windsor Woods
Hudson, Florida

Barbara remembers World War II because she met her husband, Steve, when she and her mother went to a USO dance. Steve left for the war shortly after the two met, but they kept in touch by mail. Barbara does not remember how long Steve was in the war in France before she saw him again.

Steve was injured in the service by a land mine. The incident earned him a Purple Heart for bravery, but it also left him with ear and nerve damage and burns to his body.

Barbara Ticaric
**Atria Collier Park
Beaumont, Texas**

Edith's husband, Frank, was drafted but when he appeared before the draft board he told the officials he had 150 head of cattle he had to take care of, so the draft board refused to enlist him. Cattle ranchers were required to stay stateside during the war. At that time, everything was regulated by the government. People were

permitted to raise chickens and hogs, but the cattle belonged to the government. With Frank on the ranch and no money coming in, Edith needed work. She had friends who worked in the egg breaking and powdering plant in Denison, Texas, and they got her a job. Edith worked 11 p.m. – 7 a.m. and commuted 25 miles to work, a long drive in those days. They brought in crates of 12 dozen eggs and Edith's job was to "candle" them. This means that she held the eggs in front of an electric light bulb in order to determine their freshness. Sometimes the eggs contained live chicks, so she placed them in a bucket. Sometimes they were rotten and exploded, covering her with the stench of rotten eggs. She wasn't allowed to clean up; her job was to keep on going. Many of the eggs were powdered and sent to the boys overseas. According to Edith, the only thing that kept her going was the thought that some of the eggs would reach her five brothers who were all serving in the armed forces at the time.

Edith Tolley
**Atria Cypresswood
Houston, Texas**

"I was born in 1940, so when World War II started I was just one year old. You may be asking, 'Why in the world are you in this Rosie the Riveter story? What job did you do during that period? What were you able to contribute to the wartime era?' These are good questions and I have some good answers.

I believe that everyone alive, from cradle to near going to the tomb, did something to contribute to the good of America. As a baby, I did not know anything at all about what was happening, but I was exactly following what nature intended to happen to me. That was to eat, drink, sleep and grow up. I needed to do these so that I could become a valuable citizen of our country in my time.

Slowly, I grew up and began to notice things around me. I have a very vivid memory and I remember we had two residences during the war. We had a summer home in New Hampshire and a permanent residence in Boston. We shuttled back and forth between these residences, riding buses. I used to see cars in our garages. Once in a while, my father drove the cars. We did not use them as often as we wanted because gasoline was difficult to get. My father waited in line for hours to be able to get gasoline stamps so that he could fill the cars with gasoline. He was very careful not to waste fuel. I had the feeling that we were better off than other people because we had two houses when other people had only one. Even so, we experienced the same difficulties as everyone else.

As a young girl growing up, what else did I do to help? I guess being a good girl helped my parents a lot. I did not trouble them by whining and complaining when the food I wanted was not available. I did not ask for toys and shoes and clothes when they were difficult to get. I truly feel that I have contributed my share of forbearance and tolerance during the war. Because I was just a child and my mind was simple, I was not bothered by negative emotions that the complex minds of adults experienced."

Sally Shaw
Atria Daly City
Daly City, California

Maude worked for McDonnell Douglas Corporation where it was "get to work and get as much done as possible in one day!" She worked with big sheets of metal, which were used to make parts for airplane motors. Her husband Elwin worked as a welder at another company making parts for airplanes as well. Maude was fortunate to have her mother live with them and help take care of her children and the house while she and her husband worked. Maude doesn't remember what man's job she took at McDonnell Douglas, but she does remember how happy she was to be working and helping her husband by contributing to the household income.

Maude remembers not being able to turn on lights during the war and the awful feeling of being afraid of being bombed by the Japanese. She recalls the night Elwin told the family about the sirens and the spotlight on a plane over Long Beach Harbor, which was very close to home. Maude was terrified that Americans were going to be bombed.

Maude also remembers being at her church one day when the church leader asked the different branches of servicemen to come forward and share their testimonials. After about 45 minutes, the church leader stood up and announced that President Roosevelt had declared war because the Japanese had bombed Pearl Harbor. According to Maude, that day was filled with spiritual happiness and sadness. It was quite a day!

Maude Theobald
Atria Del Sol
Mission Viejo, California

"I remember rationing well – it was very difficult! One time I got a jar of mayonnaise. I was so excited because it was very expensive and very hard to get. I was holding the jar up to show everyone and anticipating what I would make when I accidentally dropped it and broke it. I was so disappointed. Of course this was a little thing when you consider a war, but it sticks in my memory."

Verna Taylor
Atria St. George
St. George, Utah

109

Chapter 2

"During the war years, I lived in Eureka, Utah. It was a silver-mining town that had all but blown away. My husband worked in Dugway, Utah. He came home only every other weekend because of gas rationing. Gas wasn't the only thing that was rationed during the war. I remember standing in line for a bag of flour. I didn't know what to do with it when I got it. We had ration stamps for other items, too. Red stamps were for meat, blue stamps were for canned goods. We were allowed one bottle of booze, and you had to have a stamp for that too. You sure could sell those stamps!

One of the things I remember during the war is going down to the Red Cross and volunteering. We did many things including rolling bandages."

Mary McClain
Atria St. George
St. George, Utah

"At the time of war, I was too young to work but I attended school. I had a brother who served in the war. I remember my family sending him cookies and letters of comfort with prayers to follow. We prayed for the soldiers' protection as well as our country's victory.

My brother had a fiancé who was waiting for his return. My family and I took pleasure in comforting her and keeping her occupied while he was away. My brother finally arrived home safely and he and his fiancé were married."

Eilleen Dunn
Atria Meridian
Lantana, Florida

"I was living in San Francisco with my husband and two children during World War II. I had an eight-year-old child and a newborn baby when the war began. I wanted to work and help my husband with finances, but there was no way I could leave my children. My husband worked in the shipyard then and worked long hours because life was difficult. I stayed home to make sure that everything was okay. I planted a vegetable garden in my yard to ease the difficulty with food. Some items were difficult to get and we stood in line for hours to get what we needed.

Some people might say the role of wife and mother during the war may not have been important. Now think again, if nobody stayed home to take care of the basic necessities in life like cooking meals, cleaning, doing the laundry and taking care of everyday tasks, who would have done them? Would life be bearable in the face of war if the home and family were neglected? I think that there were more unsung heroes in our midst, the wives and mothers who did a wonderful full-time job of it."

Rena Ragghianti
Atria Daly City
Daly City, California

"My husband and I owned a general store in Brooklyn. We worked seven days a week from 6 a.m. until 1 a.m. My husband was too old to be drafted into the service during World War II.

I remember that certain merchandise for our store, such as ice cream and cigarettes, was hard to get because ships typically used to transport the merchandise were being used to ship supplies to soldiers. Because of not having stocked merchandise, we decided to close the store early one evening per week. It was difficult working every day for long hours, but we needed to keep the business open because jobs were scarce during the war. During this time, I had a son. My mom watched him while we worked. I often wished we could have gone out to the movies, a show or just out to eat, but money was used for necessities and there was no time."

Stella Manaker
Atria Huntington
Huntington Station, New York

Florence Inman, after graduating from high school in 1938, helped rear five younger brothers and three younger sisters, kept books for the hatchery business and clerked in Aberdeen's leading jewelry store. Times were tough on the prairie with a severe depression, terrible dust storms and drought. Then came Pearl Harbor! Young men flocked to the military services in droves. The railroads were hard-pressed to carry servicemen, supplies and commodities so important to our nation at war.

The Railway Express Agency in Aberdeen was a vital part of the rail hub, but it lost its young men to the war effort. Florence took over jobs formally held by fellows now thousands of miles away. Greeting those shipping goods out and in and preparing bills became part of her everyday routine. She even drove the little green and gold trucks and delivered and picked up shipments.

Florence Inman Anderson
Atria Summit Hills
Crestview Hills, Kentucky

Cynthia was a young woman living in England during World War II. She had a job with the British government. Her boss at the time was a major in the service. Cynthia worked in an office that tracked bombs, amongst other things. The British released bombs over enemy targets and Cynthia, along with other women who had the same duty, kept track of where the bombs landed. This enabled the British to aim better. Cynthia also kept track of where German bombs hit. When bombs from the Germans did hit, relief crews were sent out to assess the damage and help the victims.

People were very patriotic during these times, but also scared (although no one showed it).

Cynthia Reichenthal
Atria East Northport
Long Island, New York

Chapter 2

"When the war started, they needed women to replace the men in factories. That's when I started to work. I was in Michigan and I went to a movie, and in all of the movie theaters they were asking for volunteers to work in factories making war products. They showed a picture of "Rosie the Riveter." I had never worked in a factory and I thought it would be kind of fun to see what it was like to work with one of those machines, so I went to Ford Motor Company. They wanted women to work in all sorts of production aspects at the factory. They gave me a set of coveralls. They had somebody show me how to operate the machine. You had to work on one part and then pass it on to the next person, so it was real fast. I didn't like it. I lasted a day!

At that time Ford didn't pay salaries, they just paid hourly, so they asked me what I would be able to do. When I asked them what they had available, they said they'd give me a job time-keeping with time cards. When people came to work, they had to punch the time card when they came in and when they got off from work. I checked the clock machines and then figured out the amount of time they worked for the day. I liked that job. I ended up staying with the company for 30 years.

Little did I know that watching that Rosie advertisement in the theater that day would shape my life."

Bernice Altland
Atria Windsor Woods
Hudson, Florida

"I married in September 1942, and my husband went in the Army four months later on January 2, 1943. I was very upset. Of course, only being married a short time, it was very difficult. I kept our apartment in New Jersey, because I knew that when he got out, it would be hard to find a new place.

My father-in-law owned a hardware business and with my husband gone, needed help in the shop. The store supplied materials to factories that manufactured items used in the war effort. I helped my father-in-law do some of the office work. I did everything from operating the switchboard to typing and filing to checking out customers. My father-in-law picked me up every morning and took me to work with him.

I also spent much of my time knitting sweaters for the Red Cross to keep myself busy. My mother joined the Red Cross and went to many meetings. She brought yarn home and we both knitted for the boys. The sweaters were big and heavy and were sent to soldiers serving in very cold areas. I can't say how many sweaters I knitted, but it seemed like it was a constant thing to do.

At times, my husband got leaves of absence or weekend passes to come home. However, he was shipped oversees to New Guinea and I didn't see him for two years. I wrote to him every week. Like many people, we had to put our life on hold."

Dorothea R. Drumm
Atria Windsor Woods
Hudson, Florida

"I married J.C. Fouts on June 13, 1943. The first month we were married, we moved to Wichita Falls, Texas, for his Army training. He lived on the base and I rented a room off-base. It was a wonderful time being together, but sad knowing my husband would be going off to war soon. We were only married a month when he left for war. He was in Hawaii first, then the Marianna Islands and eventually in Saipan. Saipan was a very bad place to be during the war. I worried so much about him being there and wondered if I would ever see him again. I received a lot of letters from him while he was away.

After a few months, I decided to live with my sister in St. Louis. I worked at the A & P Grocery store. It was a good job at the time. I took the bus to work everyday because I didn't have a car. In 1944, my friend Christine decided to move to St. Louis and live with us while all of our husbands were away at war. Christine got a job working for the Lazure Cosmetic Company. I soon started working there, too, because the pay was better than the grocery store. We rode the bus together every day. It was fun, but also sad with our husbands being away.

In 1945, great news came: the war was over! We were all so excited and I could hardly wait to see my husband. It had been 21 months since I had seen him!"

Esther Fouts
Atria Cordova
Memphis, Tennessee

> "In 1945, great news came: the war was over!"

"I'm 94 years old now, but I was 31 when the war started. My husband worked as a post engineer at the Mauldin Air Base in southeast Missouri. Housing was provided on the base and we weren't affected by the war like a lot of people.

I remember the news about Pearl Harbor. My husband came in from work and I told him what I had heard on the radio. Of course, he didn't believe me and had to hear it for himself. My husband was proud of his country and tried to sign up for the military. Unfortunately for him (but fortunate for me), he was unable to go due to medical reasons.

An organization called the Mauldin's Women's Club that I belonged to wanted to do something, so we potted plants and gave them to women whose husbands were actually fighting in the war overseas."

Glenda Davidson
Atria Primacy
Memphis, Tennessee

"I am 86 now, but I was 23 when World War II started. My husband and I lived in Chicago; we had no children at the time. My husband enlisted in the service and was trained to be a pilot. He became a 2nd Lieutenant and was sent to Las Vegas to train gunners. He flew every day that he was training, but he was lucky and never had to go overseas. I was away from him for five months when he trained in California. I then met him in New Mexico and followed him to Las Vegas. I was very fortunate to not be away from him for very long. We lived in public housing for $65 a month. We were involved in the Officer's Club, which we visited twice a month. We had feelings of anxiety all the time because nothing was for sure. I wondered every day if my husband would get shipped out.

I remember one time Bob Hope came to Las Vegas. I loved him immediately. He was a jolly man and joked with all the servicemen. We appreciated him very much."

Pauline Mosley
Atria Primacy
Memphis, Tennessee

"When Japan bombed Pearl Harbor and war was declared, my blood ran red, white and blue. Everyone wanted to do their part to help the cause. My husband was deferred because of his job. He worked for the IC Railroad and 100% of their work was war-related. His job was to train the workers. As soon as they were trained, they were sent off to war.

I wanted to help, but I had a small child at home to care for. I found what I thought was to be a reliable nanny to care for him, so I applied for a job at the Firestone Tire and Rubber Company in Memphis, Tennessee. My job was to test the rubber that was used on military vehicles. I learned to use chemicals to test the quality of the rubber. In my estimation, I became an integral part of the safety of our armed forces. Everything that traveled on rubber depended upon the strength and durability of products we tested."

Marie Cantrell
Atria Cordova
Memphis, Tennessee

Shirley was only 13 years old during the war, but that didn't keep her from helping out. She decided that she would volunteer her time wrapping bandages at a local drugstore. She and a close friend would meet everyday after school to ride the streetcar to the store so they could do their duty. The only compensation they received were small pins from the Red Cross. Shirley says she was glad that she could at least do something to help out at such a young age.

She also aided by writing letters to young boys who had no one to write them. Shirley's uncle was in the Army and she often wrote him. In one of his response letters he told her of several soldiers that were not receiving any letters from home, so she took it upon herself to write them a quick note. This began a chain of letters that Shirley wrote twice a week to 14 different soldiers throughout the course of the war.

Shirley Popham
Atria Summit Hills
Crestview Hills, Kentucky

Maribelle was 19, attending junior college, living with her parents, constantly dancing and enjoying life to its fullest when World War II began. Six weeks after Pearl Harbor was bombed, Maribelle married her husband. After being married only two days, her new husband was drafted and would be gone for three years before finally returning home.

Wanting to help with the shortage of workers, Maribelle went to work in a steel factory. Starting off alone on a little punch press, she punched out sheets of steel. After working with the little press, Maribelle moved to the bigger punch press and worked with more people. Maribelle worked on the sheets of steel for one year.

Maribelle's father worked in the oil business, so she never kept her gas tokens. Instead, she gave them away to people who needed them. Maribelle remembers that during the war, one of the ways Americans received information was by going to the movies and watching the newsreel that played before the actual movie, which is how she kept up with news about World War II.

Maribelle Tompkins
Atria Encinitas
Encinitas, California

Flora worked at Wright Aeronautical as an inspector of propellers. She worked second shift and learned to read blueprints. Flora remembers the rationing of sugar, meat, gas, nylons, shoes and other necessities.

"Everyone dealt with the rationing as a way to support America and didn't think of it as a loss of the quality of life," Flora said. "Remember, we just had a depression and people were just glad to have a job."

Flora Rogers
Atria Northgate Park
Cincinnati, Ohio

Joyce was 30 years old and single when she worked at Eastern Aircraft in Canton, Ohio. Eastern Aircraft built military aircraft and she worked in the personnel department. Joyce worked 40 hours a week on varying shifts and made a good salary. She remembers that she and her girlfriends enjoyed spending their money buying war bonds. After some time, Joyce and her girlfriends cashed in those war bonds and took trips to Ft. Lauderdale, Florida. She recalls having fun meeting the GIs who were getting released from the service. Joyce didn't like the lack of men available during the wartime. According to Joyce, it was dull and she disliked the hard work and the long hours.

Joyce Worman
Atria Chandler Villas
Chandler, Arizona

"Everyone dealt with rationing as a way to support America..."

At the age of 20, Anna worked at the General Electric plant in Fort Wayne, Indiana, where she buffed hubcaps on planes. She worked the 3 p.m. to midnight shift for four years. Anna enjoyed her work and made good money. Anna's mother was sickly, so Anna often bought presents for her, as well as for her father.

Anna Konanz
Atria Eastlake Terrace
Elkhart, Indiana

Mary began working at the age of 17 in 1942 for International Harvester, where motors were built for Jeeps and Army trucks. Her hours were 7 a.m. to 3 p.m. She prepared parts for the assembly line. They often sang while doing this. There was no resentment of having women working at the factory, and the men were not inhibited from telling their masculine-type jokes. The room was hot and smelled of oil, but their hands were smooth from being dipped in oil so often.

Mary and her friend Rose shared an apartment in Milwaukee. They sometimes went to the Eagles' ballroom to meet soldiers and sailors, but usually they went to bed early because of having to report for work so early. Her uncle bought a hearse, converted it into a bus and provided transportation for others who worked at the plant.

Mary's boyfriend would not marry her before his tour of duty because he feared he would be wounded. It so happened his leg was shattered and he was in traction in a hospital in England for a couple of months. When he came home, he was in a body cast and was sent to California. The two married in May 1946.

Mary Wesling
Atria Mallard Cove
Cincinnati, Ohio

In 1943 at the age of 26, Dorothy was the head cashier for the Naval Air Force Base in Norman, Oklahoma. She worked six days a week, and her duties included making deposits and ensuring that the cash registers were ready for the day. Her husband worked "the line" for the Navy, signaling the planes in, refueling them and getting them ready for their next takeoff. Dorothy had heard through a friend that a job at the Air Force base had opened up because the other gals who worked there were getting shipped away to be closer to their husbands. She didn't really want to be a head cashier, but a commander said she would be good at it, and she ended up really enjoying her job. She often stayed after work to help other gals sell war bonds.

Dorothy remembers a tornado coming through the base that moved airplanes on top of one another! She said she saw a lot of wounded and it was truly a sad time.

Dorothy Cunkelman
Atria Chandler Villas
Chandler, Arizona

During World War II, Billie lived in Los Angeles, near the University of Southern California. At the beginning of the war, Billie began working at Northrop Aircraft. At the same time, Billie's husband worked at a motor company. Their son was close to graduating high school at this time, and received a draft notice one day before his 18th birthday. He was not able to attend the graduation ceremony. A flag was placed in his seat instead.

Billie recalls there were a lot of blackouts during that time. She said that whenever there was an alert, there would be a blackout. Workers at her plant formed lines to go down the stairs. It was very dark, so they had to put their hands on the shoulders of the person in front of them and follow one another to the air-raid cellar. She said some people did have small flashlights they carried in their lunch pails, but actually there was not supposed to be any light at all because light made it easier for the enemy above to see. The cellar was small and had built-in seating all the way around with a drain in the middle and an air vent. There was a soldier who guarded the door to make sure that nobody left the cellar, such as a worried mother whose child was in school.

Billie continued to work for Northrop for 15 years, and her son did make it home safely.

Billie McGlasson
Atria Fullerton
Fullerton, California

"I had been living in Los Angeles for a short time when I heard on the news that Pearl Harbor had been bombed by the Japanese. It didn't seem possible that this was happening. As time went by, we had to face reality. We heard airplanes flying overhead and hoped they were not enemy planes. We put black shades on our windows so that airplanes could not see even a small amount of light.

Butter, eggs, meat, coffee and other foods, which we had taken for granted in the past, were in short supply as they were needed to feed our troops. Everyone was given a book of ration stamps, which were redeemable for scarce food and even shoes. If we drove by a line of people, we stopped and joined them because we knew there was something that we could buy at the end of the line.

Housing was also in short supply. Once when I was doing my spring housecleaning, I had taken down curtains to wash. Someone stopped by to ask if we were moving because they wanted to buy our house."

Fern Wilson
Atria Golden Creek
Irvine, California

"We heard airplanes flying overhead and hoped they were not enemy planes."

Chapter 2

"I was a secretary in San Francisco. The company sold wire and cable during the war. It was an interesting job as each day I did something new. I had an hour commute and then walked from the train station. When the war ended, all of the office workers walked to the main street in San Francisco and joined the celebration."

Ellison Voorhies
Atria Rancho Park
San Dimas, California

"My first job after I graduated from business college was in the state capital in Pierre, South Dakota, doing secretarial work. I took the Federal Civil Service exams for employment in Washington, D. C., and I was called to duty there in April 1941. I was assigned to a secretarial position in the Army Corps of Engineers. From April to December 7, 1941, things were pretty relaxed and life was enjoyable. I lived in a room-and-board house, and I met and socialized with many new people there.

Then the bombs exploded in Pearl Harbor and the whole world turned upside down. On the night of December 7, many of the tenants from our house went down to the Japanese Embassy. In fact, a huge crowd gathered; there were searchlights and the area was policed, making it impossible to get near.

On December 8, all of the officers in our division came to work in uniform, which was a big change from their civilian garb. The number of people employed at the corps increased every day and many temporary buildings were moved into the area. I worked mainly in a two-story temporary building on Connecticut Avenue. I was fortunate that my secretarial skills were excellent and I was called on to attend and record in shorthand many important meetings and long-distance phone calls. (Those were the days before recording devices were available.) After 18 months in Washington, I was transferred to a similar position with the Army Corps of Engineers in Omaha, Nebraska. From there and in addition to being the regional secretary, I was asked to attend and record more conferences in Omaha, a one-week conference in Ft. Leavenworth, Kansas, and another in St. Louis. I was married during my time in Omaha. My husband was stationed in Ft. Lewis, Washington, so I joined him there until he was sent overseas. I then worked at Puget Sound Shipbuilding Company, where they built tugboats.

Overall, my husband was in the Infantry in the Pacific theater for three and a half years during World War II. Then in 1950, he was called again to active duty for two years in the Korean War. I was happy to stay home then in Huron, South Dakota, with two active little boys."

Rita Nenaber
Atria Chandler Villas
Chandler, Arizona

At the start of World War II, Hazel was about 35 years old. She and her husband ran a school supply and equipment business. Although business was not affected drastically, Hazel does recall how the ration system affected her home and business. At home, gas, food, sugar and shoes were rationed. Everyone had to have a stamp for everything. Hazel and her husband used their stamps to get shoes for their children because they outgrew their shoes too quickly. At work, school supplies were needed because children still attended school during the war. However, paper, scissors and other supplies were rationed, so Hazel and her husband were very limited in what they could give to schools.

Hazel McCord
Atria St. Matthews
Louisville, Kentucky

Florence worked for three years as a civilian on a naval base in Norfolk, Virginia. She maintained supplies for naval aircraft. She was single, 18 years old and worked seven days a week for nine hours a day. Florence remembers that one of the bombs fell off a plane as the soldiers were loading it. Several soldiers lost their lives that day. Florence's parents were terrified after the accident and she was not allowed to leave work until well after midnight. At that time, she was on an elevator and the elevator fell, causing injury to another elevator passenger.

Florence remembers blackouts and eating only by candlelight at dinnertime. She also remembers that women could not get silk stockings, but she and her Mom could because the soldiers would get them for her. Soldiers often invited Florence up on the ship to take a tour and have lunch. About once a month, Florence's mother cooked meals for about four sailors. Florence and her mother received several letters from the sailors' mothers, thanking them for taking care of their boys.

Florence Hartley
Atria Chandler Villas
Chandler, Arizona

At the onset of the war, Euna was 25, had been married four years and had a one-year-old. Her closest kin fighting in the war were her two brothers who served in the Navy. They were able to come home to Louisville, Kentucky, on leave on several occasions throughout the war.

Life on rations for Euna's family meant traveling from the West End of Louisville to the East End of town in order to get soap powder, meat and other rationed commodities that could not be found in her neighborhood.

Euna, as well as her husband, were vital in maintaining their home, which in turn affected the home front and the entire society. When food is rationed, jobs are scarce and air raids are feared, the family offers love and protection and carries us through those hard times.

Euna Rush
Atria St. Matthews
Louisville, Kentucky

119

Clio Webber was no stranger to the business she managed when the war broke out. She and her husband owned and operated the country supply store on Peak's Island, Maine. When her husband left to fight in World War II, she easily assumed the responsibilities of manager and did everything required to run a busy store. One might get a picture of the type of work involved if you think of the television show "The Waltons." At Clio's store, everyone knew everyone, and Clio knew when a customer was due a 10-pound bag of flour, a bag of sugar or some other daily-living staple.

Clio recalls how quiet the island became after the men and some women left to go to war and work in the war factories. The island came back to life when almost everyone returned from the war.

Clio Webber
Atria Kennebunk
Kennebunk, Maine

Betty was in her 20's when she went to work for Ellis Military Camp. Her duties included working in the engineering department where she typed charts for the military on the large keyboard. She worked eight hours a day, five days a week and was paid $100 a month. She did this for a year and a half.

Her husband Walter was in the Army and was injured twice. Betty remembers the fear she had because the Army told her only that her husband was injured, but not the extent of his injuries. She remembers spending a lot of time with her son and her family, from whom she received lots of support.

Many of the wives had loved ones in the service and they often got together on days off and picnicked together with their children. Betty's hardest times were not knowing how her husband was and if he was going to be able to survive the war.

Betty Blunt
Atria Chandler Villas
Chandler, Arizona

"My husband was an officer in the Army Medical Corps. During the war, I volunteered with many other officers' wives at the Red Cross. Although the work wasn't what you'd call thrilling– we rolled bandages, miles and miles of bandages –we all enjoyed the sense of camaraderie and belonging. It made us feel good that we were doing our part while our husbands were so far away. After the Red Cross, I worked at the armory. I was originally hired to answer phones, but once my boss found out how capable I was, I began doing the bookkeeping and writing out the checks. It was an extremely busy place and I loved the work. When my husband came home, I jumped for joy! I quit my job and became a wife again."

Margie Atkinson
Atria Kennebunk
Kennebunk, Maine

Elizabeth worked at Curtis-Wright Defense Factory in Cincinnati, as a cashier. The factory made airplane engines for bomber planes. Elizabeth was in charge of passing out paychecks, which she carried with a cigarette-tray holder around her shoulders. She also took care of the cafeteria money and counted money bags. She worked Monday through Friday, 3 p.m. to 11 p.m., and earned 75 cents an hour. Elizabeth's husband also worked in the factory as a metallurgist.

Elizabeth remembers that so many people were deprived of necessities, like food and gasoline, but she also remembers a lot of support for those overseas.

Elizabeth Burley
Atria Chandler Villas
Chandler, Arizona

"Life as usual" is how Evelyn describes life in New York during World War II. Personally, she did not experience any hardships. She worked as a secretary in a federal government building.

Within her family, however, Evelyn did experience some tragedy. Her relatives, including her aunts and uncles, were killed in Poland because of their Jewish heritage.

Life can seem "as usual" on one side of the battlefield and be drastically threatened on the other.

Evelyn Coffiner
Atria St. Matthews
Louisville, Kentucky

From 1941 to 1942, Loretta worked in an airplane factory in Erie, Pennsylvania, painting registers. They had to complete 200 of these a day. She was 30 years old, married and had children. Her husband worked at Swift and Company, a meatpacking plant. He was not drafted because he was needed more at the beef factory.

One memory she has was that coffee and sugar was rationed, which she disliked because she loved her coffee with sugar. Because Loretta and her husband had easier access to meat than most people, they often exchanged and bartered beef for coffee and sugar!

Loretta Grappy
Atria Chandler Villas
Chandler, Arizona

"It made us feel good that we were doing our part while our husbands were so far away."

"I married my husband, Will Hunt, on October 12, 1941. On December 7, my new husband and I went for a drive with his parents. The radio was on and Will started hushing everyone. He told us that the Japanese had just bombed Pearl Harbor. His mother fussed at him for interrupting the conversation in the car, and then asked, 'Who in the world is Pearl Harbor?' He explained again and then everyone listened.

I worked for Kline Auto Company at that time. The next day, my boss called us together to listen to President Roosevelt declare war. We were in shock. People were very patriotic in that day. Togetherness was the word. At that time, I resigned from the car dealership and went to work for Pratt and Whitney, a parts-assembly division for military planes. I was a 22-year-old and the oldest worker there. Will worked in the assembly on the south side of town. I worked in parts on the north side of town. I drove my husband to work and had several other riders to the parts division every day. We carpooled because of gas rationing.

We didn't have to wear a uniform, but we had to wear a badge on our clothing, a wristband and we had a special decal on our cars. Security was very tight.

Will actually worked with 'Rosie the Riveters.' He used to come home at night and tell me about how all the old men watched the women in their tight pants. I asked him if he looked and he said, 'Of course not!'

I became pregnant in 1943 and I didn't tell anyone at work that I was pregnant. I had a son and stayed home with him. We moved to Washington in 1944, and Will went to work in defense in a small town called Hanford, Washington. He came home one night and told me that something big was going on there. He described concrete walls 20 feet wide and deep. He felt that they were getting ready to build a huge explosive."

Bernice Hunt
Atria Cordova
Memphis, Tennessee

"My husband and I owned an automobile repair shop. When World War II broke out, they quit manufacturing automobiles and started building ships and airplanes, so it was necessary to keep cars in running condition for the duration of the war. As a result, my husband wasn't drafted.

I remember the blackouts during that time. Before dark, we had to draw blackout curtains across all windows, and all business and streetlights were turned off so the enemy couldn't see any buildings or activities. There was a shortage of products and the government started rationing many items, such as butter or oleo, sugar, flour, shortening, nylons and cigarettes. Gasoline and tires were also rationed. I remember standing in long lines every week to get our supplies. If they ran out of an item, we had to wait until the next week to purchase it."

Winona Davidson
Atria Rancho Park
San Dimas, California

Leslie did sales and secretarial work in her father's jewelry store during World War II. She also did a lot of volunteer work in a hospital because she felt that women should do whatever was needed to help support the men fighting in the war.

"We women were very close then," Leslie said. "We had a unity, a closeness, a common cause. We all just wanted peace and for our men to come home."

Leslie Levenstein
Atria Tinton Falls
Tinton Falls, New Jersey

"The memories of World War II are vivid to me after all these years. One of the first things I remember is how the USA pulled together. We were truly united. We had a goal to win. Most of all, our citizens did their part, starting with our military who did their all. Mothers who lost sons or daughters in the service were awarded a gold star for their window. Rationing was a way of life. Everything was scarce. Sugar was at a premium. There were those who hoarded sugar. We had stamps for meat and we saved the stamps up if we wanted beef or pork. We were asked to have no meat at least one day a week. If you were fortunate enough to have a car, you had to keep a watch on the gas stations to get in line for gas. Tires were almost impossible to get, so you kept patching the ones you had. All this led to the formation of car pools.

Bob Hope and many of the stars gave their time entertaining troops, some even in combat zones. We were asked to do without many things that we took for granted before the bombing of Pearl Harbor.

My husband, Bill, was in the Air Corps and spent six years in the service. When he was eventually stationed in San Bernardino, California, I joined him there and searched for an apartment. Luck smiled on me and I found a two-bedroom guesthouse for $48 a month. The OPA had frozen rents, so what was charged before the war was still the same rent. We rented the spare bedroom to a flight officer for $30 a month. He was a friend of my husband and we stayed in touch with him for several years, even when he was a POW in Japan. I often wrote to his mother and we became pen pals.

When Bill was shipped out overseas, I returned to Memphis, Tennessee, and went to work at the Federal Reserve Bank of St. Louis, a clearing house for checks where I ran an IBM proof machine. All checks from the military at Halls, Tennessee Air Base came through our department.

When the war ended, Memphis really celebrated. Traffic was at a standstill. The streets were full of joyful and grateful people. It was a true melting pot because no one was a stranger. Once again, we were all united – this time in gratitude."

Dorris Corbitt
Atria Cordova
Memphis, Tennessee

Chapter 3

Nearly four years after President Roosevelt declared war on Japan, the event that's been dubbed the largest, most violent armed conflict in history finally ended. With this announcement came celebrations, dancing in the streets, parades, tears of joy and soldiers returning home. Fathers met their children for the first time ever, wives communicated with their husbands for the first time in years and many women gave their jobs back to veterans in anticipation that life would be "normal" again.

From now on it's YOUR job

There is a place for EVERY woman in this nurse crisis

ARMY NURSE · NAVY NURSE · WAC HOSPITAL TECHNICIAN · NURSE'S AIDE
RED CROSS INSTRUCTOR · CADET NURSE · HOME NURSING STUDENT

Go to your local Nurse Recruitment Center TODAY

Louise used to work at Marshal Fields in Chicago. She remembers how the Red Cross came to her suburban store after hours and set up a few tables to recruit volunteers. Louise was one of the employees who stayed after regular work hours to help make scarves and bandages for the men at war. She remembers knitting khaki wool to make the scarves.

When it was announced that the war was over, Louise was in downtown Chicago. That day, Louise felt a great feeling of relief. Happiness was on everyone's face because the end of the war meant that the difficult times were over.

Louise Erlandson
Atria Bonita
Chula Vista, California

Martha recalls the day she saw the first cement structures rising up from the new construction site near her home in Columbus, Ohio. A new sign had also appeared that told Martha she was looking at the future home of a Curtis-Wright aircraft factory.

"I was only 17 years old, but I was so impressed," she recalls now, more than 60 years later. "I remember thinking, 'Gee, I wish I could work there, but I can't. I'm a girl.' After all, that's how it was in those days."

In February 1942, just three months after her 18th birthday, Curtis-Wright hired Martha

and sent her to six weeks of unpaid training before putting her to work helping build Navy fighter planes. She was paid 60 cents an hour, twice what she'd earned selling dresses, her only previous job. But in this job, she soon came to appreciate the opportunity to apply her mechanical aptitude as she drilled aluminum for fuel tanks and performed final testing and repairs on fighter plane hydraulic systems.

She appreciated the sense of accomplishment that came from supporting a valuable cause – the war effort – by doing one's job well.

"My boss kept giving me the darndest things to work on," she recalls. "Later, he told me that was because I was the best mechanic he had."

When the war ended, so did Martha's employment.

"I really loved that job," she said recently "When the war was over, we were told 'to go home and get married and have babies.' Of course, some women needed to work because they were the sole breadwinners for their families or due to other circumstances, … but that was never taken into account."

"You just fell in love with that plane," she recalls now, smiling. "It was like part of you was in it. You knew two men would soon be flying it and that their lives depended on how good a job you did, so you really put your whole being into doing the job right."

Martha Salyer
Atria Woodside Village
Columbus, Ohio

CURTISS HELLDIVER
U.S. NAVY DIVE BOMBER

Emma can tell exactly what kind of effect World War II had on families. Not only did she have to worry about her husband serving overseas, but she also had three brothers serving.

She remembers her mother crying and worrying about her brother's safe return. Emma went to work at Kodak while her husband was at war. She remembers what it was like when the war ended, with everyone joyously dancing in the streets and parading with flags. Her family was blessed by the safe return of her husband and all three of her brothers.

Emma Suski
Atria Greece
Rochester, New York

"My husband was in Europe about two years. When he finally came home, he met me at my folks' home. All I could do was cry when I saw him. It was a wonderful time. My husband was closed-mouthed when he first came home. The boys were slaughtered and he just couldn't talk about it. After a couple of years of working

in the states, he worked himself up to assistant warden in the New Jersey State Prison. He made a good husband and was a fair man. He gave the prisoners a break when they deserved one."

Mildred Abbott
Atria Primacy
Memphis, Tennessee

"I had two brothers in the war, and my mother was just beside herself. She volunteered wherever she could, and she couldn't keep herself away from the radio. On Victory Day, my mother heard shouting in the streets and went outside where everyone else was celebrating. I don't think anyone stayed inside on that day. Everyone was overjoyed!"

Thelma Burge
Atria Springdale
Louisville, Kentucky

During World War II, Mary worked in the Twinkie factory in Los Angeles. She worked on the assembly line and made sure the Twinkies were wrapped correctly. She worked six or seven days a week from 6 a.m. to 2 p.m. and earned 84 cents an hour. She wore short-sleeved shirts, pants and something to cover her hair. She was married at the time with an infant daughter. Her mother baby sat while she worked. Mary's husband, Frank, worked in the steel industry and was purposely not drafted, as the steel industry needed him. He later helped Mary get a job at the steel factory as a magnet-crane operator. The crane stood 20 feet high and Mary moved steel plates from one place to another. She wore denim at this job and a cap to keep her hair out of her eyes. She started at 59 cents an hour and worked her way up to 89 cents an hour.

Mary Molner
Atria Chandler Villas
Chandler, Arizona

A native of Canada and living in Washington, Phyllis worked for the British Ministry of Supplies as a secretary. At the time, she was not a United States citizen, but did what she had to do to become one. Her husband, Woodsen, was a captain in the Army.

According to Phyllis, everyone was involved during the war; it just so happened that she worked for the British and recalls that women worked wherever they were needed.

When the war was over, it was wonderful! During World War II, everything that was done surrounded the cause. After the war, everyone could relax and enjoy life again.

Phyllis Baldwin
Atria Buena Vista
Vista, California

"Robert G. Latham and I were married on April 14, 1941. When war was declared, he volunteered for the Air Force and was then sent to special forces. I stayed at home and helped my brother with his restaurant. I was a very lonely woman and missed my husband greatly. I made my whole family miserable because I was the only daughter and they didn't like to see me sad. I looked forward to Robert coming home on leave. When I could, I would catch a train and go see him. It was wonderful to have him home again after the war ended."

Edith Latham
Atria Cordova
Memphis, Tennessee

Twenty-two-year-old Myra worked in the war department at the Pentagon for two years. She had top clearance and read and decoded mail. She also scanned the mail and routed it to the proper officer. Her boss was a colonel.

Myra dreaded Wednesday mornings because all employees had to watch raw footage from the battlefields.

The Pentagon believed that this kept the workers' morale up and helped them maintain their desire to do a good job.

After the war, she became a librarian and teacher. Myra was grateful that all four of her brothers came home from the war unharmed.

Myra Johnson
Atria Chandler Villas
Chandler, Arizona

Helen remembers the day Japan surrendered – not because she was celebrating the end of the war, but because it was also the same day her husband left to go serve. She remembers one of her friends calling to announce the exciting news about the war being over. Helen's only reply was that her husband had just left.

Helen Katz
Atria Springdale
Louisville, Kentucky

When the war began, men who'd previously held teller positions at banks went off to war. At that time, women stepped up to the windows and took charge. When the war was over and the men came home, female workers relinquished their jobs to the veterans. Sadie returned to the bookkeeping work she'd done before the war.

The biggest change that the war's end brought to Sadie, though, was the return of her fiancé and her marriage to him. Sadie said she felt she was an important part of the women's effort to support the troops in war, and her effort was the best way she had to serve.

Sadie Short
Atria Crossgate
Albany, New York

Dorothy went to work in an airplane factory during the war. She was hired as a supervisor and made 40 cents an hour. The line workers earned about 30 cents an hour. Dorothy's job was to inspect the airplane parts to make sure they fit properly.

According to Dorothy, when the men started to come back from the war they got their jobs back at the factory. The women who were working those positions were laid off. Dorothy enjoyed working at the factory, but doesn't know how she managed it all back then because of the long hours and taking care of the house and the children, too.

Dorothy Brewer
Atria Seville
Las Vegas, Nevada

"In 1942, I went to work as a clerk-typist for Elastic Stop Nut Corporation in Union, New Jersey. The company made self-locking nuts, and it grew because of the war.

I remember listening to President Roosevelt's Fireside Chat on December 8, 1941, which was his 'Day of Infamy' speech. I also recall we had war-bond rallies at work and that our company received the 'E for Excellence' award from the government. I worked for the Elastic Stop Nut Corporation for 25 years."

Mary Oberst
Atria Cranford
Cranford, New Jersey

At age 20, Muriel packed her bags and moved to Washington, D.C., to work for the government. Muriel's parents were not pleased, but supported her. Muriel began working for the government as a clerk. Her duties included typing documents, filing and basic office tasks. After a few years, Muriel was promoted to federal financial aid attendant, making a salary of $1,440 a year. Her job entailed rationing metals, which were a limited resource due to the war. Companies had to submit their applications for the amount of metal they needed, which were received by Muriel, who would either approve or disapprove the requests. The final say in rationing the metals and approving the applications was Muriel's, a big responsibility, and a nearly unheard of opportunity, for an African-American woman back then.

After five years in Washington, D.C., Muriel missed New York, so she got a job working with the Veterans Administration, helping men who had been to war. After a few more years, Muriel got a job working for a well known lawyer in New York. She made $1,500 a year. Her job wasn't easy, but she loved it.

After Muriel met her husband on a blind date, she quit her job at the attorney's office and found her true passion in life—teaching. Muriel was a teacher until she retired. She says she is so lucky to have worked in all the various jobs she did because it helped her to find her true passion in life.

Muriel Walker
Atria Sunlake
Las Vegas, Nevada

"During World War II, I was employed at Aunt Hannah's Bakery, a subsidiary of Ward Baking Company. I took the place of a man who had been drafted. In order to get the job, I had to sign papers stating I would relinquish his job if he wanted it back upon his return.

My job was to check in 60 route salesmen daily. They would deliver their bread to the stores, return to the bakery and settle up with me. I held this job for two years.

When the men were overbalanced with me by a small amount, I put the overage in a petty cash box. My last day at the company, I threw a party for all of the men using the overage fund. They were shocked to see I had saved all of that money! And, by the way, the man I replaced came back to his job."

Lois Neubrand
Atria Windsor Woods
Hudson, Florida

Mary was 19 years old during World War II, and already working at West Coast Loading in San Bernardino, California. Her job in the factory was to powder and fold the parachutes coming off the conveyor belt. It was a difficult job. The powder from the parachutes was so strong that Mary can remember one time when she was powdering the chute and the powder got in her eye and she could not see clearly for a couple of days. This factory did not provide the best working conditions for its employees. The nearest bathroom was 20 acres away.

After a few years, Mary and her husband moved to Riverside, California. Her husband worked in the tin mills and Mary had jobs over the years in various factories. Ready for a change, Mary landed a job at the post office. Starting at the bottom, she worked her way up to become a postman. Men didn't like the idea that women were getting paid the same, so women at the post office had to stick together and not let men intimidate them. The salary for both women and men was $1,000 per year. Mary worked for the post office until she retired.

Mary Hutchinson
Atria Sunlake
Las Vegas, Nevada

"Some of my girlfriends from school and I applied for work at the Cutler-Hammer plant in Milwaukee. I got a job making electrical switches for aircraft, which I did for two and a half years. This was not the cleanest job, and it made me appreciate being in a clean home. My girlfriends and I rented an apartment and lived there the whole time we were working.

After the war, I wanted to continue working. I applied for a position at Allis-Chalmers in the purchasing department. I got the job and went to work right away. This ended up being a wonderful place for me to work. This is where I met my husband. I was in the right place at the right time."

Jane Goede
Atria Sandy
Sandy, Utah

"I worked for the Department of Agriculture in Salt Lake City, and made aerial maps of the training area in Wendover, Nevada.

Air Force pilots took pictures of the area and brought them to my department where we made the maps. The pictures were about 8" x 8". I beveled the ends toward the back and matched them up to make a map. Around 25 photos were put together and soon we had a perfect aerial map of the war training area.

After the war, I made aerial maps for farmers and industrial companies.

Now, every time I go out to one of the casinos, I look over into the desert and think I might see something I remember from those maps, and I make up my own stories in my mind.

Rowena Beratto
Atria Sandy
Sandy, Utah

Mary made her contributions during the war era by working as a cashier in the phone company cafeteria. She had to be at work very early every morning to prepare for the phone operators and see that the lines of communication remained open. She also waited and bused tables when the cafeteria was very busy. After the war, things did not change dramatically for Mary, though there seemed to be a little less urgency for everyone.

Mary Rapazzo
Atria Crossgate
Albany, New York

Helen worked for Lady Joyce, a clothing manufacturer in Lindenhurst, New York. During the war, Lady Joyce went from making women's fashions to skirts for the Army and Navy service women. Helen's job was to hem the skirts and apply the buttons.

When the war ended, Lady Joyce went back to making women's fashions. Helen continued to work there for 30 years.

Helen Manerowski
**Atria East Northport
Long Island, New York**

"My husband, Master Sgt. James Patton, was sent to war in the Pacific. I was left behind in Chicago, working for the government. I was a civilian worker assigned to the weapon unit of the Army and the Navy. I was responsible for managing the control numbers on the weapons that were issued to military personnel.

World War II was very difficult for me because I was constantly worried for the safety of my husband, who was in actual combat. The only communication we had was through letters, which were so slow in coming. I was afraid that something bad was happening to James when I did not receive letters from him as often as I expected to. I was terrified every time I heard about those who died in combat. I was so glad when the war was over – my husband came back home to me alive and whole!"

Wylodine Patton
**Atria Daly City
Daly City, California**

Ruth worked as a waitress. Both her husband and her brother served in the war. In addition to worrying about them, she was also very concerned about her mother because her mother was distressed over Ruth's brother serving overseas. Ruth had other relatives in the war as well, and she remembers how happily her family celebrated when they all returned safely.

Ruth Shoopinsky
**Atria Greece
Rochester, New York**

Kathleen began her wartime career working at an RCA factory in New Jersey. Later, she joined the U.S. Cadet Corps and was trained as a registered nurse. Most of the registered nurses were needed at locations around Europe and the South Pacific. But this left the United States short of nurses, which was a void Kathleen was happy to fill.

She received on-the-job training. A typical day included four hours in the morning and four more in the afternoon in hospitals.

After training, Kathleen was supposed to officially join the military, but the war had ended. Shortly afterward, she took the New Jersey state board test to become a certified registered nurse. She continued to work as an R.N. for many years. Kathleen's only regret is that several of her friends did not return home from the war.

Kathleen Salek
**Atria Briarcliff Manor
Briarcliff Manor, New York**

In 1942 after graduating from high school, Marie was eager to join the service. She found out, however, that at the age of 19 she was too young and had to wait until she was 20 to serve. A little discouraged, Marie followed up with different branches of the services to see which one she was interested in. After discovering that she did not want to be in the Army or Navy, and that she was too short to be in the Marines, she learned the Coast Guard needed women.

In addition to a typical physical, Marie had to take an eye examination, which made her nervous because she knew she had a weak left eye. To help ensure she made it into the Coast Guard, Marie memorized the eye chart and passed the exam with ease. Her tests also included a written test, a psychological test and an FBI interview. It was a long process and it made her very nervous, but on her 20th birthday, Marie was on a bus headed for Palm Beach, Florida, for basic training. She was thrilled to be on her way to serving her country.

After bootcamp training, Marie was stationed at the Boston Coast Guard Station, which disheartened her because she wanted to be somewhere far from her hometown of Jersey. One day, though, an announcement was made that two new stations were open: one in Alaska and the other in Hawaii. This was the break Marie had been waiting for! She chose Alaska and was soon transferred. After three hours on an Alaska-bound private ship, another announcement came. This one bellowed that the war was over and the ship should return to port. Marie remembers being elated for her country, but very disappointed personally. Moments later, the crew decided to follow through with its original plan and go to Alaska. In Alaska, the crew relieved many men on post there and sent them home.

"You had to be there. It was the best feeling in the world to send those men home!" Marie said. She was stationed in Alaska for one year working as a secretary in an office on base. It was there that she met her husband, Al.

Marie Middlesworth
Atria Buena Vista
Vista, California

Sally remembers the local grocery store saving cans of pineapples and peaches. "They issued us coupons for food," she said. "It was a very scary time."

She recalls that her brother-in-law was in charge of her neighborhood during blackouts. During blackout drills, he went door to door telling everyone to turn out their lights for security purposes. "We learned not to take anything for granted," Sally said.

When the news of victory resonated over the radio, Sally remembers her son, Dicky, who was seven or eight at the time, paraded up and down the streets with other neighborhood children, beating their little drums.

"So many peoples' loved ones were involved in the war," said Sally. "It was such a wonderful time when it was all over!"

Sally Stone
Atria Weatherly Springs
Huntsville, Alabama

Virginia was a home-front worker at Taylor Instruments assembling parts during World War II. She worked five days a week from 7 a.m. until 7 p.m., and sometimes she even worked until noon on weekends.

Virginia remembers being at work when she found out the war was finally over and going downtown with all her co-workers to celebrate. Though she was not married before the war, she did correspond with a friend she had known all her life. When he returned from the war, they went on their first date. It was a memorable date because he proposed that very night!

Virginia continued to work at Taylor for 15 years, finally quitting when she got pregnant with her first child.

Virginia Smith
Atria Greece
Rochester, New York

Dorothy worked at the Ford Plant in Ypsilanti, Michigan. The local employment office contacted her and Dorothy responded promptly because she knew she would be doing her part to help the country! "It was just accepted that women would go to work, and I felt good about it," she said. Clad in a blue-canvas, drop-seat uniform, Dorothy worked on B-24 planes.

On February 26, 1944, Dorothy married her husband, who had taken a leave from serving in the war. He then returned to the war and she continued to work until she was laid off after President Roosevelt died. Dorothy moved to Kansas City, Missouri, to live with her sister and she took a job as a typist at the Methodist Publishing House. From Kansas City, she transferred to Cincinnati, Ohio, where her husband joined her.

When the war ended, Dorothy continued working because she always felt she should do her part.

Dorothy Gilroy
Atria St. Matthews
Louisville, Kentucky

"My experiences take me back to a giggly gal of 22 entering into marriage. Oh, he was so cute! After phone calls and romantic letters from Annapolis, Maryland, I left my cozy family life for my first train ride to become a bride. After several days of 'What am I doing?', my train arrived at the station. I was met by my very handsome, 24-year-old sailor. As a scared bride-to-be, I gingerly walked on ice-encrusted sidewalks to the preacher's house. After our wedding ceremony, my new husband and I went to our one-bedroom, one-bathroom home, which we shared with others. Boy, was I green!

Later we moved to Virginia and I was amazed to learn the stork knew our address. The radio broke the news of Japanese strikes and my husband was sent overseas. Tearfully, I went back to San Diego with my parents' first grandchild. Many months later, my husband, Jim, returned. The stork struck again and Uncle Sam called again. I learned of rationing and loneliness.

After two more years, I finally I had my husband again, and he met his son for the first time. We moved to many states and mister stork found us again when our 11-pounder joined the Kellar bunch.

Being a Navy wife wasn't an easy job. It made me grow up fast. I have three children, four grandkids and (wow!) 12 great-grandkids to comfort me upon the loss of Jim."

Jackie Kellar
Atria Collwood
San Diego, California

"I lived in Memphis, Tennessee when the war started. I had two brothers who went away to war, and by the Grace of God, they also returned.

I felt I should do something to help the war effort, so I applied for work. Firestone Tire & Rubber Company hired me. My job was making the yellow lifeboats for the Navy. We spread out all of the pieces to make one boat at a time. After we assembled it, we tested it to make sure it didn't leak. I remember the night my brothers came home. They rolled ("toilet papered") Memphis from one end to the other!"

Donna Milam
Atria Cordova
Memphis, Tennessee

On the corner of Franklin and Smallwood Streets in Baltimore, Maryland was a paper-product warehouse where Mary worked. Laughing, Mary recalls that all the workers in her factory took great pride in knowing that they were supplying a necessity for the boys overseas – toilet paper. Her husband, Bob, was one of the soldiers and he was stationed in Japan. When he was on leave, Bob and Mary decided to try to have a baby in case he didn't come home. After two years, two months and three days, Bob finally did come home. He was greeted by Mary and his beautiful nine-month-old baby girl.

Mary Benson
Atria Manresa
Annapolis, Maryland

"I began working at age 16. I lived with my older sister after our parents died and I wanted to earn money. In the early 1940s, I acquired work at Wright Aeronautical, which had service contracts for airplane motors. I inspected the inside of metal cylinders for flaws. Things got to be a little uncomfortable when the Army instructor came to inspect my work. I worked the third shift beginning at midnight, so my friends and I sometimes met and had parties in the morning.

At one time, I visited a friend who was stationed in a training camp in Michigan. We fell in love the first time we met. He proposed to me in a very short time because he wanted to be married before he went off to war.
The day he shipped out was a very sad day for me. I cried for weeks. He returned after World War II, but we no longer felt the same about each other.

Things were different, and divorce was very common during that time. I later remarried and raised a family.

The decisions I made in the early 1940's made me what I am today. We made good money and there was nothing to spend it on, so we all invested."

Evelyn Stuhlfauth
Atria Mallard Cove
Cincinnati, Ohio

Imogene worked at the original Gerber baby food factory in Fremont, Michigan. Her duties included working the casing machine, which formed the cases of baby food jars. She worked five days a week, 10 hours a day, sometimes pulling double shifts. Imogene made $1.25 an hour, and Gerber averaged 550 cases an hour. German prisoners also worked at the factory, but Imogene and her fellow workers were not allowed to see them or work with them.

Her husband was overseas in the Army 71st Infantry Division. Imogene was 22 years old and had a baby boy at that time. She resided with her in-laws, who baby-sat for her. Everybody walked to work, and Imogene averaged 10 blocks both to and from the factory.

She made some very good friends and on days off, "the girls" socialized and went to the movies.

After the war, her husband came home and started working for Gerber. Imogene quit her job to stay home and care for her baby. She believed that the war liberated women as employers kept many women in the workforce.

Imogene Hayward
Atria Chandler Villas
Chandler, Arizona

The Impact Home Front Workers Made
on the Role of Women Today

Chapter 4

During World War II, the traditional roles of women, which were homemakers and mothers, were abandoned. During that time, females became active in auxiliary military groups and held strenuous jobs in American factories. After the war, many women remained in the workforce. They were faced with the same issues women are up against today, such as child-care challenges and balancing work and family. The confidence they gained during the war years helped them successfully manage their family and work issues. Their determination and their success set the stage for women today.

"Living in Birmingham, Alabama, and wearing men's modified coveralls to fit a woman of 145 pounds, I was part of a radio installation crew on a B-29 bomber. I heard there was an opening for a job, I took a test, and was expected to put in eight-hour days and sometimes longer. I remember the long hallway of the aircraft I worked on, we called it the tunnel. The tunnel was so narrow that turning around was almost impossible. Doing a back flip would have been easier.

The aircraft plant managers put up a boxing ring on the tarmac and brought in entertainment to help keep us from getting burnt out. We put in a lot of overtime. They wanted to keep people focused and a little down time did the trick.

I believe this time period was the entrance of women into the workforce. We learned about rationing gas, sugar and staples for our homes, and at the same time, we learned how to earn a dollar. We learned a lot about time management and gained a sense of value over even the smallest things. We learned about togetherness and being united to accomplish goals."

Carolyn Schlegal
Atria Sandy
Sandy, Utah

"During the war, I worked wherever the men had worked. I was a bomb inspector in defense plants in Southern California, Texas, Illinois and Pennsylvania. I got this job simply by applying for it.

The experience of being in home-front service changed my life by allowing me to travel to many states.

Traveling was fun for me because I met new people. However, it was a relief when the war was over. I was pregnant with my daughter and I was anxious to get home."

Anna Imogene Killgore
Atria El Camino Gardens
Carmichael, California

"Traveling was fun for me because I met new people. However, it was a relief when the war was over."

The war provided the opportunity for Jean and so many other American women to enter the industry field. In college, Jean changed her major to math instead of English and French, making herself a more desirable candidate to fill typically male jobs. In 1942, Jean left Kansas for California and found a temporary place to stay. She applied for eight jobs and was offered positions at five companies. She chose to work for Shell Oil Company in Long Beach in the production department.

When Jean started working for Shell, there was only one other woman there – and she was a telephone operator. Jean worked in the gas lab for two months but was soon needed in the core lab, where she labored for five years. This entailed bringing up samples of drilled earth to test for oil content porosity and salt content permeability.

Jean not only filled in for the men at war, but also set an important precedence for the future of women in the workplace.

Jean Evans
Atria Covell Gardens
Davis, California

At 18, Esther worked in the South San Francisco shipyards. She welded gun mounts and drafted and welded steel plates for ships from all over the world. She also worked as shipyard's secretary and served as the liaison between the workers and her boss in resolving problems and concerns throughout the war.

Esther typically worked 10 hours a day, five days a week. Her uniform consisted of slacks, steel-toed boots and a fire retardant leather jacket, which protected her from the hot sparks that flew off the burners and welding torches.

According to Esther, there was not much time to enjoy life the way she once did. Most of the time she was afraid of being bombed.

After the war, Esther became a manager for the San Francisco Emporium shoe department and stayed there for five years. After this, she ventured to Hawaii and became an employment placement agent, helping people find jobs. Esther took these paths because they presented her with challenges.

Working for the war effort changed Esther's life in many ways. She became more independent, fearless, confident in her abilities, open-minded and not afraid of failure. "Failure was never an option."

It was important to Esther that she attacked her challenges with ferocity, passion, dedication and love. Never expecting others to do for you what you can do for yourself. Esther wants our generation to realize that bad things occur because they are supposed to. That is the only way to learn how to do things the right way.

Esther Jackman
Atria Burlingame
Burlingame, California

Eula was 29, married, had four children, during World War II and worked at a number of companies. Eula has operated a forklift, worked at a punch press for the Navy, and worked on an assembly line.

Eula was able to work during the war because she lived in a big house that was converted into three apartments. The daughter of the tenant upstairs took care of her children.

After the war in 1948, Eula took a job at Cambridge Tile, where she stayed for 24 years.

Eula Coyle
Atria Mallard Cove
Cincinnati, Ohio

"When the war started, we were at the Polo Grounds watching a Giants game. Toward the end of the game, they announced a request that everyone remain in their seats. The president announced that Pearl Harbor was bombed. At that time, they brought out the American flag. We all said the 'Pledge of Allegiance' and sang 'The Star Spangled Banner.'

I was 19, just out of high school and a secretary for an insurance brokerage firm in Manhattan. I heard that a factory was hiring, so I applied to Sperry Gyroscope Company and was hired in the blueprint and engineering department. I became a runner of blueprints, which represented some sort of instrument to guide ships. I wore regular clothes, but the women downstairs on the line wore denim pants and big shirts. That's when women started to wear pants.

Women then were not allowed to dance together on the dance floor. It was not considered proper. They announced one evening that it was okay for the ladies to dance together. There were a lot of changes in the women's movement during those times."

Johanna Gataroska
Atria Tinton Falls
Tinton Falls, New Jersey

Born and raised in Nacogdoches, Texas, it was at an early age that Lydia found she had a passion for writing. After graduating from high school, Lydia went on to college and did side jobs writing articles for magazines and newspapers. It was during her college years that Lydia met the love of her life, Clarence Kilpatrick. They dated for three years before getting married in the small town of Nat, Texas.

Early in their marriage, the couple moved to Los Angeles. Clarence was an engineer for Northrop Aircraft and Lydia took a job traveling and writing articles for publications. But when World War II began, Lydia felt compelled to help her country, so she put away her pen and paper and went to work in Northrop's personnel office.

Lydia recalls many women feeling patriotic and coming in to apply for jobs to do anything to help America during the war. According to Lydia, there were hundreds of women doing hundreds of different jobs at Northrop. They gave up their skirts for overalls and sacrificed their dressy high heels for flat work shoes. Although she enjoyed her job of interviewing and hiring women and men at Northrop, Lydia missed writing. After three years, she returned to journalism.

Lydia Smith
Atria Buena Vista
Vista, California

As a twenty-something resident of Bowling Green, Kentucky, Margaret worked full-time at the Tennessee Valley Authority during World War II. She found some time to roll bandages and to knit socks for the troops, though she had a hard time with those needles!

Margaret remembers that everyone did many little things during the war, from knitting socks to rationing gas and forfeiting nylons.

But no one griped about the sacrifices. In fact, when you consider the sacrifices brought on by The Great Depression a few years earlier, according to Margaret, "It didn't seem like a big sacrifice at all."

"Women were able to do things that they never dreamed of being able to do!"

Margaret Harper
Atria St. Matthews
Louisville, Kentucky

Irene began her working career at the age of 15 as a housekeeper. By 18, she was working in a shoe factory in Haverhill, Massachusetts. It was during The Depression and, like many laborers, Irene put in a day's work to receive a few dollars cash payment each day as she walked off the production floor. For several years, Irene was shuffled from job to job until the war began. It was then that Irene found herself a permanent position.

Irene's plant went through a change for the sake of the war effort. Machines that once made parts for shoes were converted to make electrical parts for radios and other war-related equipment. Irene continued working at the factory for 27 years as a layout operator at the company that later became Western Electric.

Irene Denault
Atria Kennebunk
Kennebunk, Maine

At age 16, Anna worked as a floor lady in a uniform and coat factory located in Brooklyn. Anna distributed piecework and inspected the finished products. When work was slow, Anna helped sew. The factory changed its focus from making ladies' coats to manufacturing military uniforms during the war. It was very important to get uniforms out to our men in the services. After the war, the factory went back to making ladies' coats. Anna continued to work there until her first son was born in 1952.

Anna DeRosa
Atria East Northport
Long Island, New York

Living in Chicago, during World War II, Tony worked at a defense plant as a department clerk. She applied for this job after her husband, Emil, volunteered for the Air Force and was sent out almost immediately. Tony wanted to keep herself busy doing something constructive while her husband was away at war.

According to Tony, women "came into their own" during World War II, and they've come a long way since then. She hopes the younger generation will take time out to study the history of their grandparents and their part in the war.

Working through the depression and also through World War II gave Tony a sense of accomplishment. She knew she was helping her country through a difficult time in history. Though she was sad most of the time Emil was long away, she will never forget the war years - the tears of sadness and triumph.

Tony Novy
Atria Buena Vista
Vista, California

Grace worked for the Reynolds Aluminum Company in Phoenix, Arizona, as an electric-saw worker for 89 cents an hour. She sawed tubing which was used to carry gasoline and oil in military airplanes. Grace wore steel-toed boots, bib overalls and safety glasses to work. She was supposed to wear Levi's, but found that they were too hot and restrictive. After a year, Grace was promoted to forklift operator, which paid 91 cents an hour. Her shift was six days a week, Monday through Saturday. On Saturdays, she was paid time-and-a-half for four hours worked. Grace was 27 years old and the mother of two small children. Her mother-in-law baby-sat her children while she worked.

Grace saw many changes after the war as people had more money and bought more luxuries. She believes that children today do not realize how lucky they are.

Grace Quinones
Atria Chandler Villas
Chandler, Arizona

Brooklyn was Rose's home during the war. A friend helped Rose get a job doing office work and she spent her day sorting and correcting papers. Rose believes that home-front workers contributed to the war effort by doing their work and helping wherever they could. Like Rose, many women liked working and earning money, but they were also ready to get back to a normal life when the men returned. Rose recalls being very happy and celebrating when the war ended.

Rose Ferrantino
Atria Greece
Rochester, New York

"In 1943, I got married and my husband was drafted to the Army Ordnance and stationed in Aberdeen, Maryland. I got a job at the Foreign Material Museum, which was a converted barrack and housed all of the captured equipment. My job was to classify the equipment. I remember one day when the lieutenant came in and starting saying that we should 'Jew them all down.' I was furious! I tuned to the lieutenant and told him he was never to talk that way in front of me. I told him my husband was fighting for our country, my father was in the American Army in World War I, my uncle was in the Navy, my great uncle marched with Theodore Roosevelt and my husband's great uncle was with Grant at Gettysburg. I also told the lieutenant that his lousy family was in the Sudenten land where it all began. Needless to say, the lieutenant didn't make any more comments like that in front of me.

Years later, I returned to the converted barracks to find that a real museum had been built. It is now called the Cornell Jarret Museum."

Anita Freedman
Atria Golden Creek
Irvine, California

"I lived in Memphis, Tennessee, with my husband and two children when World War II broke out. When my husband was drafted in the Army, I went home to live with my parents in my hometown of Toccopola,

Mississippi. The war was pretty far along when my husband left, so I wasn't away from him very long. He went to the Philippines after basic training. I received many letters, but they were censored. My husband got wounded, but it wasn't serious enough to discharge him.

It was difficult for my husband to talk about the war when he first came home, but was able to share a few stories later on. My three sons were greatly influenced by their father, which was evident because they also joined the service.

These were hard times, but I believe those years made me a stronger person."

Mary Tutor
Atria Primacy
Memphis, Tennessee

At the age of 21, Johnnie was married. To help her husband with the bills, she took on a job at the Naval Shipyard. She made approximately $50 a week and worked eight to 10 hours a day. Her duties included carrying sheets of metal from one side of the shipyard to the other and to change the filters on the ships that were brought into the yard. Johnnie worked until she got pregnant.

According to Johnnie, jobs with decent pay were not easy for women to come by. Women at the time were still thought of as inferior. Women in the workplace had to band together to get their jobs done. If mistakes were made, they were covered by other women to ensure they all kept their jobs. At work all the women had was hope, determination and God. Johnnie said that working in the factories helped her to become a stronger woman and to understand that in life you have to have faith.

Johnnie Gilstrap
Atria Sunlake
Las Vegas, Nevada

Margaret worked at the United States Treasury's Loans & Currency Department in Washington, D.C., during World War II. Margaret's job was to search for lost or missing saving bonds. Her husband was in the Navy's construction battalion.

According to Margaret regardless of what the job was, everyone had the same purpose.

"The women who went to work showed the world they could hold down the country and gain their independence," Margaret stated. "The war made me feel more independent because I had to work."

Margaret Maupin
Atria Woodstock
Woodstock, Georgia

"In order to learn how to rivet, I had to go to school first. To be honest, I wasn't really interested in learning how to rivet, but a friend of mine talked me into taking the riveting classes. We had a great teacher, and later I found out he was in charge of hiring after training was completed. When my friend and I went down to a company in Redondo Beach, California, to apply for a job, there was a very long line. I told my friend that I didn't want to do this, but again she talked me into staying. While we were waiting in line, we noticed our riveting teacher. He approached us and got us to the front of the line with no questions asked.

My boss was so nice that when I told him I did not want to rivet, he assigned me to a different position, which was to supervise and approve all of the night-shift work. I did this for 10 months then quit. I became really exhausted because I had a young son to raise and a family to tend to.

I enjoyed what I did, but it was a hardship to work and to raise a family. I am proud of what I did even though it was for a short period of time. When the war was over it was a feeling of relief and happiness."

Martha Younker
Atria Summit Ridge
Reno, Nevada

"I did clerical work for the government in Galveston, Texas. A lot of companies went door to door to find people to work. I worked with ordinary people all making a living. I worked a lot during the war. Even with the work I put in and the sacrifices everyone made during the war, I would do it all again with my head held high. I think everyone should know that the women worked just as hard then as they do now, if not harder. I think the efforts during the war made me more independent.

After World War II there was tremendous relief, but it still took awhile to get everyone and everything back to normal. I worked for servicemen when they came and went. It was quite an experience, and I don't regret one minute."

Florence Nowell
Atria Richardson
Dallas, Texas

Rona graduated from Columbia University with a master's degree. Her first job was as a decoder with the FBI just after Pearl Harbor. Rona received many awards for her decoding abilities, and she was able to decode a very important message, which won her a merit promotion.

Her next job was with the State Department, where she worked in the Safe Haven Program Department. This department tracked down the monies the Germans were attempting to send to South America and Europe.

Rona had a one-year contract with the War Department. She worked in Berlin and Frankfurt for the Foreign Exchange Depository. There she tried to find the owners of precious metals and jewelry. It was here that Rona discovered what happened to the Dutch gold; it was sold by the Germans during the war. The remainder of the gold that was taken from the Jews in the concentration camps during the Holocaust was divided among the survivors.

After the war, Rona took six months off and traveled around Europe. When she returned, she applied for and landed her last job at the CIA. She worked for the agency from 1948 until 1956 as a case officer in Washington D.C. She provided the Washington office with information on spy cases. She was assigned some very important cases during her time with the CIA.

Rona Stoetzer
Atria Stratford
Stratford, Connecticut

"I worked in a war factory during World War II. The group of women I was a part of was responsible for manufacturing big metal plates and large-caliber shells for booster rockets. I loved working in the war plant. It gave us (the women) a sense of belonging and we knew we were an important part of the war effort."

Mary Jekelis
Atria Kennebunk
Kennebunk, Maine

"I worked at Republic National Bank in the office. I mostly did clerical work. My average day ranged from being very busy to extremely slow, depending on transactions.

World War II really opened my eyes to the people outside the United States as well as to the changes that were going on worldwide. I read the newspaper every day to see what was happening. When the war was over, it was a wild time. There was crying and parades. Most people were just happy for the soldiers to be coming home.

During World War II everyone put in an effort in any way they could. It was the real turning point for women going to work."

Barbeece Copeland
Atria Richardson
Dallas, Texas

"I lived in Klickitat, Washington, during the war and went to work first at a sawmill and then at a box company. With a lot of the men away at war, it was up to us women to learn how to work away from home. The first time in my life that I had a job was at the sawmill, where we cut lumber to make baby cribs. I was a saw tailor–someone who catches lumber after it goes through the saw. Several women tried to do the job, and the men still left at the mill laughed each time a woman failed. Then I came along and did the job just perfectly. The men stopped laughing. They said, 'Oh you've done this job before!' Of course, I had not. My father was a blacksmith and I worked in his shop as a little girl.

After the sawmill I worked at a box company, where we made ammunition boxes for the military. My position was to tally the boxes at the end of each day. In the evenings, some of the girls got together and played baseball – it was usually the box factory against the sawmill. Sometimes I was the pitcher and sometimes I played the outfield. All of us had so much fun playing those games.

We learned so much during those times and sometimes we learned things the hard way. The ones who could handle a job could continue working; the others were let go and had no income.

At the tail end of the war it was kind of a let-down having to leave our new jobs. At the same time, I was glad to see our men back home. I moved to Kennewick, Washington, and became a cook, which I did for 15 years."

Marjorie Morris
Atria Sandy
Sandy, Utah

"In December 1942, Tom and I were engaged to be married. He was with the 8th Air Force in England. He went in the service in January 1943 and was shipped to England in March that same year. It was terrible seeing him go. I didn't know if he was coming back.

I was fortunate growing up. My family was well-established, and this brought problems for me because I wanted to fit in with my friends. I had graduated from high school with an academic degree and I didn't want to go to college because my friends weren't going to college.

One night a man from a business school in Manhattan came to our home. My father enrolled me in classes. It cost $33 a month to attend a one year course. I couldn't believe my father allowed me to go there! I learned bookkeeping, stenography and typing.

My friend and I went to an employment agency after graduation to be interviewed for a job in a war plant. When I was interviewed, I was asked if I'd like to work there in the personnel department. I was thrilled and I got the job at the War Department. We had different divisions and I was secretary to one of the divisions. It was a six-day-a-week job.

Tom returned home to me in January 1946. We married in March the same year."

Jean Genovese
Atria Windsor Woods
Hudson, Florida

Bebe was old enough to be married before the war started. She and her husband lived in Brooklyn, where she was a physical education teacher. When her husband was sent overseas to work for the American intelligence, she took a job at an all-girls public school teaching PE and moved in with her parents. Some women had children to care for. Bebe carried the load of managing the rations and everything else that encompassed teaching and caring for her parents.

"The war caused me to work much harder to help support my parents," Bebe said.

She recalls the patriotism felt in Brooklyn during the war; everyone was very supportive of the military's actions. She herself was a supporter for the Army by knitting materials for the USO.

A long-overdue vacation fot Bebe and her husband came at the end of the war. But the vacation couldn't last forever; both of them had to go back to work. Bebe took a position at a new school because the end of the war gave way to better job openings.

Bebe performed her duties as a child caring for her parents, as a wife supporting her husband overseas and as a woman teaching school to provide for her family.

Bebe Schwartz
Atria St. Matthews
Louisville, Kentucky

Lorraine briefly worked at St. Louis Ammunition Plant, which made 30- and 50-caliber shells for the military. Her husband volunteered to go into the Navy as a gunner's mate instructing other allied ships on how to use American ammunition. He was stationed in San Francisco, so Lorraine moved there and got a job at the 12th Naval District Ships Service Office, a store for Navy personnel and their dependents. Lorraine's role was to portion out the goods for the naval stations on the West Coast. She allocated everything from nylons to cigarettes and paper goods to makeup. Lorraine states that her greatest contribution to the war was allocating condoms for the enlisted men and scotch for the officers! This duty prevented many unwanted pregnancies and kept the admirals happy! There was never enough scotch to go around, so she made certain the admirals got theirs first. Lower-ranking officers had to be content with the less-expensive liquors.

After the war, Lorraine and her husband went home to St. Louis and she worked as a legal secretary. Lorraine believes this time period opened the door for women's liberation. Many women were able to obtain jobs that they would never have gotten before the war.

Lorraine Ritscher
Atria Chandler Villas
Chandler, Arizona

"I got a job in the personnel office of the Saco-Lowell Defense Plant right out of high school. These were metal shops and we did a lot of work during the war. I loved working in the personnel office. I had many secretarial responsibilities, plus I conducted interviews as well. I must have enjoyed the work! I stayed for 20 years through marriage and having a baby"!

Elyce Parker
Atria Kennebunk
Kennebunk, Maine

Virginia White went to work out of necessity. She had two children who needed to be taken care of and bills to pay. So she went to work for Curtiss-Wright, a factory that had opened in Indianapolis, specifically for the war effort. Virginia got a job as an inspector of small parts for airplane propellers. She worked at the factory for a year and a half.

"I enjoyed my job there," she said. "I got a babysitter for my children and worked the 3:30 p.m. to midnight shift. I don't remember my

boss's name, but he was a little bitty guy and he was very nice and helpful."

When the war ended, so did the work at Curtiss-Wright. "In a way, I was happy to stop working. I had saved enough money to put a down payment on a house!"

Later, Virginia was hired for work at Western Electric. The company hired her on the spot because of her previous experience with Curtiss-Wright. It has been years since Virginia talked about this experience. To her, she was just doing what she had to do to take care of her family.

Virginia White
Atria Heritage
Indianapolis, Indiana

"During World War II, I worked for Southwestern Bell as a telephone operator. My average day kept me very busy. I woke up early to get the kids off to school then I went to work. During the war, it was like working all the time. Between a job, kids and keeping

house there was little free time. My husband was in the service so I had to raise the kids and keep everything running. When the war ended, the switchboard at work lit up like a Christmas tree. It was a very exciting time."

Helen Meyer
Atria Richardson
Dallas, Texas

"I met my husband, Jack, in 1940. We had been going together for about eight months when he asked me to marry him. We had a small wedding and went to live in his family's home. We had lived there for about a year when I found us a duplex. I attended the Miller Hawkins Business School and went to work for Sears Roebuck. When the boys left for the service, I went to work for Mutual Life Insurance Company as head bookkeeper. I continued to work there after the war had ended for about four years."

Ernestine Wadlington
Atria Cordova
Memphis, Tennessee

They called her "bay leader" at the defense plant in Indiana. Ida was responsible for 19 women who made relays and delays for the bombs. No special uniforms were required, but eight hours a day was expected of all the workers, who earned between 98 cents and $1.98 and hour, which was really good money at the time. Ida recalls the work she and the others performed as being very dangerous. In fact, in one instance a woman's hand was blown off.

Not only was Ida a working woman during the war, but she was a mother and a wife.

Each man who dropped a bomb on the enemy can thank Ida and others like her who stepped into a role that she probably would have never experienced if World War II had not called everyone to duty.

Ida Hubbard
Atria St. Matthews
Louisville, Kentucky

Helen worked for Western Electric while her husband, Frank, was in the Navy. She first worked in the shop factory where they built telegraph and telephone devices for the fields. When more men were drafted for the war, Western Electric needed women to run the offices, so Helen took a desk job with many administrative duties.

Every night, Helen came home after work, made dinner for her mother and daughter, did yard work and cleaned house. Late at night, she would write letters to her husband. Helen was able to save all of her allotment checks and, to Frank's surprise, had their mortgage paid off by the time he came home from the war.

Helen Mruckowsky
Atria Chandler Villas
Chandler, Arizona

Marion is a very intelligent, vibrant woman who was employed as a young person at the Shovel and Crane company in downtown Lima, Ohio. She began this job shortly after the war started, and had to compete for her position among other women. She worked for a nice mane named Bob Eckford. The majority of her job consisted of doing paperwork for the locomotive parts and paying the distributors for ordered merchandise.

One of Marian's favorite memories is of her lifelong friend, Peggy Komminsk. Peggy was also employed at the time and every week when they received their paychecks, Peggy and Marian ran right to the store to buy candy.

When the war was over, Marian married a soldier and has had a wonderful life. She will never forget the days of her youth when duty called and she went running.

Marian Klay
Atria Grapevine
Houston, Texas

Marilynn and her husband, Ben, moved from San Antonio, Texas, to Washington, D.C., in 1941. Ben was offered a job by, the mayor, so they packed up their life in Texas and started a new one in our nation's capital.

Marilynn got a job answering letters at the War Production Board. Most of the time, she wrote letters stating that they did not need any more help. She grew tired of the redundancy of this assignment and decided to contribute in a different way.

She found a new job at the District of Columbia Wage and Industrial Safety Board. She interviewed workers who had been reported as making less than the minimum wage of $30 per week, or those who were working more than 40 hours each week. Most of the people she dealt with were waitresses or maids. The majority of them were living in slum-like houses "called row dwellings," in the most dangerous parts of town. She went down the alleys between the roads to get to these people, and she usually wasn't allowed in the house. A few times she was invited inside and saw the deplorable conditions on which her clients lived. Every day, she risked her life by venturing into the darkest, dirtiest parts of Washington, D.C. and every day she went home unscathed.

"The Lord was with me because I never got hurt," said Marilynn.

Marilynn would like the younger generation to know that each and every woman has a role to play. When the war came to a close and Marilynn returned to Texas to complete her master's degree, she was a changed person. Her wartime experience had shown her that she could do anything she wanted. She knew then that she no longer had to depend on her family, that she had strength enough to make it on her own.

Marilynn Wacker
Atria Grapevine
Houston, Texas

"My husband, Joseph, was the fire chief of the San Francisco Fire Department during World War II. Shortly after the war started, he was helping control a raging fire when the ladder he was stepping on fell backwards. He fell to the ground and never regained consciousness. He passed away that day. I became a widow and I had young kids to take care of.

American Bell and Bell Telephone Company hired me soon after my husband died. My job was to give basic training to company workers on the proper use of the telephone. I was sent to different companies in different states. Some of the people I trained did not know how to speak English. I found my job very challenging but it was worth all my troubles. I had children to take care of and feed during those difficult times.

World War II was a very difficult time in my life. I am very grateful to American Bell and Bell Telephone for giving me the opportunity to earn a living for my family. I am also thankful that by working during the war, I was able to contribute to the economy by being in the work force."

Irene Cassidy
Atria Daly City
Daly City, California

It was 1943 in the small Kentucky town of Paducah when Thelma felt the urge to help her country. Thelma, along with a friend, decided to head for St. Louis, to sign up for the WAVES (Women Accepted for Volunteer Service). Two small-town girls from Kentucky arrived in the big city of St. Louis only to learn that Thelma's friend is one pound underweight to qualify for the WAVES. The plan of action, bananas and water! In the meantime, Thelma decided to sign up for the SPARs, The Coast-Guard's women's division.

Thelma successfully fulfilled all of the requirements to become a SPAR. Because her friend decided to stand by her original decision to become a WAVE, Thelma continued her journey on her own. After boot camp, Thelma boarded a troop train bound for Long Beach, California. The train carried enlisted men as well as SPARs. Thelma was of the first 12 SPARs on the West Coast. She was assigned to the District Coast Guard Office. The girls were placed according to their background and qualifications. Thelma had worked as secretary to the district manager of Southern Bell Telephone when she lived in Paducah, so she was a perfect choice for the Long Beach assignment. Thelma's days in Long Beach were spent in the mail and files department logging mail, typing, and even driving a Jeep in convoys to transport military correspondence.

After a year, she was transferred to Philadelphia. In the District Personnel Office, her duties consisted of logging the transfers of Coast Guardsmen from ship to shore and vice versa.

One of Thelma's favorite places to visit was Horn and Hardart restaurant. Not only did it have a wonderful lunch counter, it also had something new to Thelma's eyes . . . vending machines! Many years after the war had ended, Thelma revisited Horn and Hardart with her husband and was served by the very same waitress who had served her during the war.

Two years passed and the news of the end of the war brought rejoicing to the streets of Philadelphia. She had reached the rank of Yeoman 1st Class. When she moved back home, Thelma enrolled at Murray College. "Even though the men gave so much, that if I'm even just one speck of sand in the entire effort, I'm happy that I could contribute. It gave more to me than I gave to it," Thelma said.

Thelma Horton
Atria Newburgh
Evansville, Indiana

"From 1941 to 1947, I worked at the Internal Revenue Service in San Francisco. I was the chief biller of Social Security Employment Tax. Life was difficult for me because aside from my job, I was also taking care of a very sick mother. I was always in a hurry to go home from the office. Sometimes, I had to work late and go out to dinner with my boss and officemates. I was worried because there were blackouts and I was afraid of the dark. When the air raid siren sounded, we had to stay where we were."

Frances Profumo
Atria Daly City
Daly City, California

Ivis married as a young adult. Shortly after the wedding, her husband was called to fight in the war. Ivis recalls working in the Linens Thread Company in Patterson, New Jersey. Her role was to get the flax ready for processing. She remembers going with her sister looking for work in the factories because she needed to put food on the table and survive while her husband was away at war.

Ivis's typical day was anything but typical. One week she worked during the day and the next week she worked at night. "You just had to meet each day as it came to you," she said.

"I would like the younger generations to know that the role of women home-front workers was as important as the work they are now performing, and if I can do it, you can do it!" said Ivis.

She says that although the war ended and the men returned to their factory jobs, things never were as they were before the war.

Her most vivid memory about this whole experience relates to the end of the war.

"After the news about Truman dropping the bombs, I remember them declaring that the war was officially over on the radio at around noon. There were people all over the streets celebrating at that time."

Ivis Esposito
Atria Shaker
Albany, New York

"Georgia was already married during World War II. Though she was a wife and mother, she was also working full time for Upjohn Pharmaceuticals in San Francisco. Georgia's job was to fill orders for the retailers.

It was difficult for Georgia because she had to take care of three young kids, all boys, and still hold a job. Georgia was working during the day and I was on the swing shift. We each took turns watching and caring for the kids. Life was a little more difficult than in peacetime. There was the rationing of food, shoes and clothing, but we did not lack the basic things that we needed. Georgia and I rode public transportation because

gasoline was rationed. It was inconvenient, but no one was exempt from rationing. Everyone had to be patient and conserve because the situation was not normal.

My Georgia was a good sport. She was very sympathetic to our neighbors whose husbands and sons were sent to the war. She always said that we were luckier because we were together during that time. Other people were not as fortunate as we were."

Georgia Bianco
by husband John Bianco
Atria Daly City
Daly City, California

Dorothy and Edward married during the war on May 23, 1944. Edward had a three-day pass, during which the couple was married in a church and had their reception behind a bar at Eagles Nest Inn.

Many of Dorothy's friends went to work for airlines, so she went to work too. Dorothy worked at East Side Manhattan National Care Loading Corporation as a stenographer while her husband Edward was in the service. Her typical day started at 9 a.m. doing secretarial work and billing; it ended at 5 p.m. with an hour lunch during the day.

Dorothy liked seeing women taking over the workforce during World War II. She remembers that when the men returned from the service, the women were bounced out of their jobs to give them back to the veterans.

After the war, Dorothy remembers everyone cheering and then having a wave of silence, all of the younger men thinking of how fortunate they were not to have been drafted. When Dorothy's husband returned home from France, he worked as a mechanic in a powerhouse. Dorothy continued to work to help with the income.

Dorothy Graf
Atria South Setauket
Centereach, New York

"My parents were both born into farming families in rural southern Illinois. In 1940, they decided to pull up stakes and move to California. They both found work at Ryan Aircraft in San Diego.

Mama was a riveter. What fun they had! They soon had many friends and mama traded in her bobby socks and saddle oxfords for leg makeup and ankle straps. I was once told by an aunt that mama could run a perfectly straight seam up her leg with an eyebrow pencil. Friday and Saturday nights were set aside for dancing. They loved to 'Lindy' and 'Balboa,' dances made popular in San Diego and named after Charles Lindbergh and the beautiful Balboa Park. Rum and Coca Cola was the cocktail of the day. It was quite inexpensive to see the big bands – Benny Goodman, Glenn Miller, etc.

Mom got pregnant in 1941. In those days, pregnant women didn't work, so mom quit her job. Dad transferred to night shift work for an increase of 5¢ an hour. They were ready to start a family. Mama's doctor bill was $75, and her hospital bill was $100 for a 10-day stay.

Mama remembers two different times when they were at the movies and heard a woman cry out, 'That's my husband,' when they were watching the war front news reels. The streets of San Diego usually teemed with sailors, since it was the home of the Navy. But on the morning of December 7, 1941, there were no 'swabbies' on the street; mama said, You could hear a pin drop after the events at Pearl Harbor. In just a few months, Dad got his call. He never served overseas; he was sent to Los Alamos, New Mexico, to work on the Manhattan Project where the atomic bomb was developed."

Velma Rinker by Connie Betenbough (daughter)
Atria Cottage Village
Lubbock, Texas

"During World War II, I was a licensed daycare worker out of my home. Women had to work outside of the home and they needed someone to watch their children so they could provide for their families. I had two small children of my own plus six others that I kept. I also did volunteer work as a Pink Lady in a hospital in Arkansas."

Mona Kutz
Atria Willow Park
Tyler, Texas

"I had earned a degree in home economics, but married instead of taking training in dietetics. Dietitians at the University of Michigan Hospital had to spend time peeling potatoes because of lack of kitchen help.

I served as assistant dietitian at the University Health Service to be of some help in caring for students.

Toward the end of the war we moved to Tennessee, and I remember going to the train station and giving 'goodies' to servicemen and women. They enjoyed the food and friendliness and we found the effort very rewarding. I don't remember who provided the food, but it was much appreciated by those partaking.

I also served as a Pink Lady at Bristol Memorial Hospital, where I tried to do little services for patients such as delivering mail, refreshing water, reading books and running errands. This saved the nurses' time for medical responsibilities. Association with caring and helpful people is always rewarding.

My services were so small in comparison to 'Rosie the Riveters' that I feel very humble. When the war was over, women kept serving in needed places and are still doing that today. Serving my country, my friends and my fellow citizens will always be important to me, and it gave me great pleasure."

Helen Stocking
Atria Stone Mountain
Stone Mountatin, Georgia

Margaret worked in a shoe factory in Hudson, Massachusetts. A friend helped her get the job. There were several women in the stitching department where she worked, and mostly men in the cutting area. Margaret stitched on a machine all day, and sometimes the needle got stuck in her finger. Thank goodness she never got seriously injured on the job. If Margaret's sewing machine broke down she usually fixed it herself, but the machines rarely broke down. She didn't start work at the usual time because she had a son to get off to school in the mornings. No one seemed to mind because they realized that she was raising her son alone while her husband was overseas in the military.

Margaret Silva
Atria Woodbriar
Falmouth, Massachusetts

Chapter 5

Even though there seems to be no such thing as a "good war," conflicts threatening the freedoms of Americans bring about unity and patriotism. Straight from the hearts of many home-front workers are words that express pride for their country and messages for younger generations.

Alice was born in El Salvador in 1916. She immigrated to the United States in 1943 and became a U.S. citizen in 1948. "I came to the United States as a single woman searching for a purpose to serve and a direction to follow," she said. She found both when she became a factory worker during World War II.

She worked in a factory eight hours a day, Monday through Saturday. Her first factory job was wrapping food products by hand for the soldiers at the front. From this time and until the end of the war, Alice worked in shipyards for the AFL Machinists Union as a boiler maker technician. Alice worked both of these factory jobs during the day and took English classes to become a U.S. citizen. Alice's social life solely consisted of her studying English at night, so that the rest of her family would be allowed to emigrate from El Salvador.

When Alice described the end of the war, she said, "There was an atmosphere of complete and boundless utopian joy. The war's end also ended the constant fear of death that I and everyone I knew felt every day during the war."

Alice said the war caused her to develop a more complete and thorough understanding of the value of human life and to never take one day for granted, because you never know what might happen. Most important to her, and what got her through the war mentally and emotionally, was the unyielding support she received from her friends and her family through letters. The war and her family's support developed her life's philosophy: the complete and devoted love of family, country and God are the necessary elements to enjoying a balanced, complete and happy life.

One clear painful memory Alice has was her struggle to master English. Except when working, she did not feel like a complete American citizen until this accomplishment.

The primary lesson Alice hopes this generation learns is to recognize, respect and admire the immense sacrifices that her generation made to ensure the freedoms that we today hold so dear. Alice also hopes this generation learns to accept people for who they are and not what they look like.

Alice Guardado
Atria Burlingame
Burlingame, California

"I came to the United States as a single woman searching for a purpose to serve and a direction to follow."

Lois Williams worked at North American Aviation in Grand Prairie, Texas. She was a Jill-of-all-trades, working in the lathe and heat treatment departments. The factory built the Mustang aircraft for the Navy.

Before coming to work at North American Aviation, Lois was employed at a department store, making $12.50 per week. Her pay increased substantially to $35 per week when she started working at the aviation company.

Lois worked from 2:30 p.m. to 12:30 a.m., and she wore a uniform of blue pants and shirts with goggles. It was necessary that the ladies pull their hair back in nets to keep from getting it caught in the machines.

> "I was employed at a department store, making $12.50 per week."

Lois had a brother in the Marines who was shot in the hip. The heroic actions of Lois' brother made her want to do all she could for her country.

Her fondest memory of her wartime days is when one of the machines at the plant wouldn't work correctly. This machine cut little rings that dropped into a coffee cup, and the parts were needed as quickly as possible. So as not to delay the use of these parts, Lois devised a way to repair the machine with the help of a simple sewing needle she had brought from home.

Lois also remembers being at the aviation plant the afternoon the announcement came that the war was over. Everyone was relieved and excited. Six months after the war ended, the factory closed. Lois settled down and took a job as a secretary.

Lois would like younger generations to know that the riveters were very patriotic, and that they had to take over because the men were not there to do it. She said that they all worked hard and not a single person she knew was lazy.

Lois Williams
Atria Grapevine
Grapevine, Texas

Every Sunday, the Douglas Aircraft plant in Santa Monica, California, had a big ad in the newspaper looking for women to work. Eva saw an ad, applied and was hired. She was trained by a female instructor on how to safely operate the tools she would use on her job. Trained as a riveter, Eva was assigned to the assembly line. Her job was to shoot rivets while her partner held a bucking board, which smashed and secured the rivets.

There were many safety and security rules that had to be followed, such as always wearing an ID badge, which was color-coded, and not leaving your work area without a pass. Eva wore goggles, coveralls and a snood when she worked. Eva spent a lot of time with her coworkers because many were from out of state, their husbands were overseas and they had no family in California. They would go see shows at the Dug Out, where many movie stars performed. Eva was employed for one and a half years and stopped working right before the war ended.

Sadly, Eva's husband was killed in Italy while she was pregnant with their first child. Unfortunately, this was a fairly common experience among the women with whom she worked.

Eva's advice to the younger generation would be that if you feel in your heart you want to fight for your country, go for it! You have a sense of honor when you serve your country.

Eva Aguilar
Atria Colima
Walnut, California

"You have a sense of honor when you serve your country."

Anna was about 20 years old when she moved from North Carolina to take a job her friend had told her about in Oak Ridge, Tennessee. She was secretary to the purchasing agent of Union Carbide. At that time, Anna did not know that Union Carbide was in competition with Eastman to perfect the ultimate weapon – the Atom Bomb.

Anna lived in a dormitory with other coworkers. She and her workers and friends often speculated on the reasons for such secrecy in their jobs. Not only was Union Carbide a totally secured facility, but the entire town of Oak Ridge was a compound surrounded by barbed wire.

During her two years there, Anna dated one of Union Carbide's chemical engineers. She recalls that on a couple of occasions the engineer would vaguely mention what was going on at the company. However, the conversation would shift because he knew the importance of not disclosing details of his employment. They both were aware that whatever was going on there, it was not to be discussed.

Anna recalls that everything came to light the day news hit the home front that the bomb had been dropped on Hiroshima. That day, she immediately realized that it was she who had ordered the cyclotron (or atom blaster) for her boss months before. This was the key to the atom bomb's devastating affect.

"Our citizens knew the sacrifices we had to make, and we made them without complaining about it. Everyone was supportive of FDR, the war effort and our boys overseas. Some volunteered at the Red Cross and rolled bandages, others knitted and most had victory gardens to compensate for rationed goods and feed their families."

Anna is proud of her service to our country, and feels that her experience strengthened her pride and patriotism.

Anna Stallings
Atria MerryWood
Charlotte, North Carolina

In 1941, Helen's husband was called away to fulfill his obligation to his country. With her husband gone, Helen also stepped up to fulfill her obligation ... she went to work in a steel factory in Clairton, Pennsylvania. To get the job, Helen was subjected to both a written and physical examination. After passing these exams, she threw on her overalls, steel-toed boots, hardhat and name badge and tackled her job as a "hooker" on a crane. Helen was responsible for directing crane operators and repairing steel plates that were deemed defective. It was tiring work day after day, but Helen worked hard and with great pride. After completing her tour at the steel factory, Helen still saw some of her work mates around the neighborhood. Relationships were formed that lasted a lifetime.

Helen is proud to have played a role in the events that helped forge the United States as a nation. She believes that younger generations of women should be willing to step up when they are needed and go to work in whatever capacity necessary to aid in any national efforts.

Helen Johnson
Atria Virginia Beach
Virginia Beach, Virginia

"Women were needed just as much in the war as men, even if we weren't fighting. It sure was a hard time."

Effa Patton
Atria Tinton Falls
Tinton Falls, New Jersey

During World War II, Elma was a volunteer at a military base in Indianapolis. She helped the soldiers when they were hurt and stayed with them until a nurse arrived. Elma did this job because her husband was in the war and it gave her a chance to be closer to him.

When the war was over, Elma was very happy because she knew that no one else would get hurt and everyone could go back to enjoying their life and their families. She is proud of the work she did for the soldiers and her country.

Elma O'Connell
Atria Tinton Falls
Tinton Falls, New Jersey

After college, Florence decided to join the Women's Army Corps (WAC) in Tuella, Utah, in 1942. She applied for a job as a cook and was hired immediately. She prepared meals and served them day in and day out. She spent her time knitting when she wasn't busy cooking or doing chores.

When her friend, Brenda, asked her to teach her how to knit, it was a little awkward because Brenda was left-handed and Florence was right-handed. Without getting too tied up in knots, the women figured it out together. Florence recalls how funny it was to watch Brenda knit the exact opposite of her own knitting style.

When the war was over, it took a bit of getting used to. From living in the barracks to moving into a home, it all took some time to become accustomed to making changes, big and small.

"Each person had a right to choose, but all had to do something," she recalls. "People who stayed home worked too." She would also like the women of the younger generation to know that, "You always have a right to choose your life."

Florence Cimino
Atria Buena Vista
Vista, California

During World War II, I worked as a journeyman welder at Shipyard Number 3 in Richmond, California. I applied for this position and got hired through the union. I worked the swing shift and wore a leather uniform and a welding hat for protection from the hot sparks.

I became good friends with one of my coworkers, Faye Houck-Bottorf. I still keep in touch with Faye; her family and mine have gone gambling in Reno several times.

I am indeed glad that I served my country as a home-front worker. I would like for the younger generation to know that women worked hard on the home front during World War II, and we are proud of what we did.

Barbara Duprel
Atria Chateau Gardens
San Jose, California

When Pearl Harbor was attacked, Harriet was in high school. Everyone was upset and crying over the news. This altered Harriet's post-graduation plans. Instead of going on to further her education, she took a very good job as an executive secretary, which she probably wouldn't have gotten if there wasn't such a shortage of men. Harriet's dad set up the interview and when Harriet walked out of it, the manager called her dad. That call changed her life. Harriet loved her job.

Harriet wrote to many of the GIs who worked for the company before the war. One of the soldiers was so happy and grateful for Harriet's letter that he insisted on meeting her when he came home. Unfortunately, Harriet came down with hives. Her face was so swollen, itchy and sore that she didn't want to go into work. But being the trouper that she was, Harriet went to work – scratching all the way. And yes, she did meet the young man who was on furlough. Even with hives, he thought Harriet was a great girl and asked that she keep those letters coming.

It was during the war that Harriet met her husband-to-be, Marty. He was in the infantry and asked Harriet to meet him in New Jersey, where he proposed.

Harriet believes that women should help any way they can during wartime, whether it's writing letters, working in the medical field, volunteering at the USO or buying war bonds. However, if they choose a military career, it shouldn't be on the front lines in combat. Some things are better left to the men.

Harriet Roman
Atria Tinton Falls
Tinton Falls, New Jersey

Phyllis was married just before the war started and enjoyed her role as a homemaker. The chores of being a wife and mother were her job . . . then World War II started. Her husband signed up for the draft but was never called to serve. Phyllis felt she should work to help support the fact that America had just come through the Depression and now a war was raging.

In 1941, Phyllis went to work in a beauty shop for her cousin, Gladys. She recalls many women coming in to get their hair shortened to a "pageboy" style. Phyllis recalls cutting the hair of women who worked as riveters. Because of the type of work they were doing, this style was easy to manage and it became very popular.

When the war was over, Phyllis was glad to quit her job and get back to her home life and raise her son. She feels she helped during the war. She enjoyed working and being out in the public. She is thankful to all the men and women who served our country and for fighting for the freedom Americans have today.

Phillis Derrick
Atria Buena Vista
Vista, California

Chapter 5

From 1941 to 1945, Doris, worked at Consolidated Vulter. She worked in the parts department and in the general office. Doris had her own bicycle and delivered and picked up blueprints throughout the company.

Doris became a good friend with a woman named Faye, who worked the 3:30 p.m. to midnight shift. They liked to go to dinner after work and their boss, Jack Schlueter, often went along with them. Eventually, Doris and Jack grew fond of each other. There was one particular time that Doris accompanied Jack on a business trip to California. On the way there they stopped in Las Vegas and got married. After that, she followed Jack to California to live. They were married for 56 years.

Doris was in downtown Burbank, California, when she heard the news that the war was over. She remembers people honking their horns over and over and hollering in the streets. Everyone was carrying on, laughing and crying in the streets. It was a day of celebration!

Doris wants people today to know that she and her peers were very dedicated to their country and their jobs. She looks back on those days with fond memories, and the knowledge that she truly did her part.

Doris Schlueter
Atria Grapevine
Dallas, Texas

At age 23, Marie Curry worked at a war plant in Huntington, West Virginia, as a night-shift supervisor. Her duties included overseeing employees wrapping tools in paper then dipping them in hot wax to seal and protect them from rust and water before they were sent overseas. Marie worked five days a week from 4 p.m. to 12 a.m. and made $25 to $30 per week. Her uniform consisted of a regular dress, an apron and special gloves to protect her hands from the hot wax.

Marie and her two children lived with her mother while her husband served in the Army. Marie's mother worked in a children's nursery as a cook, then arrived home in time for Marie to head off to work. Marie can still remember walking to and from work, which was a five-mile walk each way. Sometimes other girls would walk with her, but most of the time she walked alone, fearing the darkness of the long distance home.

Marie remembers her mother volunteering to make medical bandages and then sending them overseas to our troops. In those days, women missed their boys and men and attempted to send them packages as often as possible, a sometimes difficult task because of the rationed items at the time.

After the war, the war plant closed. Marie remembers everyone being so excited when the war was over, but she said it was a bittersweet joy to have the men return due to the fact that many of them came home with mental and/or physical disabilities.

Marie Curry
Atria Chandler Villas
Chandler, Arizona

Pauline attended North Western College for one year during The Depression and then decided to work for the Navy. She applied in 1942 to the Naval base in Norfolk, Virginia, and worked in the commissary as a cashier for three years. There weren't many jobs to choose from, but Pauline was happy with hers because it allowed her to meet a lot of sailors.

Pauline remembers it was a joyous experience to work in the Navy commissary; she enjoyed every minute of it. Nothing was hard and she did what she had to do.

The most memorable thing that happened to Pauline during the war was meeting her husband, Robert. They were married for 38 years. Today, Pauline beams when she talks about her days in the Navy commissary and the life she had with her friends – a memorable time!

Pauline Evans
Atria Buena Vista
Vista, California

During World War II, Bernice was married and had one child. She took a job at Hughes Aircraft in Norwalk, California, because her husband told her they were hiring and that she should help in any way she could. Bernice worked the graveyard shift and her job was to distribute rivets to the other "Rosies."

Her day was typical of many housewives during that time. She took care of her home and her child, and then at night headed off to work for her late-night shift. Bernice didn't have a uniform to wear, but slacks and flat shoes were required when working.

Bernice was glad to be a part of history. She would like the younger generation of women to know that, despite the role of wife and mother, women can still stand up for their beliefs, whether it be for your spirit or for your country. Do what you can and be happy for it.

Bernice Miller
Atria Buena Vista
Vista, California

Ninagene worked at Harmen General Army Hospital in Longview, Texas, as a lab technician during World War II. She recalls how happy she was to get a job where she could help others. A typical day for her was drawing blood and doing lab tests. She laughs and says that she was known around the hospital as a "bloodsucker."

When the war was over, Ninagene remembers the excitement, but at the same time, she remembers the chaos. There were trainloads of injured men to care for. The experience made her realize never to take anything for granted.

Ninagene would like younger generations to know how important the women were who worked on the home front because they had to fill the roles of the men who were gone.

Ninagene Moriarty
Atria Carrollton
Dallas, Texas

"I am a registered nurse. I received my degree at St. Margaret's Hospital School of Nursing in 1936. In 1938, a nurse friend and I went to Honolulu, to work at Queens Hospital. When Pearl Harbor was bombed, we worked many long and very busy days. We worked for three days straight one time. Once, I was treating a sailor who had a severe back burn. He was lying on his stomach and was crying, so I went up to him and asked if there was anything I could do for him. He asked if I could write a letter to his mom and tell her that he was fine.

In addition to my hospital work, I did volunteer work with the Red Cross and took care of my family. The war changed my life and I feel I am a better person.

I want younger generations to know about the role I played during the war, and how it changed my life forever. You can never erase the memories of war; it was a time of sorrow and pain. I still have many vivid memories of my patients, friends and family. It truly was a time of sorrow and pain.

When the war was over, it was a big relief. There were many celebrations and a lot of happy times. In 1991, my family and I were awarded the Pearl Harbor Commemorative Medal by Congress."

Loretta Rogers
Atria Palm Desert
Palm Desert, California

"During the war, I worked at home on a farm where there were many jobs to be done. We all worked together as a family to do whatever was to be done, as well as with neighbors to support the cause. Our days were filled with hard, but rewarding, jobs. Crops were planted and harvested to keep food and supplies going in order to feed and clothe our soldiers and our own families. My favorite thing to do was to sew for friends and family.

We also planted victory gardens on our lawns to grow extra food so there was plenty to go around. We were even glad to go through rationing of foods and gas so our troops could have the best to keep them going and help to win the war. Between seasons of planting and harvesting, when farmers were available, my father would drive us to the air base to work there when possible. We also sent care packages to our soldiers when we could. I remember the planes from the Dyersburg Air Base in Halls, Tennessee, flying over where we lived to an area near the Mississippi River where they dropped practice bombs. We could hear the explosives.

Two of my brothers served in the military during the war. One brother was in the European Theater and was stationed in London. He was in the Army Air Corps and served as a gunner on a B-17. His plane almost went down in the English Channel, but by the grace of God, he returned from that mission and many more. He brought back a piece of flack that almost got him. This brother had a friend and I corresponded with him for two or more years. We met after the war ended and were married in 1946.

While my husband was in the service, he was a mechanic on a B-17 and was stationed in Italy. He developed an interest in radios and electronics while in the service and later received training in that area. My other brother was in the Army Medical Corps helping to care for the sick and wounded soldiers. The ship he was on near the end of the war came close to being torpedoed as they were heading toward Japan

During the war, people were all together as families, friends, citizens and church members. We did whatever we could do to bring peace to the world. It was a combined effort on the part of all to support our country and trust in God for a positive outcome. Many prayers went up daily for this to happen.

When the war was over, it was a glorious time. Americans were thankful that God had spared as many lives as He did. There was also sadness in the fact some would not come home alive. There were others who did come home, but were in bad condition from injuries, illness and other problems. Some who were prisoners of war had been treated so badly, it was hard to hear their stories. However, it was great to know that our freedom had been preserved for us and future generations.

The experience of going through a war on the home front was very sobering and helped us to grow up appreciating what had been done to keep us safe and free. The younger generations need to know the importance of patriotism, being good citizens and, in times of need, to arise to meet those needs to achieve what it takes to do so.

God bless America, land that I love. I am glad to be a citizen of the United States of America!

Vera Worrell
Atria Cordova
Memphis, Tennessee

During the war, I was training to become a nurse. I went to school for three years and graduated in 1945. After graduation, I moved to Fullerton, California, to live with my parents and I went to work at Fullerton Community Hospital. Our uniforms were white cotton starched dresses and we wore a cap to work everyday. My typical day consisted of hard and long hours, but I enjoyed it.

My home-front experience changed my life — it taught me a lot about independence. I would like for the younger generation to help out at home, and have respect for your parents, as we did when we were younger.

Mable Osborn
Atria Acacia
Fullerton, California

I lived in London with my family and worked at Norris Company, a plane factory, during World War II. This was a very hard time for my family and me because we lost a lot of friends and family. It was tough for me to deal with the war. We were not allowed to go outside at night; we had to go down in the shelter. No one could be on the streets or in their own home. There were many families that shared these shelters.

After the war was over, it was a very happy time. We had many celebrations, especially when the soldiers came home. I left the work force and started a family.

The war made me a better person; I appreciate things more than I ever did.

Hilda Isbit
Atria Palm Desert
Palm Desert, California

Marian made a different kind of contribution to the war effort. Even though her husband was a farmer and not called into service and Marian was expecting her second child, she wrote letters to many of the men from her street who were sent overseas. This kept the soldiers connected to the people at home, and let them know they were thought of often. She also remembers everyone celebrating in the street when the war ended.

Marian says no one can take their freedom for granted. It is something everyone should be grateful for and appreciate every day.

Marian Harper
Atria Greece
Rochester, New York

Ettaleen worked at Delta Star Electric Company in Chicago. Her first duties included working on the drill press. She was later transferred to the lathe, a machine that cut parts for airplanes. All this work was for the military. Ettaleen was promoted into the inspection department. She worked 7 a.m. to 3 p.m. six days a week. Her uniform consisted of khaki pants, goggles and a visor cap. She was 26 years old at the time and her husband was overseas in the Army, so she lived alone in their apartment.

After the war, Ettaleen stayed with the company counting inventory. Her husband was discharged and came home. Ettaleen's advice to other military wives is, "Stick with your guy – he is giving his life to the nation – support his efforts."

Ettaleen Patterson
Atria Chandler Villas
Chandler, Arizona

Nancy was in her roaring twenties during World War II. Texas was her home state, where she worked for the draft board. When she recalled the rationing of sugar, flour and all the other commodities the home front sacrificed for the war, Nancy simply stated, "We all did the best we could."

Not only did Nancy offer up her time and service to the cause, she had family members who served overseas. In fact, her brother served under General George Patton. Her first husband, a captain, served for three years. (Her second husband had served under the first one!)

Nancy Willis
Atria St. Matthews
Louisville, Kentucky

During World War II, I was still a student learning the basics, including history, math, English and science. My everyday life was very busy between school, homework and sports practice. We had to wear dresses to school and were only able to wear shorts when we played sports. We did make care packages for the soldiers that included bonds, stamps, envelopes and paper. I also remember men coming to our back door to ask for handouts. They would mark a tree or mailbox so the next guy would know our family gave leftovers.

When the war was over, I never heard so much hooting and hollering or saw so many smiling faces. I believe that World War II woke the United States as a nation. It made us realize how lucky we are to live here.

Dorothy Hancock
Atria Richardson
Dallas, Texas

"I am remembering, with boundless admiration, the valiant women who worked at home wherever they were needed while the men they loved fought in World War II.

One of the fresh-from-college, fresh-from-flight-training men sent to the Philippines with the American Army Air Corps 17th Pursuit Squadron was my older brother. Many months of intense suspense after December 7, 1941, brought my family American Red Cross confirmation that he was missing in action. Immediately, I left my job as proofreader for the Greenwood Commonwealth in the Mississippi Delta to be a Red Cross hospital recreation worker as long as I was needed. I was stationed at Moore General Hospital, Swannanoa, North Carolina and Fort Jackson, South Carolina. In those days, we were all passionately patriotic Americans, united in our determination to win the war and get on with our lives."

Catherine Whited
Atria Cordova
Memphis, Tennessee

Emma was a young girl, about 17, during the difficult time of the World War II era. She had an older sister and together they volunteered. Emma's family lived in the country with forestland for miles in all directions. There was a lookout tower in the forest that was used during the day to spot smoke that would indicate a forest fire might be starting.

Their duties were to go up on the lookout tower at night and watch for any airplanes that flew through the airspace around them. Airplane spotters could not use binoculars because airplanes had lights that would reflect off the binocular lens.

"In those days, we were all passionately patriotic Americans."

They would then document the time, day and type of airplane they had observed. Sometimes Emma's sister couldn't join her and some nights Emma couldn't go to the tower, so one sister would be there alone. At midnight, someone would replace them starting a new shift.

Many years after the war, Emma and her husband went to a display of airplanes that flew during World War II. Emma was surprised to find she could not remember any of the planes she had so dutifully documented while up on the lookout tower. Remembering airplanes years later was not one of the specified duties.

Emma feels strongly that the young people of today and generations to come should be made to realize what Americans did, while fighting on two fronts, to keep this land and freedom.

Emma Sackl
Atria Meridian
Lantana, Florida

"I worked as a secretary to the superintendent of the school. Then I got married, stayed at home and worked on the ranch, where we raised Hereford cattle, horses and chickens. I was typically up by 6 a.m. and sometimes as early as 4 a.m. in order to cook a hearty breakfast. I also tended the chickens and did other chores around the ranch. I cooked a big lunch and sometimes took it to family members and our other farm workers in the pasture. After doing the wash, cleaning and having dinner, we listened to the radio in the evening.

I believe World War II was a people's war and everyone did their part. All the women chipped in and worked how or where they could. When the war was over, it was wonderful."

Billie Jean Frey
Atria Richardson
Dallas, Texas

"I worked in a bomber plant and gave first aid to the men who needed help. Mostly I had to clean wounds and take care of the family. I had to wear a white nurse's dress with a cap.

I believe that everyone did their part in the war and women especially stepped up to the need. I want younger generations to know that the women worked just as hard at their jobs, and that it was okay for the women to let loose of the men.

It was a beautiful time when the war was over, and we celebrated! World War II changed my life because I would never have gotten the experience that I did without it."

Winnie Thompson
Atria Richardson
Dallas, Texas

"I believe that everyone did their part in the war and women especially stepped up to the need."

169

Anne worked for the New York State Labor Department in the Unemployment Insurance Division. She worked there until she was 65 years old, at which point she retired. Anne remembers her first daughter being born in March just before World War II began and her husband receiving some sort of special status so that he didn't have to leave in the beginning. She remembers being promoted to principal clerk when the man that had that position was called to fight. A typical day for Anne was usually 9 a.m. until 5 p.m. Monday through Friday.

Anne recalls her husband being called into service just before the war ended. At that time, she left her job temporarily so that her second daughter could be born. She recalls that her second child was approximately five months old before her husband returned from the war.

Anne has two memorable experiences from the home front. First, she remembers helping to make the "Bundles for Britain" and not being able to cast off the knitted scarves to finish them. She said she doesn't remember who finished them, but she continued to knit until her bundle was finished. Second, she remembers giving birth to her second daughter, without her husband, and trying to manage everything else. She recalls her mother being very supportive and helping whenever she could.

Anne is very proud to be an American and is very proud of her husband's service to his country.

Anne Cenci
Atria Shaker
Albany, New York

Betty worked as a secretary at the telephone company. Her typical day consisted of dictation and typing letters from 9 a.m. to 5 p.m.

Betty would like younger generations to know that the women home-front workers during World War II worked very hard. They were full of energy and happy to be kept busy.

The day the war ended was the most thrilling day of Betty's life.

Betty Borden
Atria South Setauket
Centereach, New York

"The day the war ended was the most thrilling day."

When the war broke out in 1941, Coy and Clyda McMillen went to work in the shipyard in Orange, Texas. Coy worked as a ship fitter and his wife was a sheet metal worker. Coy said that he made 90 cents an hour and Clyda made almost as much as he did – and her job was physically harder than his! The hardest part of working at the shipyard was that they had to leave their two-year-old son in Silsbee with Clyda's mother and father. They did go every weekend to visit their son until after the war.

Coy McMillen
Atria Collier Park
Beaumont, Texas

Radie was a housewife and mother-to-be during World War II. Her husband served on a submarine. According to Radie, life was difficult during those days, especially dealing with rations for food and gas. She remembers coming from grocery stores holding groceries in one hand, her youngest child under her other arm and her unborn child in the middle, so to speak. World War II mothers had much

balancing to do, not only with small children, but also trying to make the allotment of rations for food and gas fit into a workable puzzle for their families. It was not easy for the home-front families. Radie's husband was not allowed to come home for the birth and did not see their second child until he was two months old.

One memory Radie has from World War II involves her husband and the night he was nearly killed. One night it was his turn to be on lookout when the submarine was not submerged. He was so intently looking-out, that he did not hear the command to dive. A fellow crewman realized what was happening, grabbed Radie's husband's leg and, not so gently but successfully, pulled him into the submarine just before it submerged. Thankfully, he completed his tour and came home to see his wife and children.

Radie feels that citizens of younger generations do not know what it was like to do without, and that supporting your country was totally necessary in order to maintain freedom.

Radie Padmos
Atria Meridian
Lantana, Florida

I worked in a sewing factory and made field jackets during World War II. I also sang at the USO with a big-band musical group.

I was busy, busy, busy. I worked from 8 a.m. to 4 p.m. At night, I worked with the band and wrote letters to my man.

When the war was over, it was beautiful getting back to a normal life. The experience gave me a deeper appreciation of our country and its citizens.

Muriel Bontego
Atria Rancho Park
San Dimas, California

"I worked for the U.S. Engineers as a typist and a file clerk. My sister worked in the same department and they needed more help. Mary was my boss's name; she was crabby. I worked 7 a.m. to 3 p.m. and indexed a lot of files. Then I went home and cooked dinner for a family of four, washed dishes and went to bed early.

We played a very important role in defense. We were all relieved and happy to welcome the boys home."

Doris Burns
Atria Rancho Park
San Dimas, California

> " We were all relieved and happy to welcome the boys home."

"About 25 years ago when I left New York to live in California, a relative on the East Coast spotted me in a lineup of female lifeguards in the July 29, 1940 issue of Life Magazine. With time the pages have yellowed, but I have most of the article and will quote from it. The article's title is 'Girl Lifeguards Glamorize a Beach" and it says something like this:

"On hot summer days, it is pleasant to go to Manhattan Beach, New York. There if you fall asleep on the sand and the tide rises, threatening to engulf you, a pretty girl lifeguard dressed in a maroon latex bathing suit will wake you up. If you get lost, a pretty lifeguard will find you. If you are throwing bottles or digging deep holes, she will stop you. If you are about to drown, she may even save you."

In 1940, Manhattan was just another New York beach. Its 35 men lifeguards functioned efficiently but unglamorously. Then came the question: Why not have a girl auxiliary lifeguard corps? Quickly one was organized and soon became a hit. Sixteen volunteers in the corps were selected from 135 applicants.

The girl lifeguards averaged 18 years in age. We were required to be 5'4" tall and weigh not more than 140 pounds. In addition to being winsomely feminine, we had to be fully capable lifeguards and pass the Red Cross Senior Life Saving test. Most of us were in high school or college.

Although feminine, we did drills and demonstrated aquatic rescue techniques on dry land. When life saving was quiet, we did our regular lifeguard drills and practiced rescue techniques, such as the cross-chest carry, fireman's carry, chin carry and double-chin carry. We spent about 60 hours at our work.

I am proud that I was one of the female lifeguards and was able to free male lifeguards who fought for our country.

Muriel Simon
Atria Hacienda
Palm Desert, California

Chapter 6

Nearly every American family has a connection to World War II. Some are recollections of daily life straight from the "Rosies" themselves, some are detailed stories of joyous moments and some are memories that should not be forgotten. Whatever they are to home-front workers and their families, they are proudly shared here so others will understand American history more clearly and the impact World War II home-front workers made on our nation.

In early 1942, notices were posted in the local newspaper requesting help in various capacities to assist our soldiers in the war effort. At the time, Ruth was 24 years old and worked at Zuker's, a ladies' ready-to-wear dress shop. She thought about it for a short time and decided to apply. She went to Manual Arts High School in Los Angeles, and took an exhausting three-hour written examination test. She passed and was sent to Cal Tech in Pasadena, where she was trained to work on the hydraulics systems for various aircraft. Next, she was sent to work in Long Beach. She found that they needed help not in hydraulics, but in the exact science of sanding, filing and balancing propellers for both bombers and fighter aircraft.

Ruth was the only one who was able to master the machine to test governors, which determined the RPMs for each propeller. The governor had to be adjusted to exact specifications to have the propellers work properly; she used a setscrew and then locked it in place. She installed and removed Hamilton standard oil dome props used on B-17 and B-25 bombers and electric Curtiss-Wright props used on the twin fuselage P-38 fighter planes.

The work was very challenging. She and her coworkers knew they were performing a very important job and they were proud to do it. Ruth was very fit, having to pull herself up onto the plane to work on each propeller.

They all wore blue jeans and shirts. Sometimes they wore overalls or jumpsuits over their clothing. There was a coffee shop located above the hangar on the second floor where everyone took their breaks. They had sandwiches, coffee and donuts. The group felt a strong sense of camaraderie. Both military and civilians worked together, and there was a sense of excitement and urgency in their work. To relax after work, they would have dances; it seemed that everyone loved to dance!

There were many celebrities who visited the airfield and the propeller shop: Jimmy Stewart, Bob Hope, Irene Ryan and the McGuire Sisters. They even had a movie made there called "The Ferrying Command." It starred Loretta Young, Philip Terry and Geraldine Fitzgerald. In making the movie, workers saw the celebrities regularly. Ruth said that Philip Terry was handsome and pleasant; Loretta Young was always sweet and considerate. They often came up to the coffee shop and talked with the workers, sharing a doughnut and a cup of coffee. Geraldine Fitzgerald, however, never fraternized and remained aloof. Nobody much cared for her! John Payne, the movie star, also worked at the field, taxiing the planes from one location to another. He wasn't in the military but wanted to help out. It was funny, Ruth said, because he would come to work in a big black chauffeur-driven limousine along with his beautiful wife, Gloria DeHaven. In the late afternoon, the limo would pick him up again.

Everyone became accustomed to celebrities. One afternoon, Ruth had her jumpsuit on with "Tex" embroidered on her chest pocket. She felt someone watching her for quite a long time. He finally walked up behind her and said, "Well, Tex, it looks like you know what you're doing there." He smiled his famous sideways grin . . . it was Clark Gable! Ruth replied, "I'd better know what I'm doing because the boys are depending on me to do it right!"

Ruth and her female coworkers belonged to an organization called WAMS, which stood for Women's Air Mechanics Service. She proudly wore a patch with wings on it and those initials. It was navy blue with gold lettering and gold wings.

Many soldiers and sailors came through the post in Long Beach, awaiting transport to the various theaters of the war. One Navy pilot was especially memorable. He was shipping out on an aircraft carrier, but the plane needed adjustments. Mr. Zwack called Ruth late that night and asked her to come in. He told the pilot that "Tex" would be in shortly to take care of him. When she walked in and saw her approach, he shouted out, "She's a woman! I don't want a woman working on my plane!" Undaunted, Ruth asked her boss if he wanted her to do the job. He said, "Of course, Tex; you go right ahead and don't pay any attention to this guy." He instructed her to set the propeller at exactly 4,700 RPMs, which she did. Several days later, Ruth received a lovely bouquet of a dozen long-stemmed red roses. Attached was a card that read, "For Tex with my sincere apologies. It (the propeller) was set 'on the money.' I'll never question a woman again!"

When the War finally ended, there were more tears, many hugs and sighs of relief. Her own husband had been wounded by a Japanese sniper in the Philippines. They flew him to Australia where American doctors wanted to amputate his entire right leg. However, a Chinese doctor said it wasn't necessary, and after many successful surgeries, his leg healed completely.

Ruth has a photo from her home-front experience. She is standing on a P-38 fighter plane, hanging on to the propeller blade. The caption under the picture says, "She tests governors, Ruth "Tex" Wells, a popular member of this field, is claimed by the Prop Shop, lucky guys!"

Ruth Miller
Atria Del Rey
Rancho Cucamonga, California

Lillian was born March 17, 1921, in Fort Worth, Texas, graduated from North Side School and earned a Bachelor of Arts degree in Music from Texas Christian University. While she was living in Washington, D. C., she was employed by the Army/Navy Munitions Board, assisting in the admiral's office.

Lillian and her husband traveled all over the world, but the trip that stands out most in her mind is the one during which she took her 83-year-old mother to her birthplace in Monrovia in 1973. Lillian claims to be the only grandmother to ride a dromedary camel in the Australian outback and a bactrain camel in the Gobi desert in Katmandu.

Lillian Allen
Atria Willow Park
Tyler, Texas

In 1942 during World War II, Josephine worked for Grumman Aircraft Plant 14 on Route 109 in Farmingdale, Long Island, with the main plant located in Bethpage. Many people, even to this day, did not know that Plant 14 existed because the main work area was located underground, in a place that used to be a shooting range. Above ground was a garage with a dormer room. This was used as the office.

Josephine worked with approximately 150 other women. When she first began working at the plant at age 30, she soldered the ends of wires all day and placed them precisely on pre-arranged boards. After this challenging work, she tied the wires together with heavy cord and made a harness. The harnesses were then packaged and shipped. The wires and harnesses were in war planes.

In addition to doing the labor in the plant, Josephine began working in the office on Saturdays and eventually worked in the office full time. In addition to office work and dealing with all of the bosses, coworkers and workers at the main plant, part of Josephine's new duties was to promote the purchase of war bonds. One of Josephine's fondest memories was watching all of the girls coming to work each day. Due to gas rationing, many girls traveled together. One of the cars she especially remembers was a coupe that belonged to her longtime friend, Lizzie Miller. The coupe had a seat in the back that opened like a trunk, called a "rumble seat." It was built to accommodate only four people, and Josephine recalls it was something like watching a clown act at the circus when as many as eight girls piled out of it!

Although this was a very emotional and difficult time, the workers tried to keep things as light as possible. The superintendent of the plant was a stout man. When he came down each day to check on things, the halls echoed as the girls sang a popular song of the day, "Mr. Five By Five."

Working six days a week and bringing their lunches from home, workers took their breaks without leaving their workbench, and no one left the building without permission. Lifetime friends were also made along the way. Josephine still remains in contact with "Honey" Fitzpatrick Dappen, Violet Stokey Haagen and Lizzie Miller, the gal who owned the coupe. After working for Grumman, Josephine opened her own business and had a successful photography studio.

Over the years, Josephine has saved her gasoline rationing tickets, an identification card, a bracelet, a pin and a picture from a Grumman awards dinner. She will be donating them to the World War II Home-Front National Historic Park.

Josephine Heimer
**Atria Baypoint Village
Hudson, Florida**

Betty learned of the war when she was 11 years old from newspaper boys at the corner newsstand. Her uncle went into the service so she had to help her aunt run the family service station. They gave stamps to the servicemen when they were in town.

Betty Meyer
**Atria Carrollton
Dallas, Texas**

Marion is from Honolulu. Following the December 7 attack, she heard they were hiring at the Pearl Harbor Navy Yard. She applied and got a job working as a civilian in the Navy Auditor's Department. Marion was the only woman in an office full of men. She did clerical work, mainly typing requisitions for the Navy and filing. Marion worked from 1941 to 1945. Each morning, a van picked her up and returned her home after work. Marion remembers having to carry a gas mask with her to work for quite a while after the attack on Pearl Harbor. She stopped working in 1945 when she was expecting her first child.

Marion's strongest memory from the home front is the attack on Pearl Harbor. Living only eight miles away, she heard the bombing and the noise; shrapnel went right through her home! It is an event she will never forget.

Marion Au
Atria Colima
Walnut, California

"Giving blood was something I did periodically during the war. On one occasion, someone forgot that I had a needle in my arm and I passed out because too much blood had been removed from my body. In turn, I received a blood transfusion to bring me back around."

Julia Petty
Atria Sandy
Sandy, Utah

Shirley was in high school during World War II, but she felt the need to do something for the war effort. She considered enlisting in the service as she was very patriotic, but she was too young. At the age of 16, she was able to volunteer to help at the local draft board. She said many mothers from the neighborhood came into the office crying and very upset that their sons were drafted. These were difficult and scary times. Shirley remembers blackout shades, rationing and visits by air-raid wardens, who made sure neighborhoods were keeping lights from being visible from the street. Everyone was very aware that there was a war going on.

Shirley Stoloff
Atria East Northport
Long Island, New York

"My husband and I were one-year newlyweds, living in Roseland in Chicago. I confronted him with the idea that I had seen many advertisements about greatly needed volunteers to help with the war effort. Women were taught how to rivet and this helped produce fighter-bomber planes. I wanted to help and do my part as an all-American wife. My husband, Sye, consented. I could walk to the building where I was to be taught how to rivet. There were so many women there and all were in coveralls. Wow! It was so vogue!

I worked for a whole year. One day when my husband came home from work, I was in for a big surprise. He informed me that he, too, was going to do his part for the war effort and that he had enlisted in the Air Corps for three years. Boy, was that a surprise! I sure was proud of him. You see, my husband had not been drafted because he was vice president of a company that was already producing items being used in the war. I guess he always knew that it was just a matter of time before Uncle Sam sent for him.

Sye graduated from flight school and moved up in rank rapidly. He reached rank of lieutenant and I was living at home and riveting away. In a letter, my Sye wrote that he just couldn't live without me. He asked me to leave my riveting job and join him, so I did.

Shortly after our joining, the war was over and I received the honor of pinning my husband with his flight wings. What a wonderful time in our lives! This chapter of our lives will never be forgotten."

Frances Lanasa
Atria Sugar Land
Houston, Texas

"I worked at Penney's during the war. Metal tokens could be used for money and we had to take the tokens in place of money. It was so nice after the war to make change again."

Oral Anderson
Atria St. George
St. George, Utah

Florence was married with a 12-year-old son and a 10-year-old daughter, living in San Francisco when the war began. On a typical day for Florence, she was up by 5 a.m., had breakfast made and helped her husband and children get ready for work and school. After they were gone, Florence cleaned the house and got herself ready for work. She worked at the grocery with two other women, doing everything and anything that had to be done. When the day was over, Florence went home, started supper and got her children ready for bed, but of course not before the dinner was done and the dishes were washed.

When the war ended, Florence was so pleased to hear that she no longer needed to work at the store and that the men were coming back home to fill the jobs they had left behind.

Florence Rogers
Atria Campbell
Campbell, California

After she graduated from college, Virginia went to airplane school. She began working in Washington, D.C., as a radio operator for Capitol Airplane in the meteorology and flight dispatch department. It was 1942, and Virginia and her female coworkers were the first girls to relieve the men so they could serve their country. Around the clock and working eight-hour shifts, the ladies kept track of planes en route. They did this without the use of radar.

Virginia was in Washington, D.C., for many memorable events. She was there when President Roosevelt died, and watched from the street during his funeral procession. She also attended the inauguration of President Truman. She stood at the Lincoln Memorial when General Eisenhower returned from overseas in his motorcade. She also enjoyed entertaining friends and relatives who stopped in D.C. on their way overseas.

When the war ended, residents of the Capitol City were overjoyed. They had faced many hardships, like not having any meat on the table and blackouts every night. Everyone breathed a sigh of relief when the war was finally over.

Today, Virginia firmly believes that World War II was a people's war, the war of a generation. She wants younger generations to know that women were proud of their duties. She also wants women to know that they are capable of handling any job. She wouldn't trade her wartime days for anything, for they made her the person she is today. "We can prove ourselves stronger than what we really are," she says.

Virginia Rippley
Atria Grapevine
Grapevine, Texas

"I grew up and was still living in Memphis, Tennessee. I had one son during the war. My husband did not have to serve. He was an accountant, but the war didn't change his job. I tried to help the war effort by volunteering my time to roll bandages for the Red Cross. I did not consider this to be much help. I remember that we were given coupons for butter and everyone fought for coupons for bacon. I also remember the big parades in Memphis at the end of the war. That was a grand time!"

Alice Brooks
Atria Primacy
Memphis, Tennessee

Because Mary had two brothers in the Army and one in the Navy, she remembers she wanted to do her part for the war, so she gave blood every time she was able. As it turns out, one of her brothers came home because of an injury.

Mary Hurst
Atria Springdale
Louisville, Kentucky

"USO dances were something everyone looked forward to attending. When the call came for me to hostess a USO dance, I happily went and entertained the soldiers. Some soldiers had been wounded or disabled but they still made it to the dances.

We had savings stamps at the time. The more you saved, the more the stamps were worth when they were redeemed. To help raise money, I made these stamps into a bouquet of flowers and sold them in Los Angeles, and people bought them. With the money raised, I bought clothes to send overseas to Germany to help poverty-stricken families. I received a hand crocheted handkerchief from a lady I had helped in Germany and I still have that hanky to this day.

I remember one time a German ship was along the Santa Barbara coastline. That night there was a blackout and I could hear gunfire along the coast. With everything being so dark and eerie, it was very frightening. Some time later I learned there had also been a German plane flying along the Santa Monica coast and our military shot it down."

Norma Nelson
Atria Sandy
Sandy, Utah

"I lived in Memphis, Tennessee, at the time of World War II and had been married since 1938. My husband enlisted in the 872nd Airborne Engineers. I moved back home and worked in my mother's drug store. I lived with her for three years until my husband came home. He and I wrote each other every day, but when the first letter was received, it was shredded due to censoring and very difficult to read. While he was away, I received mail from New Guinea, Okinawa, the Philippines and Japan. To do my part for the war effort, I went to a few USO dances for the Navy men who were stationed at the nearby base. I also enjoyed knitting socks for the soldiers in the South Pacific.

We received ration books every month. We could have only two pair of shoes a year. Nylons were not available because nylon material was used for parachutes for the military. We used streetcars, buses or walked wherever we went because gas was hard to come by. There were a lot of factory-like buildings called defense plants in Memphis that were used for making ammunition and other war necessities."

Marty Trabue
Atria Primacy
Memphis, Tennessee

She found her place in the war at Swift and Company, a packinghouse that shipped meat to soldiers. Josephine, a registered nurse at the time, witnessed her share of severed fingers due to the dangerous knives and grinders at the packinghouse, and it was she who tended to the various wounds.

"I remember vividly that one time I was to be the next in line for the old-fashioned elevator when it suddenly beheaded the 20-year-old innocent gentleman in front of me."

Even after such a traumatic event, Josephine kept her spirits high and promised herself that from that day on not only would she heal wounds, but she would also help keep the boys happy.

It's no wonder the soldiers loved "JoJo." Oftentimes she traveled downtown to the USO amphitheater with them, where they shared dances, laughter and cocoa. At one point, JoJo traveled with the boys from Chicago to Oklahoma. They didn't hesitate to ask her for one small favor and with that, she mailed her clothes to Oklahoma and filled her suitcase with liquor for the boys. She wouldn't let anyone on the airplane come close to her suitcase and guarded it with dear life. "Well, wouldn't you?" she says. "Here I was bootleggin' for the boys!"

One of her last memories of being a registered nurse during World War II was going hungry. All of the nurses took turns stealing scraps of food from the kitchens, and one day it was her turn.

"It never fails. All my life when I do something I am not supposed to, I do it up real good."

JoJo hesitantly agreed to all the pressure from the other hungry nurses and chose a watermelon, of all things, to steal. It was quite obvious, as she tried stuffing the watermelon under her clothes, what she was doing and got caught right in the middle of it by a nun. Her nurse cap was immediately removed so that everyone would know that JoJo had done something wrong that day.

Josephine's memories of World War II are unlike any she had ever experienced.

"It was the greatest and saddest time of my life at the same time."

Josephine Krebs
Atria Lawrenceville
Atlanta, Georgia

Betty was teaching high school at the time of the war and she remembers passing out ration books to everyone. The book contained ration coupons for eggs, sugar, coffee, butter and gas. Today, she is amazed at the variety of each of the once-rationed items on every grocery-store shelf. She also remembers teaching first aid to adults and women going to the churches to make bandages.

Betty Cauley
Atria Springdale
Louisville, Kentucky

Harriet worked at DuPont and met Mercedes, who became one of her best friends. The two decided to save their money and move to California – Hollywood to be exact – where they became seamstresses for Warner Bros. Harriet remembers meeting Bette Davis and Errol Flynn, who was the nicest person she ever met.

Harriet Nixon
Atria Bonita
Chula Vista, California

"When the war broke out, I was married and I had a five-month-old daughter. I was 23 when my husband was drafted into the Army's Finance Department. He was sent to France after his training at Fort McAllen. I lived in a small duplex just three houses down from my mom and dad. I was in church services all the time.

I had a picture of my husband and I tried to teach my child about her father by telling her to say good night to daddy while pointing to the picture. My daughter was two and a half years old when her father came home, but she didn't know or understand who the strange man was. She would say, "He's not my daddy," and then look at the picture.

World War II was a sad and scary time, and I put my whole life into my child in those years."

Virginia Maners
Atria Primacy
Memphis, Tennessee

Betty remembers D-Day, June 6, 1944, because it was her son's birthday and she was trying to have a party for him.

"I couldn't concentrate on making the cake because I kept listening to the radio!"

Betty's husband was drafted, but thankfully was never sent overseas. He was sent to Seattle to work for Boeing Aircraft.

"Because they were making so many items for the war effort, Boeing stopped making electric refrigerators and other appliances. Although the refrigerators were still very new, Boeing concentrated on World War II. I was lucky enough to get one of the last refrigerators they made. An aircraft used for the war you could get, but refrigerators were scarce."

Betty started a victory garden to grow extra food even though she lived in the city.

"Going to the store you would find empty shelves. I remember bread was three loaves for a dime, but it was the worst bread. It was disgusting. The bread would be hard as a rock the next day."

Betty said that cloth was in such a short supply, she couldn't find sheets for a bed. She had to resort to using an old tablecloth for the bed.

Betty Jinx
Atria Springdale
Louisville, Kentucky

Christine married her husband, Bill, on October 1, 1943, only to have him ship out for naval duty 16 days later on October 17. After she said goodbye, Christine moved home to Northport, Alabama, to live with her mom and dad on their farm.

During the war, the rationing of food didn't affect the family much because they had many crops of their own. Christine worked in accounts receivable at a local bakery and made $12 a week. She later worked keeping up with payroll for a plumbing contractor.

Christine and Bill kept in touch during the war by writing to each other using a coding system the newlyweds developed. Christine said, "Somehow he was able to let me know how he was doing. Even when his shipmate was transferred to another ship, he still continued to write to me telling me that Bill was okay."

Christine was so happy to hear about the U.S. victory over the radio. She was tickled to know her husband was finally coming home and would be able to see his 15-month-old daughter for the first time. Christine said that when her 15-month-old saw her daddy, she went straight to him like she had known him forever. "She has gone straight to him ever since," Christine said.

Christine Ramsey
Atria Weatherly Springs
Huntsville, Alabama

"My husband was in the Navy and serving as the port director's officer in San Pedro, directing ships. I went out to be with him on the train, riding in a Pullman car the entire way. You could get a job anywhere in those days. First I helped make the badges that were required to get out to Terminal Island. Then my husband was transferred to San Francisco, before he shipped out. While there, I worked for the telephone company stuffing bills. After that, I returned home and worked for T. P. & L. While he stayed in California, my husband

lived in a boarding house. When I took the train to be with him, the lady that owned the house moved her daybed into a closet so that I might stay in the master bedroom with my husband."

Sue Prestridge
Atria Copeland
Tyler, Texas

I was in high school when World War II started. I married soon after that and lived in Memphis, Tennessee. I worked for the draft board, so I guess not too many people liked me.

My husband joined the service – 51st Engineers – and was gone for nearly two or three years. I lived with two other lady friends at that time. The naval base was full of men. I met Clyde McCoy, the leader of a big band famous for the "Sugar Blues" song.

Dean Crocker
Atria Primacy
Memphis, Tennessee

Anne's husband owned a tool and die company and she worked in the office. After the war began, a government official notified them that the business was needed to manufacture airplane parts to help the war effort. Anne became a home-front worker. In addition to her office responsibilities, Anne would often have to work in the factory.

For two years, the company was kept busy with government contracts. After the war, there was a big change in the business and no more airplane parts to be made, so Anne and her husband had to watch every penny. For the first time in their lives, they had to borrow money from the bank. But with hard work, the couple was able to build their business back up.

Working with her husband to support the war effort, Anne felt proud to support her country.

Anne Upton
Atria Colima
Walnut, California

Dorothy dated Al for part of the war and then was married to him during the later years of the war. He was not sent overseas because he was needed at home for his intelligence work. Dorothy taught school in New York during the war.

One wartime memory she recalls involves her first pregnancy, food rations and fainting. Dorothy went to the local grocery and asked for a quart of milk, but before she could finish her order she fainted right on the spot. She awoke to find people fanning her in the back storage room. She walked out of the store with several quarts of milk – more than the ration coupon allowed.

Dorothy Osse
Atria St. Matthews
Louisville, Kentucky

Pat was a secretary at Wright Aeronautical in Evendale, Ohio, which made airplane parts for the war. She wore regular office attire except nylons because they were hard to find due to the rationing.

"We sometimes got this special cream for our legs that we used instead of nylons, but I was fortunate that I could usually have a pair of nylons," she recalls.

Pat laughs when she thinks about walking in the plant area because of all the whistles she used to get.

Pat Robbins
Atria Northgate Park
Cincinnati, Ohio

184

"My husband volunteered for duty when the war broke out. In March, I went to Paris, Texas, to be with him for his basic training before he went overseas to France and Germany. This was my first time outside of Tennessee, so it was an experience for me, too. I took a bus to Nashville, 80 miles west of Cookeville, where I lived. In Texarkana, I took another bus to Paris, where my husband Vernon met me. He had a room for us with a nice lady named Mrs. Calhoun. He came home every night and we ate dinner two blocks away with another nice lady who served several soldiers and their wives. She had been at my minister's daughter's wedding in Cookeville before I left and I was pleasantly surprised to walk into the dining room and see Helen and her husband.

After I had been there for a while, I was asked to help make bandages for the Red Cross. Another soldier's wife and I would walk about a mile to town and do this all morning and hope and pray that the soldiers never needed the bandages. How wrong we were!

I later went to Nashville, Tennessee, to work in a department store, where I did bookkeeping and kept very busy. I went to church and prayed that my husband would come home to me. He came home in March 1946, and he got his old job back with the U.S. Engineers, building a dam and a powerhouse. He kept everyone's lights on for 40 years before he retired."

Harriett Oliver
Atria Carrollton
Dallas, Texas

To this day, Jennie still doesn't have a nice big aluminum pan she should have received for a wedding present. Her mother had one, but gave it away to help the war effort. But Jennie survived that sacrifice, and many others. From shortages on sugar and meat to nylons and shoes, her family lived under the ration system like the rest of the country.

Life for Jennie during World War II included a husband who worked at the Navy Yard, a brother in the Air Force, and a civil-servant job as an administrative assistant for the Army Corp of Engineers. The department she worked for was responsible for going ahead of the troops and preparing the land for them. Everything was encoded for top security.

Jennie was fortunate to be able to hang a blue star in the window, representing her brother who was fighting in the war. Other families were not so fortunate; they had to hang gold stars in remembrance of their loved ones killed in battle.

Jennie has a vivid memory of seeing what war did to people and what they went through upon returning home. One night she and her husband were at the movies. She remembers seeing a man being helped by his wife; he had a prosthetic leg and arm – obviously a veteran. The look on his wife's face was one Jennie will never forget. It revealed the pain and loss suffered by veterans and their families due to fighting for the cause.

Jennie Goldstein
Atria St. Matthews
Louisville, Kentucky

"My husband was sent to Prescott, Maine, under military contract, but I stayed in New York. My husband brought back the wounded from the war. Because I lived in an apartment and I didn't know anyone, I mostly stayed at home. I was a newlywed and my husband was gone most of the time.

My sister worked in a defense factory, and I really respect her and the other women who worked during the war. The women were a main part of the war; they took on jobs that men usually did.

I remember that we had to limit our entertainment because we couldn't just get in our car and go. Gas was rationed and we used our vehicle only for necessary trips. I remember when SPAM first came out, as well as standing in line for over an hour to get rationed items. We had a network of friends to find and tell us who had what items so we would have a better chance at getting what we wanted.

I've talked about my experiences with my kids and grandkids. One of my grandkids took a ration stamp to school for show-and-tell."

Louise Bird
Atria Richardson
Dallas, Texas

"My mother, Julia Shaw, was a full-time wife and mother. She was taking care of my elder sister and me, just a baby, during World War II. My mother did not trust anyone to take care of us, especially during the difficult moments when you did not know what would happen. My father was gainfully employed and earning well, I presume, because we had two big houses and several cars in our garages. Nevertheless, my mother was not spared of standing in line to get what we needed around the house.

My mother made sure that we were not afraid during blackouts. She would sing for us and give us things we could play with in order to distract our attention from the darkness around us. Life was not as bad for my sister, my father and myself because my mother devoted 24 hours of her time to the job of being a wife and mother."

Julia Shaw
by daughter Sally Shaw
Atria Daly City
Daly City, California

"Three of my girlfriends and I joined the Servicemen's Center downtown. We were called cadets and there were five groups of us on duty. The first floor was for meeting, greeting, relaxing and writing letters. The second floor was everyone's favorite because it had a dance floor and a jukebox. The third floor was for cards, refreshments, and conversation.

Even after our service job was over and after all of these years, I still have many happy memories of those days and all the fine American servicemen who crossed my path."

Dorothea Baurle
Atria Heritage
Indianapolis, Indiana

Arline's husband was an FBI agent. She and her five children traveled by ship to war-torn Germany to be with her husband, where they lived for five years. She remembers seeing the ruins of the warplanes lying in the streets in pieces with rubble everywhere. Arline said that on weekends people would come together and begin the process of cleaning their streets and sidewalks.

While living in Germany, Arline and her children saw the Berlin Wall. She met with J. Edgar Hoover, who was head of the agency at that time. Arline's husband was not allowed to talk about his work.

Arline Brady
Atria Stratford
Stratford, Connecticut

"When I remember WWII, I'm ashamed to realize how little attention I paid to the big picture – the terrible battles and the tragic loss of life. However, I did pay attention to the boys! I was in college and busy learning and having fun.

During my freshman year there were lots of boys around to make things interesting. By the next year, most of them had been drafted or had enlisted. We were a campus of girls, and it was dull. The following year, to our delight, the university got a contingent of sailors and marines who were studying to become doctors, lawyers and chaplains. Six weeks into the semester, five sailors entered my political science class. When they were introduced, I wondered who the boy was with the southern drawl and all of the freckles. I found out when the professor asked me to lend him my notes and help bring him up to speed in the class work. He was just back from Guadalcanal and eager for romance. Two years later, we were married. In the meantime, there were parties and dances, studies and exams, and the ups and downs of courtship.

On the more serious side, I remember the times I listened to President Roosevelt's fireside chats, laboriously mixed orange coloring into white blocks of margarine, obtained gas with ration stamps and rolled bandages. I also think about my mother taking first aid classes. And there is the sad memory of a boy and a girl who fell in love, married quickly, and within a few short weeks he was killed in battle.

Now I watch movies and documentaries about the war and learn more than I did when it was happening. Perhaps I should be grateful that most of my memories are happy ones."

Gwen Nichols
Atria Collwood
San Diego, California

"My mother was a wonderful seamstress and sewed for all of us girls, as well as for others, out of our home. She later worked at the Funsten Pecan Co., and when I was 14 or 15 years old, I went to work there. This was the time of The Depression in 1930-31. Work was hard to find in St. Louis during those years. Because St. Louis was considered part of the South, we heard about all the jobs in Detroit, and that is where I headed.

I met John Brandt at a dance. That is where most young men and women went to meet and have fun. He was quite a dancer, and never lost his love of dancing his entire life! We got married on New Year's Eve, 1936. No one had much money then and families usually lived together. John and I lived with his mother, father and sister. Things were pretty tight, but you were just glad to have a home.

Like a lot of my friends and some of my husband's family, I went to work at Dodge Main, one of the many, huge automobile production plants in Detroit. I worked in the wire room and connected wires together by hand all day. We wore slacks to work and scarves, or babushkas, on our heads to try and keep the dust out of our hair. I worked from 7 a.m. to 5 p.m. We didn't have a car, so I took a bus or trolley back and forth to work. It was a long day.

Things were happening in Europe, but we didn't talk a lot about those things. Our first baby, Betty Lou, was born in September 1940. We were very happy, but it was wartime and my husband eventually enlisted in the Army and was sent to a military base in Arizona.

I was pregnant again, my husband was still away in the service and I was living with my in-laws when, in July 1944, I went into labor and was quickly rushed to the hospital in a cab. We barely made it! Our second child, a son, Johnny, was almost born in the back seat of that cab!

Shortly after giving birth, I went back to work at the Froelich Packing House, where I worked with several other women, stuffing freshly ground sausage into long casings. I eventually became the head foreman over everyone who worked there. I had to get up at 4 a.m. each day to catch the bus down to the Eastern Market to start work at 6 a.m. I got home around 3:30 p.m., and because we still lived with my husband's parents, my mother-in-law already had dinner started.

Today, things are a lot easier for young couples. People don't have to live in such cramped spaces, everybody has cars to go places, but husbands, wives, and their children are still being separated when we send people off to war. Back in those days, we just tightened our belt and got through it somehow.

Marie Brandt
Atria Stony Brook
Louisville, Kentucky

Pearl's first work experience was at Curtiss-Wright as a janitor. "That's all they had blacks doing at that particular time," said Pearl. "I swept floors and cleaned restrooms."

Pearl's sister and brother worked at Curtiss-Wright too. The job ended when the war was over. "I worked under an older man named Walter Freeman. He was a good boss, but he died shortly after the plant closed," she recalls.

Pearl Mayes
Atria Heritage
Indianapolis, Indiana

"My husband graduated from college and went immediately into the service as a captain. He went to Hiroshima right after they dropped the bomb. He later contracted terminal brain cancer.

While my husband was in the service we managed to start a family. My little boys saw very little of their father. Whenever my one son saw a man in uniform, he would run up and throw his arms around the man's legs and holler, "Daddy, Daddy!" It's funny now, but I was so embarrassed then!"

Dolly Daily
Atria St. George
St. George, Utah

According to Bonnie, when the men went to war there was a shortage of personnel at the telephone company. Prior to the war, the telephone company did not hire married women because it took away jobs from the men, who were primarily the bread winners for their families.

When you went for an interview, you had to wear a hat and gloves or you would not be considered for the job. Bonnie was paid $12 a week and worked 40 hours a week. She took a streetcar to work that cost her 10 cents a day and she ate her lunch in the cafeteria because they did not want anyone to leave the building. She paid 35 cents a day for lunch. Workers handled about 500 calls a shift and she really enjoyed doing conference calls for companies, even though it was very stressful.

Bonnie remembers if you were caught listening, to calls you were dismissed and/or prosecuted. Bonnie said she enjoyed working for the telephone company and was thankful for the job.

Bonnie Novak
Atria Seville
Las Vegas, Nevada

The most important memory that Mary has from the war is that of marrying her college sweetheart. He was serving overseas and during a nine-day leave, the two got married. Just a few days later, Mary's new husband went back overseas for 24 months.

"I wrote to him everyday for two years. But because of the combination of the quality of the postal services and him moving around Italy, France and Germany, he sometimes would not immediately get the letters, then he would get 20 or 30 of them at a time," she recalls.

Mary McKenzie
Atria Springdale
Louisville, Kentucky

"I was too young to work during World War II because I was still in high school. I remember my brother being sent to England with the Army Air Force. He was killed in action on a plane returning from a raid and was buried in France. I remember my mother being devastated; he was her only son.

I also remember people buying stamps on the black market (after all, I lived in New York!). I remember getting off the ferry when they announced that the war was over. There was a lot of cheering and everyone was dancing in the streets."

Margaret Bolyard
Atria Cordova
Memphis, Tennessee

"I married Paul Giusti in 1939. In 1941 when World War II broke out, we were living in Daly City, California. My husband was working at the shipyard in San Francisco. My father, an American-Italian working at the California Barrel Company, got transferred to work at a laundry outside the Bay area. Just like the Japanese who were rounded up and interned at concentration camps, most Italians were discriminated against. Unfortunately, my father slipped and fell at the laundry where he was working. He hurt himself so badly that he became disabled and could no longer work. My mother was sickly and she could not take care of my father, so my husband invited them to live with us. Wartime was not easy. We had blackouts that were so scary and we stood in line for hours to buy the things that we needed.

Life was very challenging for me. I had to take care of my father, my mother and my baby daughter. Paul worked longer hours, as he was the sole breadwinner. I felt that my responsibility of taking care of the family was more than a full-time job. There were no days off for me. I was a nurse, a cook, a laundry woman and a cleaning lady rolled into one."

Eda Giusti
Atria Daly City
Daly City, California

Anne and her husband, Charlie, were both schoolteachers in California before the war. When her husband joined the Air Force and was sent overseas, Anne went to work for Lockheed Martin, where she and other women were taught how to assemble airplanes. As soon as they found out she was a teacher, they moved her to do office work. Anne remembers that both she and her husband came home safely at the same time. She returned as an elementary school teacher and her husband continued being a high school coach.

Anne Moore
Atria Encinitas
Encinitas, California

Mary was a student in high school at the time of the war. The students and teachers made and wrapped bandages. According to Mary, it brought the war closer to home for them and it was an honor for them to support the troops.

Mary Armstrong
Atria Springdale
Louisville, Kentucky

In December 1941, I was a newlywed. I had recently married a wonderful man named Charles. As soon as he heard that war had been declared, he signed up for the Navy. We were living in Memphis, Tennessee, at that time and he was stationed at the Millington Naval Base just outside of Memphis. It wasn't quite so bad until he was shipped off to Okinawa. He remained there until the war ended. Our first child was born while Charles was gone and by the first time he saw her, she was already walking. I lived with Mother and Daddy while he was away. When I heard the war was over, I was so excited and I knew that Charles would soon be home. We stayed in Memphis for awhile after the war before moving to Tupelo, Mississippi. We returned to Memphis a year later and have remained here ever since.

Lois Evans
Atria Cordova
Memphis, Tennessee

Gene's mother, Ollie Hacker, worked in Cincinnati, making airplane engines. She had to wear overalls to work. "I remember seeing mom, who was not thin, wearing the outfit!" said Gene. She also recalls that workers at the plant wanted to go on strike and threatened her mother if she did not join them. As the strike enthusiasts got physically closer to her to demand her support, Gene said, "My mother grabbed the air hose and blew dirt and air into their faces. Mom told them that she had two boys in much more danger than me fighting in the war and she was not going to strike."

Alois Gene Smith
Atria Wekiwa Springs
Apopka, Florida

"I was a beauty operator at Union Station Beauty Shop in Kansas City when World War II broke out. All those who came to the beauty shop wanted to talk and the war was their favorite subject. There were speculations about the war ending. It went on day in and day out, on and on. I was even getting tired of listening to the talks because talking about the war didn't make our problems go away. We needed to conserve energy. There were blackouts, gasoline rationing and food rationing. Other commodities like shoes were limited.

My husband, Albert, was a pharmacist and thought that to be the reason he was not called to serve. He was needed more here in America than overseas. Life was difficult during the World War II era, but we made it."

Marjorie Crumpton
Atria Daly City
Daly City, California

Before the war years, Elaine studied business. Then she worked for the Navy for 20 years and kept a journal each night of the war. In 1945, she did parades. She also traveled around the world with six ladies during that time.

Elaine Posenecker
Atria Carrollton
Dallas, Texas

"I was a housewife with five babies living in Fort Worth, Texas. My husband was drafted into the war and the day that he was to leave, I had just found out that I was expecting child number six. I was able to inform my husband before he left and they allowed him to come home for the birth of our daughter and spend two days with us. What a joyous reunion!"

Oleta Lynch
Atria Willow Park
Tyler, Texas

"I worked in an advertising company in New York on Madison and Park Avenue during World War II. I had to take the bus to the train station and was on the train for 50 minutes. When I got off the train, I had to take the subway across town, both to and from work. Whenever you were on the train, bus, subway, etc, if a solider got on you automatically gave up your seat to them.

There were several things we had to do without, but we didn't mind because it was for the good of the country. The one thing I learned during wartime was how to limit and ration myself. We stood in line for shoes, sugar, meat, butter, cigarettes and stockings.

I volunteered for the Red Cross by calling people for donations. I donated blood whenever possible and wrapped 'Bundles for Britain,' which included items for the soldiers. I learned to knit so I could make scarves for the soldiers and I volunteered at the YWCA, which held dances for the soldiers. I'm glad I could help in any way and I would do it all again.

When the war was over, there was excitement and celebration. You felt lucky to be a U.S. citizen.

Helen Thornton
Atria Richardson
Dallas, Texas

"In 1941, I worked at People's Bakery in San Francisco. My husband was working for a news company and he was also the air-raid patrol in our neighborhood. He made sure that all window shades were down and told people when it was safe to put them up again.

Thinking about the war does not bring good memories. It was very depressing then. We had neighbors whose husbands and sons were sent to war, and some of them were killed. Whenever I hear about young men being sent to Iraq, I cannot help but think about World War II."

Betty Doherty
Atria Daly City
Daly City, California

"When World War II came along, my husband and I divorced. My son and I went to live with my grandmother, who took care of him while I worked. It cost $18 a month for medicine needed for my son. His father paid a very small amount of child support, not enough to cover the cost of my son's medicine. For us to survive, I worked three jobs.

I was a secretary from 9 a.m. to 5 p.m. Lying on the sofa after work, I ate the dinner my grandmother prepared and rested. My next job was at an ice-cream parlor from 7 p.m. to 11 p.m. On Saturdays, I sold hats from 9:30 a.m. to 5:30 p.m. and worked in the ice-cream parlor from 7 p.m. to 11 p.m. On Sundays, I returned to the ice-cream parlor and worked the day shift. One day Uncle Jack asked me when I was going to quit one of my jobs so somebody else could have one."

Virginia Pearce
Atria Buena Vista
Vista, California

Dorothy lived on a farm in Springfield, Kentucky, with her family while she waited for her husband to return from war. It was a difficult time in her life, but she was fortunate to have a great family to support her. One particularly difficult period of the war was when Dorothy's husband continued writing letters stating that he would be home by Christmas.

"We waited all winter long, but he wasn't able to arrive until March. It was so difficult waiting and waiting," said Dorothy. By the time her husband returned from war, their first daughter was two years old and a stranger to him. But in no time Daddy and his little girl became good buddies.

When the war was over and Dorothy's husband returned, they moved to Louisville, Kentucky, where things went from "hard" to "wonderful."

Dorothy Blanford
Atria St. Matthews
Louisville, Kentucky

At age 22, Jessie knew that Curtiss-Wright was hiring women to work in the airplane factory. She was hired as a supervisor for the assembly line. She worked from 7 a.m. until 4 p.m. She worked on bodies of airplanes that did not pass inspection.

She worked there only during the war years; once the war was over, she did not work. Jessie met her future husband there and they were married 57 years.

One of the sad ordeals Jessie endured during World War II was losing her only brother in the South Pacific. It took two-and-a-half years for her brother's body to be shipped home. Unfortunately, her mother died just after they were told her brother's body was coming home. They had to have a double funeral. "Many people today don't realize the sacrifices American women endured during the war," Jessie says. They were all great women. We owe them all a debt of gratitude.

Jessie Bricker
Atria Woodside Village
Columbus, Ohio
194

Faye recalls that she was married during the World War II era and that her husband was stationed at Ft. Walters. He was the sole supporter of aging parents at the time. She remembers crowded housing and that she rented out rooms for anyone who needed a place to stay.

Faye Doan
Atria Carrollton
Dallas, Texas

"I worked in Detroit for Packard Motor Car Company, which made ambulances for the war. I was a secretary and took shorthand. My girlfriends who worked in the factory made more money than I did. My uniform was navy blue with gold letters and a hat that resembled an Army hat. WWMDC was printed in gold letters, which stood for "Women's Willy's Motor Defense Corps." We wore our uniforms in parades. Those are good memories!"

Beth Rosen
Atria Bayside Landing
Stockton, California

In 1941, Doris had just finished high school and went to work for an insurance company. One day she asked for a raise, complaining to her boss that her friends who were working for the government and in factories for the war effort made more money. He asked her what she would spend the money on if he did give her a raise. She said she would save it up to buy war bonds. Doris's boss gave her the raise immediately with no more questions asked.

Doris Groves
Atria Manresa
Annapolis, Maryland

Gerry worked for four years for Abbott Laboratories in Chicago. She worked five days a week, eight hours a day typing medical orders for the Army. Gerry does not recall how much money she made, but she knows that she made more money than her husband did. She remembers it being a very good job.

Geraldine Pittsley
Atria Chandler Villas
Chandler, Arizona

Aurelia's husband, Lewis, was in the service and stationed in Hawaii, so she went to work in a Navy supply company in Oakland. She typed 90 words a minute, performed typical secretarial duties and worked 40 hours a week. Though wages were frozen, her salary ran about $40 per week.

It didn't seem fair at the time that women had to go to work because they weren't treated fairly, she recalls. But it allowed our country to continue the fight for freedom. Women kept our country afloat so the men had something to come back to.

Carolyn, her sister, remembers their father saying, "With this war, we will improve our medicine capabilities and knowledge in science will sky rocket (a man before his time). War is bad, but if we take what we've learned and apply it, then it was not in vain."

After the Korean War, the words spoken by her father came back to her, much later than when they were first spoken, but with amazing impact.

When the war ended, Aurelia quit her job to be with her husband. She enjoyed the time spent working, but had no problem going back to being a housewife. After she and her husband settled in Southern California, Aurelia looked up one of her wartime friends and the two continued their friendship for a great many years.

Carolyn remembers Aurelia's experience made her sister a better person by strengthening her character.

Aurelia Corree
by sister Carolyn Ferreira
Atria El Camino Gardens
Carmichael, California

During WWII, Doris lived on a farm in Mississippi. She had two brothers who were in the Navy. Doris was in a political group in 1942 and she remembers trading stamps.

Doris Keith
Atria Carrollton
Dallas, Texas

In 1944, Liz worked at Glen Martin Airport in Baltimore. She was employed there for two years. There were three main plants on the site that manufactured B-26s and B-17s. One made the airplanes, one tested the airplanes and one repaired the airplanes.

Liz worked in the electrical division for 90 cents an hour, nine hours a day, which was good pay in those days. Liz said, "It was my responsibility to fix all drills, jack-hammers and glue pots that were used to fix the planes."

Liz worked with the most famous "Rosie the Riveter," whom Norman Rockwell made famous with the drawing of a female factory worker repairing planes during the war. Liz said, "Rosie couldn't do work until I completed her job and passed it on to her."

After the war was over, the plant closed and Liz returned to Nazareth, Pennsylvania, with her four-year-old son, Knute Claude. Her husband, Claude, was still in the Army. Liz was glad to be able to serve her country.

On November 3, 1945, Claude was discharged from the Army and returned to Liz.

Elizabeth Roth
**Atria Bethlehem
Bethlehem, Pennsylvania**

Katherine's husband worked for Shell Oil Company. Shell Oil had built five houses on the Gulf Coast for her husband and four other employees. Across from their beach house was the Sea Breeze Inn, which the Coast Guard turned into its headquarters during World War II. The Coast Guard placed markers in the ocean that looked like lampposts. The posts were placed there to alert ships, boats and any other watercrafts to not come any closer to the shore than the posts. Trespassers could be shot if they crossed the markers in the water.

Katherine did not work outside her home during World War II. She washed her dishes three times a day and would look out her kitchen window across the ocean. One day, she noticed a fourth marker post. He tried to calm her by telling her there were always four markers, but she knew better. Later that evening, the Coast Guard came to their home and told them not to open the door for anyone because a large submarine had been spotted. She told him the story about seeing something in the ocean near the markers. He told Katherine that she might have seen a smaller submarine looking for the larger sub that had been spotted earlier in Galveston.

Katherine Broussard
**Atria Collier Park
Beaumont, Texas**

Maryann was about 16 when she got her first job at Gray Stone Textile Mill in Providence, Rhode Island. She earned about $1 per hour and her duties varied depending on how much work was done the previous day. Maryann started out winding the yarn as it was fed into the machine to prevent tangles and knots. After some time, she was promoted to spinner, which was by far one of the hardest jobs in the factory. The bobbins had to be watched as they spun to make sure they didn't get tangled. She also had to make sure they did not run out of thread.

After a while, Maryann took a second job at Esmond Mill and Alandale Mill. There she was hired as a weaver, weaving and assisting in making the material. She worked in the factories for five years. Every month, Maryann saved her paycheck so that she and her sister could go to Radio City in New York City. Although they had to be home by midnight, they always found time to have fun in between their school, house chores and work.

After working in the factories for five years, Maryann decided to work for a corporate office making $2.50 an hour. She liked working in the factories, but she also liked the lighter workload in the office.

Maryann feels that she was really lucky to land a great office job. She was happy to have had all the experiences she had during World War II because it helped her learn that, if you want something you have to work hard to get it – and not to let anything get in the way of your dreams.

Maryann Inman
Atria Sunlake
Las Vegas, Nevada

"I was a government employee even before World War II started. I was employed at the U.S. Treasury Bureau of Printing and Engraving in Washington, D.C. My job was to inspect the currency that the bureau printed. When the war started, our office was converted into the War Department. I was transferred to the Bureau of Public Debt as a supervisor for the E, F, and G Bonds in Chicago. I trained other employees.

I had two brothers who were sent to the war in the Pacific. George was an Air Force pilot and flew a B-17 plane. His plane was shot down and never came back. My other brother, Cashmere, whom we fondly call "Cash," was a paratrooper. He was lucky to have survived his mission. My parents and I were always worried about my brothers' safety. When my brother George died, it was very devastating. No war is a good war."

Josephine Putkey
Atria Daly City
Daly City, California

Marie worked as a secretary at South Boston High School. Marie's husband was not in the service because he was a lawyer and considered essential personnel needed here at home.

As a secretary, Marie filed, typed and took shorthand. She had her own car and drove herself to and from work every day. The school system took care of getting her the hard-to-get gas needed to run the car.

She loved her job and especially the kids and all their problems. She remembers having to use ration stamps to buy certain items like sugar. Marie said that everyone was happy when the war ended and things started to get back to normal again.

Marie Lewando
Atria Woodbriar
Falmouth, Massachusetts

"The war broke out in 1942, and I went to school for six months to become a machine operator. I was single and after school I began working at the Texas Steel Mill in Texas. I weighed only 100 pounds. The work was very difficult and I had problems lifting the heavy pieces of steel that went into machine guns. The heat was unbearable. I had never worked before and had some real trying times. After struggling with this job for a year and a half, I was finally fired.

Next, I moved to Port Arthur and worked for Texaco making oil cans. I worked there for a year until I was laid off. Again, the work was very hard and it was extremely hot. I did shift work for 50 hours a week and made $1 per hour. My last job during the war was for Gulf Oil as a machine operator making gulf spray. I did this job for about two years.

Three of my brothers fought in the war and thankfully, all of them came back. After the war, I got a job at a bank where I worked for 12 years. I married in 1949 to a man whose job during the war was to drive a truck around and pick up dead bodies.

The war was absolutely horrible. It was a hard, trying time. Those are years I would like to not remember.

Tressie Hermsdoffer
Atria Collier Park
Beaumont, Texas

I worked at Todd Shipyard in San Pedro, California, for two years and three months. I was the payroll reconciliator. It was very busy handling cashed payroll checks, $10,000 worth a week. I worked six days a week.

The women worked very hard and were proud to serve, because our husbands had been drafted. After the war was over, we felt at peace and relieved from worry and stress.

June Relstab
Atria Acacia
San Pedro, California

"I got married in 1944 and soon went to work for the electric and gas company in Perth Amboy, New Jersey. After the war got going, there were notices in the paper for women to work in many different occupations, such as Rosie the Riveters, the cable company, bus drivers and such. Women were more accepted for these jobs after the men were called into service.

I went to the Raritan Arsenal, applied for a second job and began working there at night. In those days, computers were first coming on the market, but they weren't anything like the ones today. They had big bins of cards that were all punched in code and we had to match the order to the code on the card. It was a riot to try to match up these codes! The arsenal mostly shipped out ammunition. I would hate to think what would happen if the codes didn't match up just right!

It was difficult working two jobs all of the time, so I finally gave up the work at the arsenal. Just a couple of months after I left, there was a bad explosion.

I remember that every time the men were called up for service, they would have big farewell parades. The women with their children, little boys in particular, cried as they said goodbye to their men. I didn't like that at all. It was so sad."

Joyce Hancock
Atria Windsor Woods
Hudson, Florida

Cecile was in high school during WWII. Her father was in the Army and her mother worked in a dress factory. Cecile remembers the rationing. She would take a street car in Los Angeles to the Clifton Café to eat meat on Tuesdays. She also fondly remembers dancing the jitterbug at the Palladian Civil Auditorium with the sailors when they came home.

Cecile Middleton
Atria Carrollton
Dallas, Texas

During the War, I worked on Wall Street as a statistician. There were many people who applied for this position, but I was chosen because of my speed. After a while I was promised a raise when the market improved.

A good memory I have involves acts of kindness. A good friend and I used to send hooch in hollowed-out bread loaves to the soldiers to comfort them!

When the war was finally over, we had the day off to celebrate. We hugged and kissed with great joy. I think that I was more appreciative after that experience.

Lydia Maples
Atria Meridian
Lantana, Florida

"I worked for three different companies during World War II. My first job was as a merchandiser in the ladies' department of the Emporium in San Francisco. I also worked at Metropolitan Life Insurance as a clerk and at the Pacific Telephone and Telegraph Company.

I had four brothers. Three of them were servicemen even before the war. When the war broke out, my other brother was drafted, and all of them went to war. I needed my brothers to go with me to dances, to play baseball and to do other things families do together. I missed out on all of these because my brothers had responded to the call of duty. We were constantly worried about my them.

During the war, there were things that were difficult to get. I remember that we were allotted only one pair of shoes per year. I played tennis then and I needed tennis shoes often, but I could not get them as often as I needed. We were lucky when it came to food. My mother, who was a full-time volunteer for the Red Cross, developed a nerve disease when my four brothers were all sent to the war. Because of her medical condition,

we had more allocations for meat, eggs and milk. We were all so glad when the war was over and my brothers came home. Wartime was a difficult period. The good thing was we became more neighborly. We became more conscious of other people's needs."

Norma McCrellis
Atria Daly City
Daly City, California

"I worked in San Antonio, Texas, at Joskey's Department Store full-time during World War II. I had been married for 18 months when my husband was sent overseas. I did not get to see him again for two years and four months. I missed him so much!"

Eleanor Patrick
Atria Willow Park
Tyler, Texas

Virginia remembers working as an 18-year old in a women's clothing factory in New York. She would get clothing that was already cut and she sewed them together. She lived in Brooklyn and took the train into work every day. Virginia worked five or six days a week, eight hours a day. Her uniform consisted of a smock to protect her clothing from other fabrics. Virginia had to work to support her entire family. Her two older brothers were in the service, and her two younger brothers lived at home.

After the war, Virginia met her husband, who had been discharged from the Navy, at a church dance. Virginia was very fortunate to have all of her friends and brothers return from the war. One brother did lose an eye in the war, but Virginia was so thankful that he came home.

Virginia Delucci
Atria Chandler Villas
Chandler, Arizona

Evelyn began her work for the war when a family friend, who was also a doctor in their small community, told her that his receptionist was leaving and asked her if she would be interested in the job. Her typical day consisted of filing, typing and dictation. She had to wear a white nurse's uniform.

She recalls everyone being very patriotic. Though everyone was so happy and grateful when the war finally ended, Evelyn's happiness was clouded by grief for her brother who was killed in Italy shortly before the war ended.

Evelyn Plutchak
Atria Greece
Rochester, New York

When World War II started, my first husband and I were in Fresno, California. We decided to move right away to San Francisco and I started working as a manager for 680 Ellis Hotel.

It was also in this hotel that I met someone who later became my second husband. Even before the war, my first husband and I were having trouble, and the everyday difficulties during the war added to our friction. Soon we decided to part ways and I got married to the most wonderful person in the world, Albert Quinto.

During the war there were food items that were so difficult to get. We could not have as much coffee and sugar as we wanted and even butter was rationed. People stood in line for hours to get cigarettes. Oh yes— those were difficult times that I will never forget.

Edith Quinto
Atria Daly City
Daly City, California

Dorothy was married to her husband, Gene, during the war. He had a punctured eardrum and he tried three times to join the service but was refused. Dorothy also recalls that she traded her car for a bicycle because she could not get enough gas stamps. Dorothy also entertained troops at the USO center on Governor's Island.

Dorothy Aiello
Atria Carrollton
Dallas, Texas

Alva began serving the country in the ways that she was able. A local farmer would take Alva to his family's victory garden and she would work in the fields. She also met a young soldier who was in charge of the Army ordnance and the two of them sold war bonds in St. Louis. Alva's family lived near a prisoner-of-war camp and her mother picked up a hitchhiker one day. As she listened to the radio, a report came through that a prisoner had escaped. She realized the prisoner was riding in her car! He was released without a problem and she never picked up a hitchhiker again.

Alva later married Glenn Kerr, a colonel in the Army who served all over the Pacific. Glenn and Alva were patriots doing anything and everything they could to bring peace to all.

Alva Kerr
Atria Cypresswood
Houston, Texas

Dorothy went to work for Allison's during World War II. She was pulled back and forth between the jobs of inspector of parts for airplanes and secretary. Dorothy said, "I liked the inspector position better. It paid more!"

After the war was over, Dorothy went back home to start a family.

Dorothy King
Atria Heritage
Indianapolis, Indiana

"I lived in Tyler, Texas, was a housewife and had my children during the war. My husband was sent off to the war while I waited patiently for him to arrive home safely!"

Marie Bowman
Atria Willow Park
Tyler, Texas

"All the women that I knew during World War II worked. I did bookkeeping at the National Casket Company in Dallas, Texas. I spent the day at my desk with a bunch of paperwork.

I think the war effort was an effort by everyone and for everyone. Everyone did what they could. It was a happy time when the war was over, but a sad time for those who had lost loved ones. I still keep in touch with a few of my fellow workers. I think my loyalty and that of others kept the USA working during a time of great crisis."

Mary Bonner
Atria Richardson
Dallas, Texas

"In April 1942, my husband, Stan, went to the South Pacific with the 32nd Division Infantry of the Army. It was horrible being home alone. I lived with my grandmother and grandfather, yet I missed Stan so much.

I got a job at Standard Steel, which furnished the steel for the tanks. I ran the teletype machine and kept track of the steel shipments. It was my duty to inform plants when the shipments would be received. It was a very secretive deal at that time and all communications were guarded. It was also my duty to send the tanks to the distribution location. I never sent a tank to the wrong place.

During dull moments, we did gossip on the teletype. I would talk to girls in other cities, find out what they were doing for the night and ask them about their weather. We used to have more fun with those teletypes!

I also ran a Western Union machine, which was fun. I would type out the messages being sent. Even the messages were secretive and I had guards around me. They were guarding against sabotage and were mostly concerned with what was happening overseas.

I worked at the steel company for three years. Stan was released from the service in January 1945. We have been married 62 years. I still love everything about my husband. As we grow older, we get in less trouble with one another. The first three years of our marriage was the greatest. Stan was overseas and I was home collecting his $28 monthly allotment!"

Doris MacDonald
Atria Windsor Woods
Hudson, Florida

> "I never sent a tank to the wrong place."

"I worked at the clothing factory in Red Bank, New Jersey. There we sewed Army uniforms and field jackets for the soldiers. My typical day was rough. I want others to know that women had to work because the men went to war. When the war was over we celebrated."

Louise Talerico
Atria Tinton Falls
Tinton Falls, New Jersey

"There were many things we did not have, but we did not feel deprived because everyone else was in the same situation. We remember in great detail the misery of The Depression. We were taught and we believed in duty, honor, frugality (we still do), courage, service, love of family and country and responsibility for oneself, above all.

Edith Tapp
Atria Copeland
Tyler, Texas

"My husband was drafted in the Navy and he was gone for three years. We had one son at the time. My husband returned to give something back to our little town of Turrell, Arkansas. He promoted progress by bringing a women's clothing factory to town. He later became mayor. People liked him because he got things done. I am proud of what my husband became and what he accomplished after the war."

Maxine Baer
Atria Primacy
Memphis, Tennessee

Mavis was a nurse for 30 years. She was a charge nurse on a major surgical floor, working different shifts for eight to 10 hours a day. At times she worked 18-hour shifts when she was on-call for a surgery. The Navy paid her $175 a month. Her husband was in the Army stationed in Texas.

"When I checked in at Great Lakes, I was given directions and mistakenly ended up in an area where the chief nurses' offices were," she recalls. I was swinging my suitcase down a hall when I collided with a chief nurse. The next time I saw her after this incident, I almost knocked her over! I had to check in with the chief nurse when I came on duty. When I saw the chief nurse that I had collided with, she said, 'Oh no, not you!'

"One Sunday morning, we were expecting more than 500 from California. Our ramps had screen doors and my ward was in charge of keeping the doors closed. A corpsman came in and said that we needed a fly watch. I told him that I was busy several times. The corpsman was the captain! Shortly after that incident, the captain retired and a big party was held in his honor. He went around the room and said goodbye to everyone. When he came to me, he gave me a big hug and said, 'I like your style.' You could have heard a pin drop!"

Mavis Farina
Atria Chandler Villas
Chandler, Arizona

"During World War II, I was married and lived in Newark, New Jersey. My husband was in evacuation hospital care for the Army in Texas. While he was away, I went to work in New York City for John and Fredericks Millinery Company. My husband and his family owned a wholesale banana company, so I also worked as the company's bookkeeper. When my husband was discharged, we were able to start our family."

Hannah Barr
Atria Cranford
Cranford, New Jersey

"In January 1943, I enlisted in the Woman's Auxiliary Army Corps, or the WAAC, as it was known then. I thought that I could contribute to the war effort with my knowledge of several languages. I was assigned to Fort Oglethorpe in Georgia. I was put through a few weeks of basic training without having a chance to use my specialty because I became ill and was assigned to a transit barracks, waiting to be discharged. That was where I met another girl like me, a New Yorker, and we became friends. After we both received our honorable medical discharges, we renewed our friendship in New York. That is where I met her brother, who became my husband shortly after when he was inducted into the Army Air Corps."

Hortense Berman
Atria Mallard Cove
Cincinnati, Ohio

In 1942, Sarah applied for a government job in Washington, D.C. She started off as a secretary, then was promoted to editor and sent to school to learn editorial work. Her typical workday consisted of editing journals for the Army, Justice Department and the state. When the war was over, Sarah moved to Maryland and continued working.

Sarah has fond memories of her job, especially all the perks and promotions. "I had a wonderful experience working and learning all the new aspects of my job. I enjoyed the promotions and the hard work," she says.

According to Sarah, her home-front experience changed her in positive ways, "It strengthened me and gave me a broader perspective of life."

Sarah Singer
Atria Buena Vista
Vista, California

"I took a job at Bell Aircraft in Niagara Falls. I didn't know what to ask for, so I became a "Rosie the Riveter." That was quite a job! I had to crawl under the plane to put it together. Sometimes you crawled over here; sometimes you crawled over there. You couldn't hear anything – it was a noisy job! The riveting gun was very loud and it wasn't just me riveting. There were about six of us riveting at the same time. We had coverall uniforms that were navy blue with white collars. It was quite a place!

One day, one of the girls borrowed my new set of wrenches that I had just purchased. She was one of these 'la-dee-dah' girls. Instead of getting my new wrenches back, she brought me a set of old ones. She had given my new wrenches to her boyfriend! Of course, I raised cane, but it didn't do me any good – I didn't get anywhere. There was another girl there who was really something. If she was sweeping the floor, she would try to ram the broom handle in your face if you didn't move out of her way fast enough. I sort of got sick with my nerves and with that job, and the doctor said that I should take time off."

Blanche Lynch
Atria Windsor Woods
Hudson, Florida

"There are so many little things that stay in your mind as you remember the World War II era. Here are a few:

- Crossing the Atlantic on the Queen Mary – sleeping in a stateroom designed for two – and there were nine of us! Good thing the trip only lasted five days!
- Being quarantined in Glasgow in small Quonset huts.
- Being sent out on detached duty to a small town 20 miles from London and having time to explore both the area and London.
- Being called back to Glasgow to reassemble and be off across the English Channel, a rough crossing at night.
- Spending several weeks in a little village in Belgium, where the village priest came out and stood on the church steps to give all the villagers news of President Roosevelt's death.
- Setting up the 126th EVAC six miles from the Czechoslovakian border. It was summer and the countryside was beautiful with only an occasional sound of guns firing.

After about a year, we were told to pack for the South Pacific – via Texas. Thankfully, the war was over before we could be sent"!

Pauline Hill
Atria Copeland
Tyler, Texas

"My husband Paul and I lived in Miami, Florida. He was working as a machinist when war was declared. He volunteered for the Coast Guard and was stationed in Key West. I remember flying out to visit him in a plane with the windows blacked out.

A very funny thing happened one night while he was on guard. He spotted some movement in the water close to the shore. He called out for it to stop . . . but it didn't. Thinking that it might be the enemy, he shot at it and hit it. It turned out to be a very large otter. He actually took it, had it skinned and brought it home to me. I made a Halloween costume out of it and wore it the following Halloween.

I wanted to do something to help during the war, so I filled out a petition to work with the Coast Guard also. I was hired as a file clerk. I remember a little boy polishing my penny loafers every morning when I reported to work.

I had a very dear friend who lived in Annapolis. Because of gas rationing, I didn't get to see her very often. I remember one visit, though. We went to the commissary and bought a milkshake. Because of the circumstances, that was probably the best milkshake I've ever had."

Katherine Barnard
Atria Cordova
Memphis, Tennessee

"In 1942, I think it was at Northwest Airlines, we had a shell of an airplane and we had an instructor instructing us how to rivet inside the plane. This seems like 100 years ago! Of course, you had to take tests in order to do this work. We spent many hours on our knees – there was no sitting. All I remember is just riveting. It was a good-paying job and I was single at the time.

It was easy back then to get work. The jobs didn't pay, but there were plenty of them.

It was only six months that I worked there, for I had a boyfriend in Bremerton, Washington, serving on the U.S.S. Enterprise carrier. He wanted me closer to him, so I relocated to Washington. It was amazing to see all of the ships come into port. One day, a woman and I were walking around Bremerton when all of a sudden the roofs of many of the houses opened up and big guns came out. It was a practice drill. When battleships and carriers came into port, they conducted these drills in preparation. It was fascinating to see.

We had blackouts, where all shades had to be closed and stay that way. I ended up working at J. C. Penneys, but that was ok because I could be with my guy."

Carol Baker
Atria Windsor Woods
Hudson, Florida

Maggie was born in London, England, on March 7, 1923 and was in school at the outbreak of Word War II on September 3, 1939. The first few months of the war were fairly quiet, but in 1940, the Blitz on London began and living was extremely dangerous with air raids going on both night and day. The Lawrence family began living in their air-raid shelter, which was an underground, sandbagged bunker in the corner of their backyard. Because travel to and from school became quite dangerous, the children were moved en masse to Harrogate, Yorkshire, and lived with families in the area. Filled with homesickness, the children never knew from day to day if their parents had survived the air-raids the night before in London.

After graduating from school and working for the post office for a year, Maggie decided to join the Royal Artillery. After basic training in Wales, Maggie passed various tests and became a 2nd lieutenant radar technician on a heavy artillery/anti-aircraft gun site. The next few years were spent moving around coastal sites from Scotland to Southern England. Conditions during those years were, to say the least, primitive – living in tents and using a latrine surrounded by canvas for privacy! Maggie kept up this job and these conditions until she was demobilized in 1946.

Maggie Lawrence
Atria Copeland
Tyler, Texas

"I worked in a war plant where they made parts for smaller fighter airplanes. I was a tabulator at Tightflex. I did key punch and sorters. They are the cards that described each part that came. It was like keeping an inventory of all the parts.

No, it was too long ago. I'll tell you one thing, we couldn't keep the women at work. They'd all leave to go see their husbands at Camp Stewart in Georgia. I went to see my husband down there one time and had to sit in the train station all night because he couldn't get off duty. He finally showed up the next morning.

Another time we were working overtime and all the girls were in the office and the weather was really scary – it was pitch black outside. We saw this thing moving really slow back and forth past the window, so we all started screaming and ran. It was a big dead leaf caught in the screen. We thought we were being invaded. I learned to drive a car at work because the boss would take us out and teach us.

I lost my brother in the war. Raymond was 25 and was in the 8th Air Force. He was an aerial gunner and he was shot down over the North Sea. It was really sad.

When the war was declared over, we just stopped dead in our tracks. It was a stillness I will never forget."

Alice McDevitt
Atria Regency
Mobile, Alabama

Beulah was living in Bakersfield, California, with her husband and children. Soon after the war started, Beulah remembers a day when soldiers came to her house asking for food. After that, Beulah became the soldiers' angel. She would give food to every soldier that the USO sent to her house. Beulah helped feed so many soldiers that when one of the big grocery stories found out what she was doing, it started donating food. Not only would Beulah cook for the soldiers, but she would also make things for them in her spare time.

Beulah had to get up very early to fix breakfast and help her husband and children get ready for the day ahead of them. After that, she and her mother started cooking the meals for the soldiers. Beulah was happy that she was making a difference helping all those soldiers.

When the war ended, there was happiness and joy all around. Beulah remembers soldiers from all over coming to her house to clean it in order to thank her for all of her generosity. She remembers a special visitor who came all the way from Chicago. It was one of the soldier's mothers coming to thank her for everything that she had done for her son. This lady was so pleased to know that there were still people like Beulah who helped so many people. When Beulah moved to New York after the war, she continued to help anyone who showed up at her door. She would always find something to give them. To this day, Beulah still gives and helps out wherever she can.

Beulah Melvin
Atria Campbell
Campbell, California